ALSO BY SAMIR SHAWA

Gaza, Where to? (Arabic)

Charlie Khalil of Gaza

Popcorn Dementia

Ghazawi Disappearance (Arabic)

LOBBYING FOR PALESTINE

LOBBYING FOR PALESTINE

A COLLECTIVE STRUGGLE FOR THE FUTURE

SAMIR SHAWA

ALHANI CULTURAL

First published in Great Britain 2022
by ALHANI CULTURAL

The moral right of the author has been asserted.

ISBN HB 978-1-7396875-0-2
ISBN PB 978-1-7396875-1-9
ISBN EB 978-1-7396875-2-6

Most photos in this book are from the author's collection,
Al Hani Books photo archive and family & friends albums.
Every effort has been made to identify copyright holders;
in case of oversight, and on notification to the publisher's
email, corrections will be made in the next edition.

A CIP catalogue record for this book is available from the
British Library.

Printed and bound by CPI Group (UK) Ltd, Croydon, CR0 4YY

info@alhani.org

To Hani, who urged me with encouragement and eagerness to continue writing about Palestine, which he never set foot on, with my heartfelt thanks and love.

Contents

Throughout history many nations have suffered a physical defeat, but that has never marked the end of a nation. But when a nation has become the victim of a psychological defeat, then that marks the end of a nation.

— IBN KHALDUN (1332-1406)

Introduction

*"The history of memory includes the writing of memory...
Who should we study? Should we study heroes, the great
events of the past or should we study the people whom
history doesn't speak about? ...so we could see ourselves
more honestly and clearly."*

— EDWARD SAID

Most individuals have their untold stories. Often they are simple stories, ones that can be told in a number of ways; some exquisite and dreamy, while others realistic and closer to the heart, but there is a fundamental difference in the case of the embittered Palestinians, particularly those living in Gaza. Their stories always consist of trauma and loss, as if in constant and continuous mourning. Their narrative is inherently a story of dispossession, bombardments, siege and exile.

Naturally, deep pain takes time to be overcome and to be accepted, but some inexplicable pains endure, never fading, and touch the innermost fibres of our being.

The Pain of Losing One's Home

The 20th century began traumatically for Palestine: First World War devastations, the ominous Balfour Declaration, the notorious and biased British Mandate, the Nakba and the painful journeys of exile that began as temporary, but the fear was that they would become permanent. Periods of dazed, angry bewilderment and sadness followed those who wandered in strange and new places, their only concern was to return home. With the long wait for a desired good piece of news, most Palestinian children were born immersed in politics, mothers breastfed their babies with the milk of politics and adults lived a life of politics, believing that from the depths of calamities, hope is born.

Life in the 1940s seemed promising for many small ordinary Palestinian families who had a secure and stable future. Once they crossed the borders of neighbouring countries, they became refugees, a status attached to all of them; it wasn't merely a deprivation of a homeland, a future, or a passport. Rather, a lump stuck in their mind and conscience, violating respect as human beings and swallowing all desires of goodness and hope in the depths of their hearts. Anger, anxiety and feelings of revenge among the children of those displaced families, which became their destiny. This led to a wide array of reactions: some turned to loud demonstrations, others to violence, some to diplomacy and progressive initiatives, and a few to reading the Qur'an and the teaching of the Prophet's biography and his openness to the concepts of reason, the foundations of purpose of life, mercy and coexistence.

The intellectuals among them continued the search for knowledge of the resurrection of the prophets, the contents of the Gospel, the Torah, the teachings of Buddha and others. Also, the study of what the ancient Arabs said and inscribed by the Greeks, what philosophers have said for thousands of years: that most of what we say or do is taken from the opinions and actions of others and the product of their ideas.

Myth is created by man, a long-standing one becomes embedded in people's minds whether they believe in them or not; they become woven into their preconceptions and beliefs. In the complex issue of the Israeli-Palestinian conflict, these myths are enforced by the history of tendentious and inaccurate media propaganda led by media outlets supporting Israel, aimed at completely erasing the rights of

Palestinians in the remainder of their land, and avoiding the implementation of international resolutions.

The phenomenon of Arab Nationalism, as an idea for political unity, spread quickly during the days of President Gamal Abdel Nasser, who ignited the enthusiasm of the masses with bold promises to realize their dreams of unity, progress, victory over colonial powers and to fulfil the promise of liberating the expropriated Palestinian lands. Displaced masses, who lost their homes, adhered strongly to these slogans, they relied completely upon the progressive Arab armies to restore their homeland, trusting the virility of the young enthusiastic new Arab leaders.

Unfortunately for the Palestinian people, the Arab leadership, after a long and deep slumber, discovered that they were not ready for war; they decided to launch a Palestinian body that would be solely entrusted with fulfilling these amazing slogans, hence the establishment in 1964 of the Palestine Liberation Organization "PLO" headed by a lawyer named Ahmed al-Shuqairi.[1]

One year later, a group of exiles in Kuwait formed the Fatah movement, headed by Yasser Arafat, who ultimately managed later on to replace Shuqairi as leader of the Palestinian Liberation Organization (PLO); another group, the Popular Front for the Liberation of Palestine (PFLP) was formed by a doctor named George Habash.[2]

The centrality of Gaza is clearly evident in this book; after the Nakba, Gaza was the only part left to bear the name "Palestine". The struggle for Palestine was first revived in Gaza, almost a decade before the founding of the PLO.

Over the years it hosted dozens of dignitaries, including Nehru, Nasser, Sadat, Che Guevara, Malcolm X, Sartre, Simone de Beauvoir, Nelson Mandela and Bill Clinton amongst others. Gaza also sparked the first intifada in late 1987.

There are always challenges in life, particularly to refugees in their adopted countries; their lives are mostly filled with paradoxes and contradictions, some endured prejudice against their ethnicity among other difficulties.

Fortunately, one of the calming sedatives in exile is the rumination of memory with its pure, beautiful, and authentic storage in their minds. Therefore, it is a compelling necessity in studying the past, as our present and future is in many respects the product of historical factors that led to the miserable situations and complex problems we have dwelt in. Thus ensued the arduous journeys of those creators in exile who refused to surrender to defeat, the loss of their homeland, and the humiliation of living in refugees' camps, who embodied the indomitable, moral and patriotic spirit of Palestine during those long and critical early years.

There were those who kept thinking and trying to present initiatives, participation in public affairs became a necessity despite being a personal point of view and vision; but in the Palestinian case, it became a national duty that could not be neglected. Despite that tragic catastrophe, many pioneers emerged, including creative academics and historians who were able to occupy the highest positions at the most prestigious universities in the world; top-ranked doctors who brilliantly operated in the most famous hospitals; great scientists in the fields of physics and chemistry, economists and founders of the Arab banks in the region, highly qualified engineers and architects, who designed the most iconic buildings, entrepreneurs who succeeded in developing mega projects worldwide.

The failure of the Camp David talks that resulted in igniting the second Intifada and a devastating siege imposed by Ariel Sharon on President Arafat in the Muqata'a, regrettably, was met with complete silence and indifference by most world leaders.

The situation had become significantly critical and dangerous, and the fear of losing the opportunity to achieve the anticipated Independent State of Palestine became entrenched and was growing at an amazing speed.

A group of young businessmen, most of whom were born to parents who were expelled from their towns and villages, set out to form a committee in order to contribute to helping the besieged authority improve the deteriorating economic situation and to encourage administrative and political reform. They formed a committee called "PBCPR". The group embarked on a complex and difficult mission, "lobbying for Palestine" in America, an endeavour which was described by many Palestinian officials as a "Daring Adventure"!

The Arabic dictionary has no word synonymous with the English word "lobby"; such a word has become a unique phenomenon in recent years, distinctly associated with the invigorating description of the extremely powerful Israel lobby in America.

Among their first appointments was a visit to The Aspen Institute's Wye River which culminated in the formation of a special Middle East Strategy Group (MESG). Other scheduled meetings on subsequent visits took the members to the White House, the Capitol, the Pentagon, the State Department, the World Bank and surprisingly to the offices of AIPAC.

Fortunately, there were active global campaigns for Palestine led by many great and faithful people, political parties, artists, sporting figures, academics and students, football fans and incredibly, many Jewish public figures. In an unremitting search for justice, their noble ideas, powerful and supportive voices, campaigns and actions represented a distinctive and explicit statement of "lobbying for Palestine."

Finally, due to the extensive details of events and experiences that had been shared with others over many years, that gave me the honour of meeting many distinguished people whom I recognized, with absolute admiration, and whose bold opinions and valuable achievements became deeply ingrained in my memory,; they all contributed significantly in identifying some of the priorities for the relevant contents of this completely different book, which is also a retrospection of Palestinian lives, and how our previous realities were impacted by such significant events, as well as to emphasize that the interest in reaching a just and binding solution to the Palestinian cause at the global and popular levels is far from fading away. On the contrary, it enjoys growing support among younger generations of graduates, academics and artists around the world.

It is a true reminder of the power of our existence and resistance. I used to admit without shame that I was not well versed in the English language, not even in Arabic. Some people focus on linguistic errors and forget the purpose of the topic.

With the emergence of Islamic movements in the region, including Hamas and Islamic Jihad in Palestine, does this lead to their prevailing belief that Islam is the future of mankind? Is there in fact a doctrine called "The Chosen People?" Are the Palestinians among these people?

In our daily life, there is an expiration date for everything including food, drinks and medicine; the Israeli occupation too must end, just as colonialism has ended around the world. Will the strong stay strong forever?

This book conveys the deepest gratitude that emanates from within the hearts of the children of Gaza and Jerusalem to all the good people in the world who reject injustice, oppression, and the killing of innocent civilians, some of whom have been subjected to attacks, blackmail, and loss of jobs as a result of their principled and courageous stances.

Are we really prepared for future events?

Are we allowed to think about a one-state solution as a possible option in the end?

Of course, the discussion is complicated and long. With the lingering state of waiting that haunts us, mainly due to the uncertainty of what tomorrow will bring, and the absence of a rational leadership on both sides, the perplexing question arises: Where are *We* and *Them* going?

Will the answer depend on which direction Israel and its future governments go? Or does it depend entirely on a new position taken by the present or future US administrations?

Or in which direction will the Palestinians eventually go?

CHAPTER 1

A Palestinian State on Probation!

"Panic from a catastrophe is another catastrophe."

Peace of the Brave

"Among the misfortunes of life, one has to see an enemy
whose friendship is of utmost necessity."

— AL-MUTANABBI

The option of peace talks and negotiation with the old enemy usurping the homeland, whether directly or through mediators, has been discussed numerous times among the leaders of the Palestinian resistance groups. Two major events dealt a powerful blow to the resistance, making it necessary for the leadership to review its strategy and methods of resistance. The first was the military and political retreat from Lebanon during the summer of 1982. This led to the disengagement of their forces from the borders of historic Palestine, and a dispersal to the most remote areas of the Arab world, Tunisia, Yemen, and Sudan. The second event was the brutal Israeli airstrike on the Fedayeen camps in the Hamamat district of Tunis in 1985. The assault left some seventy Palestinian and Tunisian martyrs. These events and the resulting deteriorating political relations with the Arab regimes necessitated the launch of a massive campaign seeking global support.

A group that would be supportive of the idea of peace and nego-tiations with Israel emerged among Fatah's leaders, who tried to per-suade others, including their scattered and weary warriors to accept the idea of peaceful struggle due to the impossibility of achieving a military victory under the adverse circumstances. At the head of this movement was Mahmoud Abbas and Khaled al-Hassan, who managed to outperform their comrades, the hard-line leaders Salah Khalaf, Khalil al-Wazir and Farouk Qaddoumi.

They adopted new slogans such as "Take and Demand" and the "Establishment of our state on any inch of our homeland", which were significantly floated on the surface and clearly expressed by the public. Some even talked and criticised Yasser Arafat's refusal to enter into negotiations on the future of Gaza, which Egyptian President, Anwar Sadat, called for during the last episodes of the peace talks with Menachem Begin, before concluding the peace treaty under the principle "Land for Peace" that led to the complete Israeli withdrawal from the Sinai Peninsula.

The outbreak of the first Intifada (uprising) that erupted from Gaza City and became known as "The Stones' Intifada", saw the hard-liners regain their breath. They saw an opportunity to push for armed struggle as global support poured in for the Palestinian up-rising, particularly the many children who protested peacefully and unarmed, with nothing but stones. Amazingly, Arafat's popularity rose rapidly again.[1]

Less than one year after the popular intifada, King Hussein of Jordan made a sudden announcement concerning Jordan's disen-gagement from the West Bank and East Jerusalem, thereby ending a relationship that lasted for exactly forty years, and thus placing the responsibility of all occupied Palestinian land squarely on the laps of the PLO. In parallel, there were intense but indirect contacts between the American Administration and the PLO under the auspices of Secretary of State George Shultz, and communication through Am-bassador Richard Murphy[2].

Events accelerated in the fall of that year, at the forefront of which was the historic declaration in Algiers of the independence of the State of Palestine in November 1988.

The significance of choosing Algiers as the platform for the declaration was the 8-year long Algerian revolution against the French colonial occupation in the 1950s, which had received massive Arab popular support, and was a great motivator for the Palestinians to gather their ranks and begin resisting the Zionist colonial occupation of their country. Ahmed Ben Bella was the bright public figure of the FLN (National Liberation Front), who became president of the newly independent Algeria, and a favourite among millions of Arabs and Arafat's supporters[3].

On a previous visit to the Algerian capital, Arafat asked his ambassador Munther Dajani to search for a book written by General Charles De Gaulle on the negotiations that led to Algerian independence. It was a strange request, as everyone knew Arafat did not read books, but rather, invoices, reports, and personal requests from his fighters for financial assistance. The following day, Dajani returned without a book, but with a copy of the front page of a newspaper dating back to 1962 with the bolded headline *"De Gaulle annonce la Paix des Braves"* [De Gaulle announces the Peace of the Brave].

The Madrid Peace conference of 1991 was convened by President George H. Bush, under the direct supervision of Secretary of State James Baker. The Israeli Prime Minister, Yitzhak Shamir[4], objected to the PLO's participation in an independent delegation and threatened to boycott the conference, therefore, Arafat was forced to agree to the Palestinian delegation, which was headed by Haidar Abdel Shafi, and to participate in a unified delegation with Jordan, that was headed by the Jordanian prime minister Abdel Salam Majali[5].

There were two significant events that profoundly disrupted the old Israeli strategy in dealing with the Palestine problem, the first being the intifada serving as a disturbing and horrific internal shock for the Israeli public.

The second event that threatened to upset Israel's strategic foreign policy was the loss of a valued partner, namely, the declaration by

South African President F.W. de Klerk of the end of the apartheid regime and the release of Nelson Mandela. Hence, Rabin thought of offering a peace deal to Arafat and the PLO that would provide self-rule for the Palestinians while maintaining Israel's grip on the territories, in the full knowledge that Arafat's difficult financial situation and lack of funds from the Gulf states following his support for Saddam Hussein, would make him accept this fantastic offer.

The Declaration of Principles was concluded and welcomed by then President Bill Clinton, who sponsored the signing of what became known as the Oslo Accord, in a magnificent and historic ceremony in the courtyards of the White House on September 13, 1993. News Channels broadcast live coverage of the ceremony to all parts of the world. Arafat called this agreement the peace of the brave, he used to repeat this phrase on every popular or official occasion. The image of Rabin and Arafat shaking hands, became a distinctive symbol of the coming peace.

Many exiles, mostly professionals and businessmen, rushed to seize on the historical opportunity granted by this event. After a forced absence that lasted for decades, and taking advantage of their experiences and savings acquired during their work in the diaspora, they could now participate in building their homeland.

My friends encouraged me to return home from London and play an active role in the building of a new Palestine. The most confident of a promising future was Nasser Al-Din Nashashibi[6], a veteran journalist who worked for King Abdullah of Jordan and President Nasser of Egypt. He was scornful of my political information, accusing me jokingly of being an outsider and intruder in the publishing trade, and urged me to stick to practising my original profession of engineering and contracting. He was applauding Rabin's move toward true peace as bravery on the part of an inspiring Israeli military leader.

Family members, as well as most of my close friends, were against any thought or desire of going back, some advised me not to make a rash decision about something that I could later regret, as they were sceptical of Israel's true intentions and did not believe Rabin was serious about the peace process. So, I decided to wait.

A few weeks later, Saida Nusseibeh, a friend and activist, who is also the wife of my friend, Jawad Ghussein, arrived at my publishing office "Al-Hani Books" accompanied by a man: "Dr Mark Ellis, a distinguished professor at Maryland with an idea of publishing his new book." I learned later with humble amazement that Dr. Ellis was a Rabbi who taught theology at Maryland university and had previously published a number of books. I also felt he was sincere in showing sympathy towards the Palestinians and their right to live in peace and security on their land. His book focused largely on restoring Palestine back into the Jewish memory. "Golda Meir, a former Israeli prime minister, was calling on all Jews to delete Palestine's name from their own memory before demanding that others forget Palestine and recognize Israel instead", he explained to me. A few weeks later, the book was published by Alhani under the title, *The Renewal of Palestine in The Jewish Imagination*[7]. It was a move that angered most of our Jewish customers. However, and in spite of this, my determination continued to grow with the idea of returning home. On one rainy July day the following year, Nashashibi came in waving a page from *The Times*, wearing a large smile and said, "Samir, please, read what Yitzhak Rabin said yesterday in a joint session of the Congress." I re-read Rabin's speech again and again, looked at Nasser:

"Now I'm convinced that Rabin is definitely sincere in making peace with the Palestinians, he has had great courage to announce it in Washington." Rabin's speech:

> Today we are embarking on a battle which has no dead and no wounded, no blood and no anguish. This is the only battle which is a pleasure to wage: the battle of peace… In the bible, our book of books, peace is mentioned in various idioms, two hundred and thirty-seven times. [8]

A few days later, Arafat arrived at the town of Rafah from Egypt accompanied by President Hosni Mubarak. There, he crossed into Palestine, where he was received by a large crowd signalling the establishment of the Palestinian Authority.

Finally, I decided to liquidate all my business in London and book a flight *via* Cairo to my hometown of Gaza. Dreaming all the way of the "peace of the brave". When I arrived at my father's house on October 14,1994, I had an overwhelming and indescribable feeling as I kept saying to myself "How sweet it is to come home".

During that same evening, my cousin Aoun, the mayor of Gaza, came to greet me and said he had just returned from the temporary residence of President Arafat, who was very thrilled to hear the announcement that he had been awarded the Nobel Peace Prize! What an amazing coincidence it was. Yasser Arafat a Nobel Laureate? Can anyone believe it? [9]

But of course, it is the affirmation of the world's welcome to the Peace of the Brave.

Auspicious Return Home

July 1994 witnessed a historic landmark in the long march of struggle with the first meeting in Gaza of the newly-formed government of National Authority, as the Palestinians call it. Israel, and the USA, described it as Self-rule (or autonomy) of the Palestinian Territories, etc.

The beginning saw a modest and timid government with limited authority over the two oldest ancient cities in Palestine: Gaza on the Mediterranean coast and Jericho over the Dead Sea. Yasser Arafat chose his new headquarters inside a small social club building on the seashore called "*Al-Muntada*".

The cabinet's responsibilities included the preparations for the next phase of receiving additional Palestinian cities that were to be evacuated by the Israeli army during the transitional period. Most members of the cabinet were from his comrades in arms who lacked previous practical or administrative experience. Although very excited, they found it extremely difficult to adapt to their new jobs as ministers of a democratic government, dealing with its people for the first time.

From his new office window overlooking the sea, Arafat appeared to be staring at the distant horizon as he tried to recall some historical events; he even admitted once that he was not deeply familiar with ancient history, but that he firmly believed that he was one of the makers of modern history of the region, especially as an architect of the "peace of the brave". He also began to review his personal memories about his father, Abdel Raouf Arafat Al-Qidwa, who was born in Gaza but lived and worked in Egypt most of his life, before returning back to Gaza in the 1950s and was eventually buried in Khan Yunis, a few miles south of Arafat's new headquarters.[10]

This historic city was built on the land of Canaan on the Mediterranean coast, almost five thousand years ago. Gaza was home to many ancient civilizations, including the Egyptian Pharaohs, the Phoenicians, the Greeks, the Romans, the Muslims and the Ottomans. The city also revolted against the British Mandate forces, resisted the Jewish settlements during the mandate and ignited the first intifada against the Israeli occupation in 1987.

In the evening, Arafat would spread the prayer rug and pray four *rak'ahs* of praise and thanks be to God, his dream of returning to this beloved land had been fulfilled, while remembering the Indian astrologer with a wide smile.

His close adviser, Marwan Kanafani, told this fascinating story:

"Adnan Khashoggi, the Saudi entrepreneur, made an amazing offer to send an astrologer to Arafat to find out what fate had in store for him, in that critical period after the Gulf War! Persuaded by his wife Suha, Arafat agreed. I received the astrologer who arrived in Tunis on Khashoggi's private plane in February 1992: a tall Indian who claimed to be a spiritual advisor to a number of world leaders including Ronald Reagan, Giscard d'Estaing and the Sultan of Brunei.

"When meeting Arafat in the presence of Suha and myself, the Astrologer confirmed that Arafat suffered from non-serious diseases and no one was plotting against him. With great confidence he predicted that Arafat would succeed in returning to Palestine and becoming its president within two years! Provided he survived what might happen to him in the fourth month, without specifying the year."

On the 7th of April that year, Arafat's plane crashed in the Libyan desert due to a severe sandstorm, killing two Palestinian pilots and a Romanian flight engineer, and Arafat miraculously survived! [11]

Many people returned to Gaza and Jericho imbued with a new sense of hope. For some, it was a journey of self-discovery, but for many they returned to their old cities, where they could see the people carrying the heavy burden not only on their shoulders but also their faces. Despite the myriad complexities and traumas of life in exile, they were equally joyful and brimming with affection.

People were entering the Palestinian side of the Rafah border crossing, coming from Egypt, and being greeted for the first time by a Palestinian flag flying over the passport office building adjacent to the border. What a wonderful sight! The few numbers of Palestinian Police welcomed returnees with warm greetings and sometimes with hugs! Many of them were overjoyed with the realisation that their return would be the beginning of a new journey in their lives. A journey of searching for an identity they had lost in the years of alienation. They were back to their cities hoping to embrace their memories of childhood. The spirit of hope filled many with a strong belief of a bright future for Palestine. Businessmen would certainly be able to participate in building economic and social institutions that would eventually lead to the establishment of the Independent Palestinian State.

My decision to return was extremely difficult, as I was returning without my wife and children, who preferred to remain in London to complete their studies. The lack of a close family atmosphere compounded matters. My older brother, two sisters, and numerous old friends now lived outside of Gaza. And of the family that remained, I had not seen them in many years. Most of my friends were urging me to think seriously and rationally about my hasty decision to return, and a few firmly advised against returning.

The words of my Iraqi friend and poet, Buland Al-Haidari, whose wife, Dalal, worked as director of Al-Hani bookshop, echoed in my mind: "The Oslo agreement is still under trial, it is fragile and most probably will not withstand much in front of the typically known arrogance of all Israeli leaders."

He also warned of what he predicted was a new reality in which Palestinians returning under the terms of the Oslo agreement would be compelled to live under Israeli occupation for a considerable period of time, if not permanently. The prospect of a Palestinian State could take a much longer time than what we'd imagined.

On the first day inside our house (my father's) in the Rimal neighbourhood, which was in dire need of repairs, my cousin Aoun, came to greet and welcome me back to the city of our ancestors. He insisted on taking me to his home in Shejaiya, the old city, to spend a few days until the repairs of our house were completed. I spent several wonderful days in his hospitality together with his generous wife, Rawya, a committed writer and political activist "who was subsequently elected to the Legislative Council for the first time in 1996 and was re-elected for the second time in 2006."

During my stay there I made some new friends, and met many family members in addition to a few officials of the National Authority, including a congratulatory visit to President Arafat as insisted by Aoun. After the usual hugs with Abu Ammar, I had a strange feeling that this seemingly simple and ordinary person was the same leader of the Palestinian revolution who survived several bloody battles, difficult and critical confrontations in Jordan, Lebanon, Syria and most recently attacks in Tunisia. Now he was sitting behind a desk littered with dozens of files, in front of me in my city in Palestine!

Somehow, I could notice a sparkle in his eyes that would dissipate any anger toward him! I promptly gifted him some books that Alhani had published in London, including *The Renewal of Palestine in the Jewish Imagination*, and the Arabic translation of Princess Diana's biography, *Her True Story*, which I suggested he give to his wife Suha Arafat. But very quickly he pushed the books aside without caring to look at or even read the titles.

He then asked me: "Aoun told me, you are also a civil engineer and a contractor specialising in large projects. What do you have in your pocket for Gaza?"

"Well, under your leadership, we are all willing to do our utmost to build Gaza. There are many infrastructure projects. I can check with Aoun on the most urgent project, then call on my Palestinian and foreign colleagues, consultants and investors abroad to participate. May I report to you next week?"

"I will be waiting for you next Thursday morning."

The return of eligible families continued auspiciously and densely to the West Bank as thousands of Palestinians crossed the Jordanian border through the Allenby Bridge. Many businessmen started forming private companies, while others introduced a new concept of establishing public companies, offering their shares for subscription by the public, an uncommon practice in Palestine under occupation.

Some notable returnees included Munib Masri, who was born in Nablus. Historically, Nablus was one of the most important Palestinian cities for industry and trade, especially known for its soap industry, made from pure Palestinian olive oil. Masri succeeded in attracting a group of investors and formed the first public company "PADICO" with a capital of $200 million. He was followed by Omar Aggad coming from Saudi Arabia with sizable investment in a new company.

The Arab Bank reopened its branches which it had kept closed since 1967, and appointed Shukri Bishara as the director general in Palestine. He is currently the PA's Minister of Finance. Sabih Masri also decided to open his bank, Cairo-Amman in Palestine. Zahi Khouri, who returned from a long journey in Saudi Arabia and Florida, to Jerusalem to restore his family's home, successfully acquired the Coca-Cola agency exclusively for Palestine and established the largest beverage facility for bottling soft drinks. Mohammed Sabaawi, returned from Toronto, and managed to form the first public owned insurance company in Gaza. Mahmoud al-Farra, upon his return from Los Angeles, began planning to build the first wheat mills and storage silos in Khan Yunis.

The manifestation of that period was clearly active as indicated by these returning businessmen and their respective investments. The early years of the fledgling National Authority heralded an actual urban renaissance. In anticipation of a promising commercial, trading, financial, agricultural and industrial economy. This economic renaissance was accompanied by a wide spread of newly established newspapers, and magazines. The Palestine TV channel started broadcasting its somewhat modest transmission for the first time from its office in the homeland. Gaza, being the headquarters of Arafat and the government, also witnessed unique media coverage from the important visits of many world leaders[12].

The presence of permanent representatives of the European Union and Russia and other friendly countries added to the extensive coverage. Diplomatic activities increased when some Arab countries such as Egypt, Jordan, Tunisia, Qatar, Oman and Morocco opened embassies in Gaza. Media offices of international news channels: CNN, BBC and Al-Jazeera were opened, their correspondents and cameramen were clearly visible in the streets of Gaza[13].

Significantly, most of the businessmen overlooked the PA's mistakes and accusations of corruption. They considered them minor details and acceptable at the time due to the lack of administrative experience of their officials, who were returning from their arduous journey of struggle and exile, very far from the homeland.

Most of them sought to achieve their national aspirations regardless of the success of their investments. Despite the hardship and ruggedness of the current road, a period of excitement and optimism prevailed.

A Beginning Shrouded in Mystery

During the second meeting with President Arafat in the presence of my cousin Aoun, I explained that my ambition was mainly to contribute to future infrastructure projects, as my engineering experience was in oil and gas, as well as electricity and water projects. Most work was conducted in Libya. When he heard "Libya" he laughed, seriously frowned and said: "Gaddafi is the biggest international thief! You have lived in Libya? Over $136 million of our money Gaddafi refuses to transfer to us, under the pretext of my approval of the Oslo Accord without informing him in advance".

I said there is also a possibility for a grant to fund the construction of a printing press affiliated to the Authority, which in future can print official permits, passports, ID cards, driving licences and any confidential and secret documents. I noticed he began to listen carefully when the press project was mentioned, and especially the secret documents, he definitely liked that idea. He picked one of the three pens from his front pocket and wrote a few lines on a piece of paper, folded it, and gave it to me to present to the Minister of Housing. He stood up, rang a bell, and Omar entered the office carrying his camera to take a souvenir photo with the President to mark the end of the meeting.

On the way back to the municipality building, Aoun asked me to read Arafat's note. It was addressed to Minister of Housing Zakaria Al-Agha, a doctor from Khan Yunis, who was married to Feryal El-Banna, also a doctor and very close friend to my late sister Wijdan. The note asked him to urgently allocate a suitable plot of land for the establishment of a proposed Government Printing Press. Aoun sent the paper with his driver to Zakaria who was unaware of the nature of the project — namely it being a public printing press. The note was promptly sent back with a comment that read: "Your family owns a lot of land in Gaza and does not need any public land from the nascent authority!"

Suddenly, I realised with amazement that a President's instructions to his ministers were shrouded in vagueness and not carried out promptly or treated with respect.

With sadness and utter denunciation, many owners of farms that were close to the Israeli settlements were unable to reach their farms, which were given a new description "C Area". It was agreed to divide the Palestinian Territories into three areas: A, B, and C. Whereas Area A shall be controlled solely by the Palestinian Authority, Area B was to be jointly monitored, and Area C would remain under the sole authority of the Israeli forces.

This strange, thorny and unfair demarcation applied to Gaza and the West Bank, which meant that over 60% of Palestinian land would be subject to full Israeli control! The PA negotiating team accepted the Israeli terms restricting movement of Palestinians between the Gaza Strip and West Bank. This meant a complete ban on vehicles except for those of Chairman Arafat and forty of his senior officials, who would be granted special VIP cards. Arafat's only response to this precarious situation was an insistence to raise the number of cards to a hundred! Regrettably, at that time, Arafat woefully underestimated the Israeli forces' brutally restrictive and oppressive subjugation of Palestinians that would ensue. Unfortunately, ordinary people were subjected, on all Israeli checkpoints, to systematic and humiliating searches that generally ended with rough treatment. An Israeli General, who was involved in the VIP negotiations said, during the Pugwash Berlin conference:

"We believed that Arafat and other PLO leaders cared about their personal interests, without paying much attention to the needs of their people, a carbon copy of almost all Arab dictators, such an unexpected attitude encouraged the cautious Israeli army generals and the opponents of the Oslo Accord alike, to treat him with extreme contempt and suspicion of his future and hidden intentions."

This distinction was a major factor in creating a new class of citizens, known as the "Privileged Ones". The term VIP became very popular, although ordinary people were using it with envy, without knowing its meaning. "It could be an English password that means safe passage," someone explained. "Or is it intended as a secret sign of a surrendered person?" People soon observed with astonishment that the person who held that card would be treated at checkpoints with respect and even cordiality by most of the soldiers and officers of the Israeli occupation army. They were regrettably described by some of their relatives as "*Very Israeli Persons*." People suspected that their skill mostly lies in their amazing capacity for frivolity and hypocrisy.

The PLO leadership became the first in history whose members carried VIP cards provided to them by their enemy, in order to cross the Israeli checkpoints with safety and respect, while their people were tormented and humiliated at those barriers. Expectedly, Fatah dominated almost all important political and security positions in the Palestinian Authority, as it did in the PLO Executive Committee. They were not prepared for a truly democratic system of government. The ambiguity and confusion stemmed from the large number of security services that were set up by the Authority in agreement with Israel. The conflict of responsibilities between these security institutions was clearly visible, especially between the heads of these services, significantly, all of whom were members of Fatah. In many cases, citizens were unable to realise who was actually in charge of the internal security, as various forces appeared to impose additional taxes informally on merchants to facilitate the transit and entry of their goods to and from the Israeli ports.

Of course, it was a sad and painful beginning, but the situation on the ground seemed more difficult and complicated than our previous and high expectations.

Probation: A Challenging Road Ahead

The prevailing belief was that the Oslo Agreement provided for the establishment of the independent State of Palestine, starting with the well-rehearsed phrase "Gaza-Jericho first", which officially began with the arrival of Yasser Arafat to Gaza and the establishment of the National Authority in July 1994.

Because so few people were aware of a five-year probationary period, inaccurate narratives frequently dominated discussions on the timing of the establishment of the promised Independent Palestinian State. Consequently, the Palestinians had to earnestly prepare for this massive and significant transformation, during that transitional period. Since many businessmen had no desire to participate in any governmental position, they turned their attention to the advancement of the local private sector that was rising from the obstacles of the occupation. The developed countries that practice democracy were keen to preserve the independence of the three fundamental authorities: the legislative, executive and judiciary. Among the most important and basic duties of the executive authority is to protect its citizens, respect the judiciary and implement its rulings.

Most of the local jurists, judges and lawyers praised the integrity and competence of Palestinian judges who worked for many years during Mandate, Egyptian or Jordanian, or even Israeli rule, some ex-judges expressed their fear for the future of a fair and independent judiciary in an era of power led by ex-revolutionaries, who may demand that judges obey their orders, so that their rulings are not implemented fully.

A cycle of repeated disappointments greeted generations of the Nakba. What had happened was not expected, and what was expected never happened. The liberation of Palestine, Arab Nationalism, Arab unity, freedom, justice, and true independence, never materialised. Palestinians were hoping for a national government that would not repeat the experiences of other ruling dictatorial regimes in the region and their poor peoples who were celebrating imaginary victories. Many were absolutely thrilled when they entered a ballot box at their old schools and cast votes in their own constituencies during the 1996 elections of the Legislative Council. There was an overwhelming feeling of excitement for their first experience exercising their electoral right in their own country.

The Legislative Council was chaired by Ahmed Qurei, who was a prominent participant in the secret negotiations of the Oslo Agreement. In line with the traditions of other parliaments, several committees were formed, including economic, legal and foreign. The Foreign Affairs Committee, chaired by my friend Marwan Kanafani, was the most I was engaged with, as the majority of the projects I was involved with enjoyed significant foreign participation and funding, particularly the Palestine Electricity project. Representative Ziad Abu Amr included me as a member in the newly formed Palestinian Council on Foreign Relations, alongside Hanan Ashrawi, Raji Sourani, Samer Khoury and Munib Al-Masri.[14]

The Paris Protocol on Economic relations, written by some Israeli experts and signed by the Palestinian representatives, proved to be a disaster for the poor and tormented people of the Gaza Strip and West Bank. There were numerous examples highlighting the damning effects of this criminal and unjust agreement. One major area was gas prices. Palestinians filling their cars with gasoline would be left in a fit of astonishment and resentment, as they'd find a price of one litre was three times its price in New York! And four times its price in Cairo or Beirut! This was done in the full knowledge that the average per capita income in Gaza was one tenth of that in Israel. Ironically, the poor citizens of Gaza — mostly unemployed — would pay the same price as Israelis, not only for gasoline, but for all other goods and services including electricity, water, food, and cigarettes. This injustice extended to wages wherein a Palestinian worker inside Israel would receive three times the equivalent of a worker in the Palestinian territories, effectively meaning that citizens under the Authority were doing two-thirds unpaid work!

The financial policies defined by the Paris Protocol[15], which subjected the Palestinian Authority to the control of Israel and international donors, stripped it of the necessary legitimacy to communicate with Palestinian society directly and freely. Thus, those agreements forced a sizable majority of the Palestinian people to live completely dependent on the aid provided by foreign donors.

Surprisingly, the Authority officials were not aware of the great calamity that awaited them as a result of their completely uninformed signing of the Protocol. It seemed the agreement wanted Palestinians living under the PA to turn from proud, productive, and self-reliant people — even before the establishment of the Authority — to a people of beggars waiting to receive conditional aid, in a consumer society that depends solely on what Israel allows.

Despite all of these concerns, many returnees had great confidence in the ability of the elected "Parliament" in enacting legislative laws and monitoring the performance of the future governments. I worked hard to strengthen a good and practical relationship with many members of the council, with an absolute belief that it represents the most important institution of the upcoming nascent state.

Optimists of a successful return experience, accepted most of these mistakes whether deliberate or unintentional, and justified finding excuses for every misconduct: that we are in the probationary phase, which is full of potholes and obstacles, but should be preserved to the end.

Ziad, in his position as Minister of Culture, wrote a foreword for a book in Arabic published by Alhani in Gaza on the first anniversary of Edward Said's death, with the title *Edward Said, Courage of Thought and the Authenticity of Belonging.*

> Everything we know now about what happened in Oslo suggests that the Palestinian leadership believed that it easy getting a state, whereas the Israelis in fact were planning exactly the opposite. The question then

is if this situation was made by human beings, and is
not an act of God or a fact of nature, is there any way of
dealing with it that does not perpetuate the injustice?
I think the answer is yes.[16]

Palestinians in the diaspora did not agree with serious criticism
of the Oslo Agreement, which was echoed by many academics at the
time. They decided to return home insisting on hope not fear. They
only read the headlines, but the devil was in the details. Nearly twenty-five years after probation, they would likely agree that the critics
were absolutely right, and their political farsightedness surpassed
many leaders of the Palestinian factions.

Guardians of the Eternal Memory

"If you feel pain, you're alive.
If you feel other people's pain,
you're a human being."
— LEO TOLSTOY

Writing history is both a science and an art. A limited number of historians and academics have the ability to combine the mention of the
incident, and the invocation of its spirit, to the point where it makes
others feel the event itself and live out its details while understanding
and accessing its depths.

Yet, there are many, and sometimes conflicting, accounts of
the history of Palestine, and repeated historical claims that certain
false narratives are true. One of the leading Palestinian scholars,
Professor Nur Masalha, traces Palestine's heritage, uncovering cultures and societies that stretch back to the beginnings of recorded
history. The history of Palestine itself, unlike the myth-narratives
of the Old Testament, has multiple "beginnings", and the idea of
Palestine has evolved over time from these multiple "beginnings"

into a geo-political concept and a distinct territorial polity.[17]

Masalha's explanation about the distinction between Palestine as a country and Palestinian nationality:

> The ancient term Palestine (country, *balad* or *bilad*) and modern Palestinian nationality are not identical or synonymous; the latter has existed for millennia while the former has come into a modern use and was the product of the emergence of modern Palestinian nationalism. [18]

Palestinian Christians constitute an important pillar in the history of Palestine and their active participation in the national movement, as generations of talented Christian patriots have made themselves models of sacrifice and redemption. They are true guardians of our eternal memory.

Intellectuals constitute the conscience of a nation as they preserve its identity, dignity, and national practices. In Palestine, there is a dual mission; they must defend the legitimate rights in international forums and the outside world and also confront mistakes and internal political corruption at home. They have an important national duty in adhering to their vanguard role in facing the concerts and aches of the nation.

History is neither abstract or absolute, and is usually written by the victor. Edward Said expressed the need to write about others, stating:

> The history of memory includes the writing of memory… Who should we study? Should we study heroes, the great events of the past or should we study the people whom history doesn't speak about? … so, we could see ourselves more honestly and clearly.[19]

Local historians attempted to write about events with truthful, primary verbal testimonies, to collate a comprehensive biography combining events that some of us lived through and witnessed. They narrated biographies of individuals who had suffered the inexplicable pain and the experience of exile and alienation, many outside and some inside their own homeland, in which they were deliberately marginal-ised and neglected. Not many of them were lucky enough to document their personal experiences. Collective memory is a powerful weapon in achieving justice. Ideas, like weapons, evolve over time. Will overcomes firepower, which is the ultimate description of resistance.

After the inaudible declaration of the *"All-Palestine Government"* in Gaza in September 1948, a National Council convened at the end of the month and declared the Independence of the state of Palestine, affirming its historical borders to the north: Syria and Lebanon, to the east: Syria and Jordan, to the west: the Mediterranean Sea and to the south: Egypt. It called for the establishment of a free, democratic and sovereign Palestinian State. More than one hundred national figures signed the document, including: Emile Ghouri, Amin Akl, Khalil Sakakini, Rushdi Shawa, Haj Amin Husseini, Michel Icarius, Anwar Nusseibeh, Talaat Ghussein, Ahmed Helmy Abdel Baki—who was appointed prime minister, Musa Sourani and Issa Nakhleh. Arab and later Palestinian leaders unanimously agreed to abolish this conference and completely sideline it from the national memory, as it demanded the declaration of the State of Palestine in 1948, when the armies of Egypt and Jordan still controlled the remaining parts of Palestine: this must be preserved as an important testament to our eternal memory.[20]

Saad al-Hashwa, a Palestinian engineer who splits his time be-tween Abu Dhabi and Canada, is one of the Guardians who collect-ed coins, postcards, stamps and photos of old Palestine. People are amazed at his close emotional and physical connection to the land of his parents and grandparents, who lived in Jaffa for over two cen-turies.

Whenever asked about his bond to Palestine, he would insistently answer:

We have lived in many countries and have travelled and visited hundreds of cities, but Palestine remains in our heart. Jerusalem, Jaffa, Gaza and Bethlehem do not lose sight of our imagination! If you ask us why or how?
The answer is really "We don't know."

Another historian, Hisham Sharabi, tells us:

In Chicago, I learned serious reading, and I understood what Nietzsche meant by saying that reading was *"the art of chewing, which only a cow knew well."* Previously, reading to me had been something I wanted to finish with quickly in order to turn to other, more enjoyable things. The custom of looking at the book instead of reading it and memorizing the lesson instead of understanding it was the simple result of the authoritative method of instruction we had grown up with.[21]

Growing up in families consumed by strife, many Palestinians overcome hurdles in their remarkable journeys into the unknown, enduring a difficult test; but some people always envy others for things that are not worthy of envy, only to escape their own reality that you once shared with them.

Mahmoud al-Ghefari, nicknamed *"We Meet in Jerusalem"*, who had never attended high school, undertook a personal project of collecting scattered pieces of Palestinian narratives of pre-*Nakba* Palestine through live recordings, and documenting many unrecorded historical events. He had a divine gift for preserving national memory, being one of the unknown soldiers. A distinguished guardian of memory.

Most exiles often have conflicting feelings about their newly adopted societies, especially for those who immigrated to far-away lands, their lives were filled with paradoxes and contradictions. Luckily, in a world that is constantly evolving, resilience was the key to the success of many who embraced the opportunities that were available. The world of alienation has its different social, psychological and cultural impact on the lives of immigrants, its images also vary in several places where they are related to the reality of people, their identities and their roots. Diaspora stories are complicated. Alienation is painful. No one feels it except for those who have tasted its bitterness. Yes, it affects their personalities, their thoughts and their life. Humanity has not yet discovered reasonable solutions to the crisis of minorities among peoples. It is a chronic and sustainable problem, many people in our region have inherited it with great persistence. In most countries of the world there are majorities and minorities. The young Caliphate Al-Ma'mun, the son of Haroun al-Rashid, recalls that when he was a young student, his teacher hit him for no reason and every time he asked why he was hit, the teacher replied, "Shut up", and so on. After twenty years he took over the Caliphate, and immediately summoned the teacher and asked him angrily: Why did you hit me when I was a young boy?

The teacher exclaimed: "Have you not forgotten?

The Caliph replied: No, by God, I have not forgotten.

The teacher smiled: "In order to learn that the *oppressed* do not forget" and returned to advise him: "Do not wrong anyone, because injustice is a fire that does not extinguish in the heart of the oppressed, even if many years have passed." [22]

Palestinian historians believe that what the Nazis in Germany did to the Jews is tragically what the Israelis were doing in return to the Palestinian people; as the Jews will never forget, thus we will also never forget.

In late 2005, a Swiss mission led by Marc Haldemann, the Governor of Geneva Museums, and other archaeologists visited Gaza on a mandate to search for Gaza wine pottery vessels. They found nine jars of Gaza wine under the ruins of a demolished Church in Geneva. They also had reliable information that there were other treasures of antiquities from the Crusaders' era on the shores of Gaza. [23]

The old port of Gaza was connected to a large piece of the coast called *Blakhiya*, where most of the ancient Mediterranean civilization have left their traces on its sand.

Nur Masalha explained the history of Gaza wine: Gaza wine was famously known in the Byzantine era as "*Vinum Gazetum*" bottled in the famous Gaza pottery jars. The fame of the great "*Gazza Amphorae*" was mainly due to its location in the Byzantine province "Prima *Palestina*". [24]

Indeed, after a few months of excavation, they found a dozen of those jars, thus creating a special relationship between Geneva and Blakhiya. They enjoyed exploring the mysterious landscapes of Blakhiya beach, discovering how people have been finding solace and well-being amongst its extraordinary scenery for many centuries. They also inspected one of the first monasteries built in Palestine during the Byzantine era, the St. Hilarion in Gaza; its remains were discovered in Tal el-Ojoul. The existing St. Porphyrios Orthodox church was also built in Gaza by the Greek Bishop "Porphyrios" over a thousand years ago.

The Mayor of Geneva visited the site carrying an invitation to President Abbas to visit Geneva and a pledge of Geneva's readiness to contribute to building a modern museum on the Blakhiya site in addition to holding a six-month exhibition in Geneva to show Palestinian archaeological artifacts. Indeed, an exhibition was held of Jawdat al-Khudari's rare antiquities that he has collected from the same site over many years, it was inaugurated by Abu Mazen in April 2007. [25]

During that visit, Geneva agreed to help in building the proposed Gaza Museum at a cost of 30 million dollars to preserve antiquities and historical memory. Another national goal was to recover all the artefacts that had been confiscated and seized by Moshe Dayan, then commander of the Israeli army during the first year of the 1967 occupation. [26]

In addition to these calamities that continue to descend on Gaza, less than two months after the exhibition, the situation was going against the trend, a new path had emerged on the scene, which did not recognise or accept museums or antiquities. Hamas has established its military control, which was followed by a complete Israeli blockade over the entire Gaza Strip, all the dreams of building a museum have gone unheeded, except for the *"eternal memory"* that will be preserved by future generations.

The Phoenix at the Crossroad

The phoenix and the ghoul are among the best-known imaginary characters in the Arab world. The more famous Greek myths that have invaded our ancient history were replaced in recent times by tales of *Abu Zayd Al-Hilali, Kalila wa Dimna* and *Sharazad* with *king Shahryar*, who remained silent about permissible talks every morning for a thousand and one nights. There are periods we experience which are full of variables, moments at crossroads whose trajectory we cannot predict; maybe they lead back to the starting point.

Gaza also has a long experience of war; Nebuchadnezzar, Cambyses, and Alexander the Great were all there; Antigonus and Ptolemy, Judas Maccabee and Alexander Janneus took the toll of its wealth and life. Saladin and his army built the old neighbourhood of Shejaiya. Turks and Mamluks rode over it and Napoleon slept in its castle in 1799.

In the early weeks of the *Nakba*, the remainder of unoccupied cities such as Nablus, Al-Khalil *"Hebron"*, and Gaza received the influx of expelled families. Gaza was the centre of many painful chapters: the withdrawal of British forces that was immediately followed by the entry of the Egyptian army and the huge influx of refugees from the surrounding villages. The atmosphere was fraught with a lot of pain, suffering and anticipation.

Sheikh Mustafa Abdullah, in his Friday sermon, tried to alleviate the horror and enormity of the catastrophe that afflicted Palestine by an analogy that is identical to the *Hijrat* of the Prophet Muhammad, *peace and blessings be upon him,* from Mecca to Medina. "The people of Medina were the *"Ansars"* who greeted him with songs and flowers until God granted him victory in the conquest of Mecca. You, the people of Gaza, Hebron and Nablus are the *Ansars,* may God grant us victory, what happens to us except what God has written for us." [27]

In classical mythology, the phoenix was a unique bird that lived for six centuries in the Arabian desert (or close to Gaza). At the end of its life, after burning itself on a funeral pyre, it would rise from the ashes with renewed youth to live through another cycle. Gaza experienced devastating destruction in the First World War by the invading British forces from the east, led by General Edmund Allenby, and the British fleet with its destroyers and their indiscriminate cannons.

Following each battle, Gaza would rise up again, shake off the dust, and reconstruct its destroyed buildings with a genuine resolve and determination from its residents to preserve the architectural structure and unique social fabric of their glorious city. Gaza has an amazing instinct of determination to survive against continuous adversities.

This imaginary bird resembles in its return to life what the besieged Gazans wish for — fulfilling their eternal dream of freedom and a dignified life. The new Palestinian generation is addressing the chronic national issue in its own developed language. Time will not stop for anyone, the young will grow, the strong will weaken, the oppressed will triumph, and the oppressor will be held accountable in the end. Life and empires all go through times of rises and falls, that is an inevitable end. The phoenix has been adopted as the old emblem of Gaza Municipality. The young Palestinians are the ancestors of their future: a generation that will either be celebrated for its activism or blamed for its apathy. They hope to act as their symbol: the phoenix rising from the ashes. A monumental time in their own growth experience.

Gaza is known as *"Ghazzata Hashim"*- Hashim's Gaza, as it is the burial place of the grandfather of the Prophet, peace be upon him, Hashem ibn Abd Manaf. It is also historically and Islamically famous for being the birthplace of Imam Muhammad al-Shafi'i, one of the four Imams of Islam and Islamic legal school of thought. Gerald Butt once commented that "because of its position as a strategically important town, in a matter of only a few decades, control of Gaza had passed from the hands of the Crusaders to the army of Salah al-Din and his successors, back to the Crusaders, then to Turks, followed by the Mongols and finally to the Egyptian Mamluks. Gaza was destined to be trampled over by succeeding armies." [28]

The most famous historical event that was captured on the hills of Gaza was the intriguing love story of Samson and Delilah. The remains of the temple that was supposedly destroyed by Samson according to Biblical narratives, and a phenomenon that personified by Cecil de Mille in a film directed by him, based on a story written by Ze'ev Jabotinsky, one of the earlier Russian Jewish settlers to Palestine, who became a leader of the extremist Zionist *Irgun* gang. The site of the temple is called "*Abu el-Azm*" meaning father of strength. A few hundred yards north of the temple is Samson' tomb, which remains to this day.

After the February 1955 attack on Gaza, led by Ariel Sharon, massive demonstrations followed in protest against the Israeli attacks This was led by Mnin Bseiso of the Palestine Communist party and the youth of the Islamic Tawheed group, demanding Egypt allow them military training in weapons to be the nucleus of an army to liberate their stolen homeland. These shocking events that took place on 1st of March, forced Gamal Abdel Nasser[29] to visit Gaza, accompanied by Field Marshal Adel Hakim Amer and other high-ranking officers, promising the demonstrators to fully meet their legitimate demands. Maher Othman, a Palestinian writer explains: "Following the attack on Gaza, the British General Staff prepared a report classified as 'Top Secret' in April 1955 to be shared with the Americans who believed the existence of a possible plan by Israel aimed at occupying the Gaza Strip, partially or completely. The British General Staff, on the contrary, believed that Israel's target would be to occupy the West Bank, where it would secure its Eastern geographical and natural borders." [30]

The British military expectations did not materialise, as Israel deliberately delayed its withdrawal from the Gaza strip, refusing to implement Security Council resolutions. Under pressure from President Eisenhower, it withdrew in March 1957. A United Nations peacekeeping force was deployed on the common borders. A state of calm prevailed, which produced an economic and social renaissance for Gazans.

During that unique stable period, Gaza witnessed several exciting visits by many distinguished public figures; being the sole destination that bears the name of Palestine, since the West Bank became part of Jordan in 1950. It is an open duel between the will of life of a people whose enemy is trying to usurp their right to exist by plundering their land and confiscating their present, their future and self-capabilities. Israeli attacks have taken a new direction, a new character, land siege and indiscriminate airstrikes, by rockets and sometimes by cluster bombs. The enemy and its bombs now come from the sky, from the air.

A Life Wrapped in Dreams

"The history of the World is but a biography."
— THOMAS CARLYLE

Palestine before the Nakba was a largely tribal society wherein a families strength and numerical abundance allowed it to play a significant role in the economic and political spheres. In an agricultural society, the nature of land ownership is a central factor influencing not only the economic development of the country but also its social and political formation.

Rashid Khalidi notes that, "socially, Palestine was still heavily rural with a predominantly patriarchal, hierarchical nature, as it largely remained until 1948… the sense of identity of large parts of the population was also evolving and shifting. My grandfather's generation would have identified — and would have been identified — in terms of family, religious affiliation, and city or village origin." [31]

Of course, flaunting one's origin and belonging to these families was an important matter in daily dealings with others. Despite my desire and conviction not to write about personal or family virtues in this book, I find myself compelled to mention some important roles that our family played as an authentic example of the reality faced by other similar Palestinian families during that period. I'm learning to swim in the waters of memory, which is nostalgia for childhood days when we were free to own our minds and dreams.

Despite the large numbers of our family and its social status, my great secular mother was against ostentation. She always warned us not to use such offensive phrases, and repeated that most kings, princes, military leaders, and even her beloved creative artists and singers, including Umm Kalthoum, were peasants and sons or daughters of poor farmers.

She strongly believed that all religions were great, even more so for those individuals who believed in them.

My mother was skilled in creating hope, she mastered the fabric of joy and wished to spread it in all corners. She was a rare breed in her honesty, her delicate sense and her good spirit, turning the earth into a thriving garden. She loved books, music, and jasmine. The scent of jasmine instantly takes me back to my childhood and the picture of my mother picking her favourite flowers from her beautiful garden.

"*The mind grows by reading and thinking*", was her daily lesson to her children. She taught us to question and search for the sources of things, whilst being tolerant. She carefully reminded us that "Tolerant people are the happiest in their hearts, they know the value of life, and therefore do not care about the mistakes of others. Their lives are full of forgiveness."

My father lost his trading business in cars and agricultural equipment when they were stolen from Haifa port, along with his farms after the second armistice in Rhodes between Egypt and Israel. This gave Israel an additional area of more than 200 square kilometres of fertile land east of Gaza city, which unfortunately included his farms.

He used to recite quietly and reverently, almost daily, Surat Ad-Duha *"The Morning Hours"* from the Holy Qur'an. Listening to him, I memorised it by heart as it has become a constant for me as a guide in my dealings with others, especially its divine commands: *"Thus the orphan must not be exploited, never repulse the needy, proclaim the grace of the Lord and tell about his favour, the Lord will give you all good so that you shall be satisfied."*

He strongly believed that life is a journey, not a race. You must go on your journey and have the determination to deal and coexist with what life brings. The years usually change many things, they certainly change the terrain of the highest mountains, they drain lakes and rivers. How can they not change our conditions? Be thankful.

My older brother, Sufian, along with two of his friends, loved historical films. They used to eagerly wait for such movies to arrive at the *Al-Samer* cinema, the only showroom in Gaza, and race to buy their tickets in advance. They became madly in love with the iconic movie *Spartacus*, a film about the attempt to break slavery from the clutches of the Roman Empire starring Kirk Douglas and Tony Curtis. They even used to compete among themselves, to imitate the voices and movements of these two mighty actors.

Their history teacher in high school noticed their unbelievable attachment to their two idols could distract them from studying. He claimed that both actors were Jewish, in the hope of deterring them from following the two actors, but they did not care, as they insisted that religion would never be a barrier preventing them from watching their beloved Jewish American stars.

The first, and only, time that my father took me to a mosque was in the early morning for *Eid Al-Adha* prayers, which was typically followed by a visit to greet the dead. At the cemetery, I discovered that my grandfather died at the age of thirty, his elder brother also died at thirty. My elder sister, Wijdan, sadly died at the age of thirty, and five years later my brother Bassam also died at the age of thirty.

I had a constant struggle with that number and a strong desire to escape from reading it, or even find a way to delete it from my memory. That sick-inducing number always reminded me of an early death, constant sadness, and growing pessimism. My favourite month is February because it never ends with 30. Actually, my relationship with that obnoxious number was not full of hate, but rather a feeling of pain and admonition.

After recovering from my peculiar arithmophobia, my new phobia turned to the colour black! My mother remained dressed in black for nearly three years after the death of my sister. My father wore a black tie as well, where the colour was symbolic of pessimism and sadness. Hundreds of Palestinian mothers mourn in black for many years, mourning the loss of their martyred children or widows, grieving the loss of their husbands who were brutally killed by the occupation forces.

My close friend, William Sayegh, once complained of his mother wearing black all the time. His cousin, May, the poet, used to describe black as a mysterious, rebellious and significantly attractive colour; it reflects the deep secrets of life. In their poems, ancient Arab poets praised and flaunted their black colour, especially when describing the black veil, black eyes and long black hair being the ultimate beauty of their lovers.

My earlier dreams began to revolve around a fascinating character called "*Sinbad*" and his fantastic land travels and his amazing sea voyages. I kept dreaming of becoming a traveller imitating *Ibn Battuta* or an explorer similar to *Marco Polo*.

One of my favourite, and hilarious, dreams that continued for a few weeks on end involved *Abbas ibn Fernas,* the father of aviation, an engineer, and inventor who lived in Qortoba, Andalusia, and was the first man to fly. In my dream I was flying over Jerusalem, but quickly descended landing in front of the Church of the Holy Sepulchre. Each night I would travel to other landmarks like Al-Aqsa Mosque, Dome of the Rock, Mount Abu Ghunaim, and so on. Whenever I revealed the secrets of my dreams to my mother, she would laughingly recite verses of "*Lastu Adri*", *I don't know,* a poem by the Lebanese poet Elia Abu Madi:

> "*Where have my dreams gone?*
> *They used to go wherever I went.*
> *They are all lost.*
> *But how did they get lost?*
> *I don't know.*" [32]

The nightly dreams continued to dominate my thoughts until one day in 1955, I was struck by a pandemic that Gaza had never heard of or faced before. I was thrown to bed, started to lose a lot of weight and became severely emaciated. The family doctors at the time were Haidar Abdel Shafi and his younger brother, Mustafa, who diagnosed my disease as one of the first cases of the Asian flu that suddenly spread in Gaza. They kept me at home isolated, and took turns treating me for 14 days of vaccination with an injection of vitamin B. Fortunately, after two weeks I recovered completely, although sadly, many residents had lost their lives as a result of that deadly epidemic.

Regrettably, that damn flu destroyed my beautiful and cultural nocturnal habit! My mother continually praised the brothers' abilities, "they were brilliant doctors, graduates from America!"

As I grew up, she was persistent in reminding me "*Alhamdulillah,* the two brothers saved your life from certain death, therefore, you must carry their favour forever". I admit that I had an overwhelming feeling of gratitude towards them, always bowing to them respectfully every time we met. [33]

Giving injections for any disease was fashionable treatment for Palestinian families, it was customary for the doctor to give an intramuscular injection and write a prescription for the patient, regardless of whether medicine was needed or injections were required. My mother was happily relieved that I was getting better, and even took extra care of my eating regime with additional special healthy dishes followed by her direct interference in the path of my dreams, calling them "*obedient dreams*" after my latest health malaise. She began demanding I study science in order to become a doctor in recognition of the role of her friends, the two brothers, who had a pivotal role in my survival.

A year after the miraculous recovery from the flu, Gaza fell into the hands of the Israeli forces during the 1956 Suez War on Egypt. Israel kept procrastinating on its withdrawal, until US president Eisenhower demanded all three countries including Israel implement the UN resolution, but eventually agreed to the deployment of a peacekeeping force stationed on its borders with Egypt and Gaza.

The UN force, consisting of armed soldiers from six countries including Sweden, Canada, Brazil and India, arrived in March 1957 under the command of the Canadian General Burns. The logistical and administrative staff were mainly civilians from several countries.[34]

My father's three empty apartments were rented by the UN to house their senior staff. The first for a Yugoslav doctor, Izedin Mavic, and his Egyptian wife, Suad. The second for a Swedish accountant, Borgman and his Dutch wife. The third was the largest and taken by a Greek mechanical engineer Costa, his wife, Zoe, and their young daughter Maria. Thus, our home became a lucky house that brings together residents of five nationalities and multiple languages.

A few years later, influenced by Costa's wife and Maria who became a close friend to my elder sister Wijdan, my interests shifted to Greek mythology after I finished reading the Arabic translation of "*The Legend of Sisyphus*" and his amazing rock that rolls down from the top of the highest mountain in Athens. The Trojan War, where the tales were apparently myths and fiction, but they delved into the depths of man and history to reveal the struggle for survival.

Dr. Mavic told us about the heroic story of a young Yugoslav girl, Lepa Radic, a resistance icon, who was executed at the age of 17 for shooting at German troops and not revealing her comrades' and leaders' identities to the Nazis, after her capture, during their occupation of Yugoslavia in the Second World War. Apparently, Lepa was born in the same village as the doctor, though he was a Bosnian Muslim.

Wijdan, listening attentively to the story of a young girl's determination in fighting the invading forces, broke down in tears
and in the evening, she asked her mother to start calling her Lepa!
Among her focused readings of historical books, she studied the
Russian revolution, and the heroism of Fidel Castro. After meeting
with the revolutionary hero Che Guevara in Gaza, she decided with
resolute determination to join the resistance movements. Following her graduation from Cairo University, she ran a care centre for
Palestinian refugees.

A few months later, fate intervened, where she was subjected to
a tragic accident in a collision with an Egyptian Army truck on the
Cairo-Alexandria Road, she died at the age of thirty. [35]

The American film star Yul Brynner, on his visit to Gaza, was
surprised by the great popular welcome from hundreds of Gaza's
residents. Bassam was among the crowd of fans, hoping to interview
him and quickly file a report to his newspaper in Jerusalem. He only
managed to take a photo. The crowds were excited to meet the hero
of an iconic western movie "*The Magnificent Seven*", which tells the
story of Seven heroes helping and arming the poor residents of a
Mexican village terrorised by bandits.

While discussing his role in the film, Brynner was deeply moved
that Palestinians wanted the other six heroes to join him, hoping to
turn fiction into reality, in order to help them recover their homes
and farms from the occupation forces.

For a strange, painful and distinct coincidence, my younger
brother Bassam, had a similar accident when his car collided with an
Israeli Army truck on the road between Gaza and Jerusalem, he died
at the age of thirty too. Bassam was driving from Gaza to Jerusalem
to meet editors of the Daily newspaper "*Al-Quds*". He worked as its
Gaza correspondent for seven years. His press reports were mainly
on the nature and geography of Palestine:

"Palestine's natural and picturesque advantages added to this holy
place a tremendous material wealth and religious deity. Its people
were famous for their artistry and effective progress in the cultivation

of agricultural produce. Its natural beauty and wealth were coveted by its neighbours and by invaders from faraway countries who aspired to seize those bounties throughout the ages."

In the morning of his tragic accident, he told his bride Fadwa about his dream of the night before, in the form of a poem or a song that calls for liberating Gaza and the homeland:

> "The blessed land of Palestine,
> a crucible of vast variety, the sanctified
> country of eternal peace, anchored in faith
> in the one God who commands justice,
> compassion and benevolence.
> One day the sleeping homeland woke up,
> and saw a bright ray of light, but fell asleep,
> woke up once more, fell asleep again,
> then came a leader with an awakening
> that raised the nation from its long deep sleep,
> a cry like fire, like a stubborn fate
> that ignited the enthusiasm in the hearts of
> the people and resurrected the nation…" [36]

The surviving members of our immediate family deeply hate and mourn *armies*, any *army*.

The Keys in My Pocket!

"Time changes everything. The search for survival."

The dreams of ordinary Palestinians revolve around a return to their liberated homeland. These deeply personal journeys explain the impacts of the *Nakba* and explore the meaning of return and belonging and the challenges of maintaining resilience and hope. This is symbolised by the unique phenomenon of many displaced families keeping the keys to their homes, which they had shut in a panic behind them without even thinking of securing them tightly with heavy locks — such was their absolute belief that they would return within a few days!

Nazih al-Khalil was born in Jaffa, his father enjoyed a prestigious position as the director of customs at the port of Jaffa. Most of the Jewish merchants courted and respected him greatly for the extreme accuracy in his work clearing imported goods without discrimination. The family was enjoying a financially prosperous life, their children were enrolled in English schools and looking forward to a promising future. Suddenly, the father was forced to escape the 1948 catastrophe and expulsion with his family, leaving all the contents of their home, except for his passport; as their evacuation was believed to be for a few days or weeks at most.

They took refuge in Ramallah, then moved to Zababdeh, the birthplace of their parents, in which the majority of its inhabitants were Christians. After Israel was established, he received several messages from Jewish merchants asking him to return to Jaffa and resume his work in the port, but he refused with condescension and defiance: "How can I be content with myself working under people who have usurped my country since I was higher than all of them in status, knowledge and position?"

Life as a refugee was hard, as Nazih used to carry a large jar and walk for two miles to fill it with water from an old well that was over four hundred years old. He would walk the two miles back to their temporary home. A few years later, the father took the family to Amman, where he established a trading company.

Nazih al-Khalil successfully graduated as a civil engineer from Cairo University, which enabled him to become a contractor in Saudi Arabia, working on joint projects with his colleagues Zain Mayasi, Walid al-Qattan, Sabih Masri and Rafik Hariri [37].

His journey continued moving to work and live in California for several years, after which he and his family moved again to London, where he managed to establish a real estate company that owns a hotel and a collection of apartment buildings. Nazih proudly retains his father's passport, which he never used since their escape from Jaffa, and proudly bought the land of the old water well that he used to carry water from during the early days of the Nakba, to preserve its legacy.

Charles Zacharia, an architect born in Jaffa, recalls his cousins, who owned three wheat mills and an ice making factory, located between Jaffa and Tel Aviv. Jewish militias forcibly seized all their properties, including the three mills and their homes, and subsequently displaced Hanna to Gaza and his father to Lebanon at the end of April 1948.

Subhi Alhashwa was a successful businessman in Jaffa, who had great confidence and belief that the Arab armies would easily eliminate the diverse Zionist militias within a few days; with this conviction, he had bought a luxurious car only a few months before he and his family were forcibly expelled by those militias, who stole his new car: a "Chevrolet Fleet Master."

His only consolation was preserving the purchase receipt issued by the dealer in Jerusalem, as proof of ownership that would get his car back after the liberation of his beloved city. His son, Saad kept all his father's photos and papers including that preserved historical receipt. There was an incredibly amazing surprise when his grandson Eissa Alhashwa googled the Motor Number and found the car online! [38]

Roald Dahl once said: "Above all, watch with glittering eyes the whole world around you because the greatest secrets are always hidden in the most unlikely places."

Najati Ayoubi, manager of the Telephones and Telegraph office in Jaffa, which was also called "Post and Telegraph" during the British Mandate. He lived in a house in the upscale Al-Nuzha neighbourhood in Jaffa with his wife Umm Adnan, born in the Syrian city of Hassakeh to Kurdish parents, and their five children.

During this time, Jaffa was considered the artistic and cultural capital of Palestine, housing famous musical bands, theatres, cinemas, newspaper and magazine publications, and book printers.

Umm Adnan was a skilled *oud* player, a devoted fan of the famous singer Asmahan; she memorized all her songs, while her younger son Muhammad harmonised with her melodies as she played her oud, with songs by Farid al-Atrash, the younger brother of Asmahan, whose father was a Druze Prince in Syria.

The Ayoubi family, like many others in Jaffa, lived in a cheerful atmosphere, reassuringly full of music and rapture. Their house was full of singing nights, sometimes with the participation of young local musicians and singers. The artists' visits were also interspersed with the National Anthem, that was written by the Nabulsi poet Ibrahim Touqan, who was also the director of the Al-Quds Radio station:

> "*Mawtini .. Mawtini..*" My Home.. My Home..
> "*Oh my home, Oh my home,*
> *Glory and beauty, grace and majesty*
> *Are in your hills, in your hills.*
> *Life and relief, felicity and belief*
> *Are in your love, in your love.*" [39]

On a Friday afternoon, Umm Adnan was excited to be invited by one of her Syrian friends to meet Asmahan at the King David Hotel in Jerusalem. Umm Adnan played and sang some of her songs with inspiration and merit, a performance that impressed Asmahan greatly to the extent that she gifted her *oud* to Umm Adnan in a kind gesture.

That special oud was made in Aleppo, the old capital of music and rapture in Syria, masterly encrusted with pure and distinctive mother-of-pearl.

Remarkably, Asmahan gave that gift as if she knew she would not return to Jerusalem. Indeed, she died by drowning in her car in a Nile canal the following week in mysterious circumstances on her way back to Cairo. [40]

Despite her deep sadness over the death of Asmahan, which lasted for several years, Umm Adnan carefully preserved the oud.

With the intensification of clashes and daily attacks on Arab homes by the Zionist forces, it became clear that there was a secret plot by the British forces' commander to hand over the city, including public buildings, police stations, and the telephone exchange building to the Jewish militias.

In the meantime, Najati realized the impossibility of staying in Jaffa under future Jewish rule, but he wasn't sure whether the Palestinian population would be expelled by force or, at most, that Palestine would ultimately be divided according to the United Nations' partition resolution of 1947.

There were rumours that Gaza City was the safest place in Palestine, due to the fact there were no Jewish settlements or kibbutzim there, in addition to the presence of some organised resistance in the Southern District that also included the city of Bir as Saba' "Beersheba".

When the sounds of bombs and gunshots approached the nearby Al-Ajami neighbourhood, he rushed back to his house, carried some papers and his passport, instructed his wife and children to carry some light clothes and to lock the outside door as he muttered to his wife: we'll be back in a few days, until the military situation becomes clear, keep the keys.

They all set out for the port of Jaffa, hoping to board a ship heading to Gaza. It was a sudden and hasty act, without planning as he would have liked. The ship did not stop at Gaza, but kept sailing to the Beirut port that housed the Karantina "Quarantine" which kept all arrivals for a period of three days. The Ayoubis were transferred by bus to a small village in Southern Lebanon called *Mieh wa Mieh.*

On the way south, Umm Adnan thought they were returning to Jaffa and kept shouting "the keys in my pocket".[41]

Years later, the young Mohammed was fortunate to get a scholarship to study at the American University of Beirut, from which he graduated with a degree in political science.

Ramzi Kayed and Fuad Abu Gheida are two friends living in London, both were born in Haifa, where their parents were partners in two companies that built roads and housing units. Their last shared project was a luxurious apartment building on the famous Abbas Street in the centre of Haifa, for their own families' residence.

The occupation of Haifa was early and preceded other cities to seize its strategic sea port. Both families were expelled among thousands of other Palestinian home owners. Kayed was famous road contractor in the Galilee regions, his road construction equipment included heavy trucks, that he used his own car to escape the intensifying attacks from the Zionist militias that approached their homes without any protection form the British Mandate forces stationed in Haifa.

At first, both partners took refuge in Lebanon, and a few months later Abu Gheida moved to Damascus taking the main keys to their building, while the Kayed family moved to Beirut, preserving their ownership papers "*Koshan-Tabu*".

Fortunately, after a short period of time, the two partners were able to travel to Jeddah in Saudi Arabia and continued their work in the field of contracting and buildings.

Years passed, Fuad became an outstanding footballer in the famous Egyptian club "Al Ahly", and eventual commentator on sports for several Arab TV channels, he had a huge following. One of his followers was a lawyer from the 1948 Palestinians who contacted Fuad and invited him to visit his old house in Haifa. Apparently, the lawyer managed to buy the building after the death of the Israeli family that was housed in it some sixty years earlier. Indeed, Fuad and his wife were given a great reception from the neighbourhood residents.

Surprisingly, the lawyer presented a key to one apartment for Fuad to live in for life.

Raeda Taha, born in Jerusalem and raised in Beirut, a well-known playwright, wrote a book about her father, the martyr Ali Taha who was killed by the Israelis in 1972 during a hijacking operation; he was 34 years old. Raeda wrote and performed a one-woman play that was staged in Beirut about the legendary building on 36 Abbas Street in Haifa, based on the story of Fuad Abu Gheida's trip to his old parents' home.

She also told the story of how her aunt, Suhaila, kept lobbying for the release of her brother's body that was kept in an Israeli morgue for two years and finally managed to meet Henry Kissinger in 1974 in his hotel during his visit to Jerusalem who promised her to make the Israelis agree to her demand.

They did.

Raeda believed in collective work being the spirit of theatre arts.

Lebanon, like Palestine, was blessed with a moderate and beautiful climate, and in the 1950s enjoyed an economic and social renaissance. Beirut was a focal point for Arab culture, arts, paintings, songs, and theatres.

In this environment, Ramzi Kaed's father, like many Palestinian businessmen, professionals and artists began to feel that they were embarking on a new phase of their life, and quickly realized that there are increasing opportunities for profitable businesses waiting for them in the future.

Years later, sadly many Palestinian exiles noticed strange social interactions which began to unfold in Lebanon and the unthinkable behaviours started surfacing, where people started to deal with each other on a sectarian basis, Maronite, Orthodox, Druze, Sunnis, Shiites, etc.. Such terms were unheard of and definitely unpalatable in Palestine, as their social fabrics did not differentiate between people on the basis of their religious beliefs. Palestinian families didn't care much about the religion of their neighbours or friends.

The children were strictly and justly raised to love others without knowing their religion.

As for Ramzi Kayed, he followed his father's dream to carry on working in the housing sector as he developed apartments and still keeps the "*Koshan-Tabu*" papers.

CHAPTER 2

America & World Disorder

"If a law is unjust, a man is
not only right to disobey it,
he is obligated to do so."

— THOMAS JEFFERSON

"America Meen"? America Who?

There are events that may seem trivial or happen by chance, but their importance lies in the decisive and unexpected changes they make. The ancient history of Palestine, spanning thousands of years, witnessed many significant events that had a lasting impact on mankind's historical, social and religious transformations.

Palestine was the scene of distinct historical events and an advanced site of the making of our history; the birth of Jesus Christ in Bethlehem for example - this small spot that became known as the Holy Land. A beautiful, calm, dreamy oasis surrounded by barren deserts, which ignited the ambitions of its poor neighbours who drooled over it to seize and acquire some of its many bounties, and also to live on its picturesque plains, its moderate climate, which God endowed with three seas, lakes, rivers, forests and fruitful trees, all of which contributed to the multiplication of its natural wealth.

The year 1492 witnessed two significant events that changed the course of modern history as we know it today. The first happened purely by chance when the Italian explorer, Christopher Columbus, set foot on a newly discovered continent far away from the ancient world, it was later known as America. Upon returning to Spain the following year, Columbus brought presents to Ferdinand and Isabella including some plants that were unknown to the Europeans; most importantly, the tobacco plant, the turkey bird, and the pineapple fruit.

Columbus never admitted his discovery of the New World came by accident, as he thought that he reached the East Indies. Thus, his description of the inhabitants of the lands that he visited as "Indios", Spanish for Indians. A group that would later be portrayed in Hollywood western movies as the red Indians or American Indians.

Five years later, another great Portuguese navigator, Vasco da Gama, discovered the sea route, via the Cape of Good Hope, to India, using giant commercial and war ships they had won from the Muslim Arabs after the fall of Granada. The result of that discovery was a complete interruption of historical land trade routes passing through Egypt, Palestine and Syria, which led to a sharp decline in their income.

Almost seven centuries prior to Columbus' voyage, the city of Baghdad rose to prominence as the greatest centre of learning in the known world, welcoming all religions, philosophies, and sciences to its universities and libraries. For five hundred years, the outpouring of scientific innovation that flowed from the city was like nothing the world had ever seen, and its influence is still felt today in modern culture. As the author, Dan Brown put it, "To this day, more than two-thirds of the stars in the sky have names from [the] Arabic language because they were discovered by astronomers in the Arab world." [1]

The second significant event was the official surrender of Granada, and with it the end of the Arab-Muslim rule over the Iberian Peninsula that had lasted for more than seven centuries (711-1492 CE). The victory over the Arabs led to a rapid and comprehensive renaissance by Spain and Portugal, especially what they inherited from the Arabs, the art and mastery in the manufacturing of ships, which enabled their fleets to cross the oceans and occupy huge lands of the new Continents, almost completely in the south and partially in the north. They were able to exploit the natural wealth and minerals of gold and silver, which enhanced their status as a new world force.. Their languages spread to become the vernacular of the indigenous people to this day.

In the year 1517, exactly twenty-five years after those significant events, that is, the discovery of America and the Arab surrender in Granada, the Ottoman armies attacked and easily occupied the Levant and Palestine. Within a few years, the Ottomans were able to extend their control over all Arab lands, including Egypt, Iraq and the Maghreb countries, in addition to large parts of Eastern Europe.

The ordinary Arab citizen became accustomed to seeing Turkish soldiers, obeying their orders, accepting life under the command of the current invaders, and coping with this strange new reality. The gradual collapse of the Ottoman Empire that began in the mid-nineteenth century, was interspersed with Napoleon's short-lived campaign against the Levant in 1799, which ended in failure and defeat on the walls of the besieged city of Acre. The Ottomans' decline resulted in the fall of huge parts of the Arab world into the hands of a new European colonialism spearheaded by Great Britain, France and to a lesser extent by Spain and Italy.

Before the advent of the *Nakba,* and the announcement of the establishment of the state of Israel that was followed by an immediate American recognition, there was no clear image of America in the eyes of the vast majority of Arabs and Palestinians in particular. There was no visible or audible presence of that giant state, far away from the ancient world, of which Palestine, the Holy Land, was an integral part.

The absence of any visible — American "invaders"— presence in Palestine was a negative factor in establishing a relationship with that distant country, unlike the rest of the neighbouring "European Invaders". There was no American presence whatsoever in Palestine;

for example, there was no American university in Jerusalem, nor any recognised investment in education similar to the American university in Beirut and the American University in Cairo, nor an American hospital in Jaffa or even an American "Evangelical" church in Bethlehem, the cradle of Jesus Christ and Christianity.

Views differ in defining the United States of America, the superpower that controls many aspects of the lives of millions or perhaps billions around the world. Who is that modern and mighty empire? And how did it achieve its prestigious position in modern history? A few nations express their gratitude and admiration for the help and prosperity it offered them. Many European countries are allied with it militarily and economically, and appreciate its vital contribution in saving them from the clutches of the Nazis. Other smaller powers look at it with envy and rage for their inability to keep up with America in several strategic areas. Many others look at it with the inherent hostility and hatred for the tragedies and devastation it brought upon them.

Of course, no one can deny its beneficial contributions to the world at large, with significant inventions that have altered the ways of our daily life. The discovery of electricity, the invention of the telephone, aeroplanes and aviation, medicine, development of oil and gas production, cars and ships. American film producers succeeded in their access to the eyes and minds of the world's youth through the cinema and television, which they developed and controlled through their global monopoly. They also overcame the elimination of several European industries, including food and beverages' brands. French and Italian style clothing almost disappeared and was successfully replaced by American jeans.

Among its diabolical actions, which include the dropping of nuclear bombs on Hiroshima and Nagasaki, which contributed to the surrender of Japan, the United States has entered more wars nearly non-stop since the end of the second world war. More recently is the war of revenge that was waged against Afghanistan in what was claimed to be a state-based retaliation for the 9/11 attacks.

The most ugly and intransigent war was on Iraq, based on flimsy claims of the existence of weapons of mass destruction. These were accompanied by the heinous crimes of their soldiers, especially in Abu Ghraib prison. There are American forces in North East Syria with a declared purpose of protecting the Syrian Kurds and fighting ISIL, others believe their presence is to control the Syrian oil and gas fields there.

As for the timing and location of the next war, it has not yet been announced, and one can surmise it is being planned in the Pentagon; history has documented the CIA plot to kill Allende in Chile, the Bay of Pigs invasion to topple Fidel Castro in Cuba, the capture of Che Guevara, and the cold war years with the Soviet Union.

The image of the American cowboy that stuck in my memory and others, was the cowboy character in the John Wayne and Clint Eastwood films.

Like many Palestinians, I had never met an American in my entire life until the night of November 22, 1963, when I was quickly climbing the stairs of my friend, Basil Dajani's building in North London, and was frightened and shocked when a young woman came rolling down the stairs, screaming with anguish: "They killed him... They killed him, yes they killed him... Yes they killed our president... John F. Kennedy is dead."

I had not heard the news of the assassination that evening on the radio, but I sat anxious and shocked next to her on the stairs and tried to comfort her and calm her down and even wiped her tears. An hour later, Basil told me that she was an American student in her final year at the university of London, studying philosophy. That was my first meeting in a sad and poignant situation. Kennedy's assassination, and the student's crying, came to mark a moving and sad event in my life which made me somewhat follow the political news of America, despite my deep and strong hatred for their heinous crime of dropping the nuclear bomb on Hiroshima. A month later, I met a new student, who joined us to live in the same building. His name was Khaled Al-Ghussein, an accomplished guitarist and admirer of the works of the Persian poet Omar Khayyam, everyone called him "Abu Khayyam", he was born in Ramleh. One day, while I was following up on Jacqueline Kennedy's news, Khaled told me casually that his older brother, Talaat, was Kuwait's ambassador to the USA; he had a picture of his brother with Kennedy at the White House. It was a pleasant but an unexpected surprise to see a Palestinian sitting in front of John F. Kennedy and his rocking chair!

I was impressed by Kennedy's address in which he showed leadership, with his famous, albeit somewhat borrowed phrase from the Lebanese Christian poet, Khalil Gibran, stating: "Ask not what your country can do for you, ask what you can do for your country... We shall pay any price, bear any burden, meet any hardship, support any friend, oppose any foe to assure the survival of liberty."[2]

After a few years, those unexpected circumstances would come to mark the beginning of my working life in Libya for a Palestinian company that carried out major projects for two giant American oil companies: ExxonMobil and Occidental Oil. Throughout my work with these oil giants, I developed long-standing and distinguished friendships with a number of American engineers and oil experts. Occidental had just completed a large water contract in the desert oasis of Kufra, impeccably managed with the incredible negotiating skills of its owner, Armand Hammer[3]; it was surprisingly awarded a large concession to explore for oil. He hired another American company, Bechtel, to build the field facilities, a pipeline and an oil terminal on the Mediterranean coast.

The workforce included dozens of technicians, operators, accountants, administrative staff and engineers, many of them were Palestinian refugees. Each had detailed accounts of the forced displacement of their families from their towns to the refugee camps in neighbouring countries, mainly Lebanon, as locals used to call all expats "Lebanese".[4]

I felt that I was living in these cities and villages of my occupied country which I had never visited before, through the tales of these employees: Joseph Hayek of Jaffa, Ali Harb of Haifa, Anwar Hassouna of Lud, Azam Nimr of Nablus and Hisham Alami of Jerusalem.

Joseph Hayek, born in Jaffa and a graduate of AUB, was the chief engineer in charge of five oil field working sites. The relationship between us strengthened as he was cultured, cheerful and much admired for his vast experience and smooth dealings with clients and workers alike.[5]

On one occasion, I had a special short meeting with the president and founder of Occidental Armand Hammer, when he knew that I was a Palestinian from Gaza. He asked me about the future of Gamal Abdel Nasser and the prospects of peace between the Palestinians and the Israelis.

Libya was part of Greater Maghreb, where I learned from Floyd Cullop - an American engineer who had great interest in history - that when America declared its independence from Britain on July 4, 1776, Morocco was the first Arab country, or probably the first in the world, to recognize the newly independent United States, and allowed American ships to use its ports by decree of Sultan Mohammed III in 1777 (believed to be the great-great grandfather of the present King Mohammed VI). Morocco then signed a peace and friendship treaty that is considered to be the longest unbroken relationship in U.S. history.

President Harry Truman, who was believed by some to have opposed the creation of a Jewish state in Palestine that might expel its original inhabitants, Christians, and Muslims, was, surprisingly, the first American President to recognize the state of Israel.

There is a saying often repeated by leftist Arab writers and supporters of the resistance movements, whenever an anti-American revolution triumphs in the Arab region in particular, and the world in general: "If your cover is American, then you sleep naked." *[Inta Erian iza metghatti be Al-Amrican]* meaning, never count on American protection.

This is echoed in a satirical song, entitled *"Amreeka Meen"*, by the popular Lebanese singer Ziad Rahbani , the son of the icon of Arab singing, Fairouz:

"Amreeka Meen? [America, Who?]
The chorus replies: *Shayteen.[Demons]*
Amreeka Wayn? [America, Where?]
The chorus replies: *With "John Wayne."*

The song resonates with most Arab youth rejecting American involvement in Iraq, Syria, and its blind bias towards Israel. Rahbani wonders about the extent of America's adherence to its Arab or foreign allies, and how it leaves them easy and palatable prey to their enemies without protection:

"Look at Vietnam, Taiwan, the Shah of Iran, Mubarak of Egypt, Lebanon and Afghanistan. There are more inevitable defeats in the future. The Gulf States should be wary of what happened to America's former allies in the region." [6]

Abu Abed, an elderly refugee in the Jenin camp, was told that two American policemen would be coming to carry out an inspection as part of a training program (known as the Dayton Mission); this pertained to Gen. Keith Dayton, who was in charge of overseeing the training of Palestinian forces as part of an agreement for security coordination between the Palestinian security police and the Israeli army.

Abu Abed asked with amazement: "Do they come on horseback? Are they all cowboys? Wearing their big hats? I haven't been to a cinema or seen a movie for fifty years since the occupation of 1967."[7]

Balfour, Churchill, and the Mandate

"The whole history of the world is summed up
in the fact that when nations are strong they
are Not always Just, and when they wish to
be Just, they are often no longer strong."
— WINSTON CHURCHILL

The dreaded Sykes-Picot agreement had plunged the Arab nations into a deep disorienting period, and transformed their story into a fiction, despite it becoming a de facto reality in which they lived alone in a forest full of falsehood and deceit. As noted by the British historian, James Barr:

> In the secret Sykes-Picot agreement they split the Ottomans' Middle Eastern empire between them by a diagonal line in the sand that ran from the Mediterranean Sea coast to the mountains of the Persian frontier. Territory north of this arbitrary line would go to France, most of the land south of it would go to Britain, for the two powers could not agree over the future of Palestine. The compromise, which neither power liked, was that the Holy Land should have an international administration.[8]

A Turkish diplomat discussing the subject of Jewish immigration to Palestine during Ottoman rule in the late 19th century, strongly confirmed that Sultan Abdulhamid strenuously rejected offers to allow the purchase of land in Palestine by Jewish immigrants in return for a very generous financial sum that was urgently needed to fill the Ottoman Caliphate's empty treasury.

The Zionist movement began emerging in Europe through its leading figures, mainly Theodor Herzl, a Hungarian Jew living and working in France. He took up the 'right to return' argument, writing:

> Shall we choose Palestine or Argentine? - Argentine
> is one of the most fertile countries in the world, it
> extends over a vast area, has a sparse population and a
> mild climate. It would derive considerable profit from
> the cession of a portion of its territory to us. Palestine
> is our ever-memorable historic home - If His Majesty
> the Sultan were to give us Palestine, we could in return
> undertake to regulate the whole finances of Turkey. [9]

Historically, there was never even a remote equivalence in the struggle between the Palestinian National movement with its very limited resources on the one hand, and the vastly well-armed, supported and organised Zionist militias on the other. In fact, the Palestinians fiercely resisted but sadly were unable to meet their expectations and form a strong and effective rival against the Western-backed Zionist led movement, with its extremist religious ideology, at the beginning of the conflict.

A few months prior to the outbreak of the First World War, the Ottoman army launched a call for arms that was known by the Turkish phrase "*Safar Barlek*", which translated to Arabic means a 'Forceful Conscription'.

The call to arms was targeted at men between the ages of 15 to 35 from the remaining nations under the shrinking Ottoman Empire; Egypt, Petsomnia, Palestine, Arabia and Syria.

Palestinian peasants working in orange groves, hid their grown-up sons in ditches next to water wells and graves in cemeteries in order to escape their *Safar Barlek's* arrest by the Turkish soldiers. The lucky families were able to flee to Arabia and join Sharif Hussein's forces in their revolt against the Turks that was led by T. E. Lawrence, generally known as *Lawrence of Arabia'*. Tens of thousands were forcefully recruited to fight in a war in which they didn't know their enemy. None of them came back home. [10]

Gerald Butt, a former BBC correspondent and author, described the First World War as a scene of sad desolation:

> In the early weeks of 1917 only a handful of people knew about the existence of the Sykes-Picot accord. Sir Archibald Murray and his advisers were working out how they might dislodge the Turks from Gaza and cities to the North. As the Allies advanced northwards they set down a railway track and a pipe to bring water from Egypt.

The Right Reverend Rennie MacInnes, the Anglican Bishop of Jerusalem from 1914 to 1931, commented wryly that, "when our armies, with the magnificent assistance of the Egyptian Labour Corps, began to make a railway, they called it the '*Milk and Honey Railway*'."

The pipe alongside the track eventually brought water from the River Nile, when the railway was extended, all the way to Gaza. Bishop MacInnes recalled that there was: "an old tradition in South Palestine that the Turks would hold to the country '*till the waters of the Nile flow into Palestine*' — i.e. an almost impossible contingency." [11]

The entry of British forces, led by General Allenby, into Gaza from Egypt during the First World War, initially incurring heavy losses due to the fierce resistance they met, led to their victory and the beginning of a new chapter that inflicted a decisive defeat of the Ottomans and their German allies.

The Gaza cemetery for over 5,000 British soldiers who had been killed in the three battles that had taken place in 1917 bears witness to these losses. At the entrance, there is a large marble sign that reads: "*The land where the Allied soldiers have been laid is a gift from the people of Palestine.*"

Lord Balfour, the British Foreign Secretary, in his letter on the second of November 1917 to Lord Rothschild, stressed that nothing should prejudice the rights of the Palestinians:

His Majesty's government views with favour the establishment in Palestine of a national home for the Jewish
people... It is understood that nothing shall be done
which may prejudice the civil and religious rights of
existing non-Jewish communities in Palestine.

Sir Edwin Montagu, the sole Jewish member of the British cabinet, opposed the Balfour Declaration. He denounced, "the mischie-
vous political creed of Zionism" and asserted that "there is not a
Jewish nation". He believed Zionism "forces a nationality upon people
who have nothing in common" apart from a shared religion and that
this meant Jewish supremacy in Palestine rather than "equality with
the inhabitants of that country who profess other religious beliefs." [12]

In response to his objections, a paragraph was added to alleviate
the concerns of European Jews of being sent to their new and only
'homeland': "*Or the rights of and political status enjoyed by Jews in any
other country*," Bernard Regan wrote:

During the mandate period the laws which had been
introduced under Ottoman rule were augmented by
the imposition by the British of further legal con-
straints. The high commissioner introduced a series of
measures which had an especial effect on land ownership... that facilitated the sale of lands which aided the
purchases by the Zionists... and prevented Palestinian
farmers from extending their lands.

A congruent biblical narrative linking a Jewish identity,
as articulated by political Zionism, with an imperialist
perspective imbued with a Christian millenarianism,
was invoked to legitimise the denial of the rights of
the Palestinian people. This narrative was intertwined
with ideas promoted by secular ideologues arguing

that *res nullius* applied, permitting the occupation of notionally ownerless property by whoever asserted that claim. "*A land without people for a people without land*" has its roots in the philosophy of the classical liberalism of John Locke. [13]

In his article 'Zionism vs Bolshevism,' Winston Churchill advocated Zionism for imperial interests, as a bulwark against a rising socialist threat, stating:

> Some people like Jews and some do not; but no thoughtful man can doubt the fact that they are beyond all questions the most formidable and most remarkable race which has ever appeared in the world. Disraeli, the Jew Prime Minister of England, and Leader of the Conservative Party, who was always true to his race and proud of his origin, said on a well-known occasion: "The Lord deals with the nations as the nations deal with the Jews." The conflict between good and evil which proceeds unceasingly in the breast of man nowhere reaches such an intensity as in the Jewish race. The dual nature of mankind is nowhere more strongly or more terribly exemplified.

> … First there are the Jews who, dwelling in every country throughout the world, identify themselves with that country… Regard themselves as citizens in the fullest sense of the State which has received them.

> …There is no need to exaggerate the part played in the creation of Bolshevism by these International and for the most part atheistic Jews. With the exception of Lenin, the majority of the leading figures are Jews.

It has fallen to the British Government, as the result of the conquest of Palestine, to have the opportunity and the responsibility of securing for the Jewish race all over the world a home and a centre of national life. Of course Palestine is far too small to accommodate more than a fraction of the Jewish race, nor do the majority of national Jews wish to go there. But if, as may well happen, there should be created by the banks of the Jordan a Jewish State under the protection of British Crown, which might comprise three to four millions of Jews, an event would have occurred in the history of the world, which would be beneficial and in harmony with the truest interests of the British Empire. [14]

That was the British road to disaster, as Gerald Butt explains:

The root of the problem facing Britain, though, was the fact that the Balfour Declaration also promised that nothing would be done which may prejudice the civil and religious rights of existing non-Jewish communities in Palestine. In other words, the British had made two self-contradictory promises. From the first day of British Mandatory rule Hebrew was declared to be one of the three official languages along with Arabic and English. The whole period is overshadowed by the unsuccessful attempts by the authorities in Jerusalem to reconcile the two irreconcilable promises made to the Arabs and the Jews.[15]

Albert Einstein in response to the Deir Yassin massacre commented that: "A most disturbing political phenomena is the emergence in Israel of the "Freedom Party", closely akin in its organization, methods, political philosophy to the Nazi and Fascist parties...led by Menachem Begin. A shocking example of their behaviour in the village of Deir Yassin, terrorist bands attacked this peaceful village, killed most of its inhabitants (240 men, women, and children) and kept a few of them alive to parade them as captives through the streets of Jerusalem." "When a real and final catastrophe should befall on us in Palestine the first responsible for it would be the British and the second the Terrorist organisations build from our own ranks. I am not willing to see anybody associated with those misled and criminal people."[16]

On 16th September 1948, the UN's Swedish mediator for Palestine, Count Folke Bernadotte declared that "No settlement can be just and complete if recognition is not accorded to the right of an Arab refugee to return to the home from which he has been dislodged…" Sadly, the following day he was assassinated by an organization led by Yitzhak Shamir, who reputedly played a role in planning the assassination: however, he was not tried and years later was elected as Israel's Prime Minister.[17]

By 2017, the centenary of the Balfour Declaration, much of the world 'viewed with favour' the establishment of an independent state for the Palestinian people alongside a secure and recognized Israel. Yet the prospect of an equitable two-state solution being agreed voluntarily by both sides was extremely dim. The impasse remained. [18]

The New World Disorder

A person's life is measured by the extent of their ability to explore their freedom and to the extent to which they are able to enjoy and be creative in their life.

Freedom is the most gracious gift that God has given to us.

Between the years of the *Nakba* and the *Naksa* [Setback], and despite the armistice agreements, Israeli attacks on Arab lands have not stopped or abated, causing destruction and great loss of life.

It is also strange when considering that the victims, out of the intensity of their anger, demonstrate in protest against these horrendous attacks; and while they were never met by any military response, in an odd and suspicious way they were usually confronted by security forces that violently and forcefully suppress the innocent demonstrators. We need now to rethink courageously and objectively some of our assumptions and ideas, even if we must take a bumpy road.

I met for the first time with then British Foreign Secretary, Douglas Hurd, a writer and intellectual, accompanied by the Saudi ambassador Ghazi Algosaibi, a well-known poet and intellectual. Secretary Hurd at the time was president of the European Union Council of Ministers, and when he learned that I was a Palestinian who owned an Arabic publishing house in London, he smiled and whispered: "Would you be able to publish one of my books in Arabic?"

Indeed, Al-Hani Books published two of his books. The first, *The Last Day of Summer,* (in Arabic) tells of his personal experience helping to end the Balkan war between the Serbs, Croats, and Bosnians. The novel had protagonists: a Bosnian Muslim, a Croat, and Serbian neighbours. With the intensification of the battles and the killings, the Serb shouts to the Bosnian, *"If you don't like to live in our country, you can go to Mecca!"*

Some readers considered that sentence racist. Serbian forces committed violent war crimes by killing tens of thousands of innocent Bosnian Muslims of Srebrenica.

And the second book, *A Suitcase between Friends*, rejected the idea of the New World Order:

> We have gone to war to prevent aggression against a country attacked from the outside; in 1914, when Kaiser invaded Belgium; in 1939, when Hitler invaded Poland; and in 1991, after Saddam Hussein invaded Kuwait. In each case, our obligations were less than to a formal ally but we acted to maintain collective security.
>
> …it is impossible to guarantee order everywhere. That is why talk of a New World Order was not helpful.[19]

As for the Ambassador, he published a new poetry book that included a poem entitled, *The Tale of the Colt of the Winds,* which took up the story of one of the young Palestinians of the first intifada, the *'Children of the Stones'*.[20]

To illustrate the significance of his active involvement in the Palestine problem after the Madrid talks in 1991, and being the President of the European Council of Ministers for the next 6 months, he called for the acknowledgement of Palestinians' right to self-government and recognizing the role of the PLO in future peace negotiations.

Tony Benn, a Labour MP for 51 years, and a staunch supporter of the Palestinian right of return, complained about world disorder: "An educated, healthy and confident nation is harder to govern. There's an element of people's thinking that we don't want people to be educated, healthy and confident because they will get out of control. The top 1% of the world's population owns 80% of the world's wealth. It's incredible, people put up with it, but the majority are poor, demoralized and frightened, and the safest thing to do is to take orders and hope for the best." Benn also said: "There are two flames burning in the human heart… The flame of anger against injustice, and the flame of hope you can build a better world." [21]

The Palestinian scholar, Ali Issa Othman, discussing the role of Islam in the World Order; *We have not sent thee O Muhammad. Except to mankind entire.* Qur'an (34:28)

Each of us is given the will to become in the course of our vocation in this life either "one of the grateful" *Shakir* (the Islam of the human being chosen individually, consciously, knowingly and willingly) or "one of the ungrateful" *Kafir.* Each of us comes with the same attributes, and it is the proper development of these attributes that is the primary objective of Religion. *"He has laid down for you as Religion that He charged Noah with, and that We have revealed to thee, and that We charged Abraham with, Moses and Jesus."*[22]

Layla Moran, the UK's first MP of Palestinian origin (Liberal Democrats) submitted a bill calling for the recognition of a Palestinian state. "Given the UK's role in the Balfour declaration, it is vital that Britain would go some way to reigniting the spark of hope that has gone out in the hearts of Palestinians across the world. There is no table to go back to." [23]

This assumed that the Palestinians could one day obtain a public apology from the British government for the Balfour Declaration with an official recognition of Palestine as a State. Balfour was a promise and declaration that the Palestinians were not a party to.

Tony Blair further elaborated about the Palestinian Dilemma:

> I believe the creation of a state of Palestine is both desirable and feasible. Most commentators now greet the idea with a hollow laugh. Many Israelis and Palestinians have given up on it. I haven't, because of my conviction-perhaps irrational — that reason ultimately prevails. The Israelis should not want to govern Palestinians in perpetuity. The Palestinians need freedom from occupation and the dignity of statehood.[24]

The assassination of British Labour MP Jo Cox — who was a member of Labour's Friends of Palestine, and supported the humanitarian movement that defended peace and the right of people to self-determination — was a horrific incident that resonated with the peoples of Gaza and Jerusalem; they mourned the death of one of their committed supporters.

Crispin Blunt, MP and a Foreign Office adviser, stated:

> I am done with empty statements of "concern" and my country's willingness to offer Palestinians every sort of rhetorical assistance short of actual help to address breaches of international law, in language that hasn't changed for a quarter of a century.[25]

President Carter said the following with respect to the worst example of deprivation he knew:

The occupation of Palestinian land-the confiscation of that land that does not belong to Israel- the colonization of that land and the connection of those multiple settlements by a highway on which Palestinians cannot even travel nor cross is the worst example of apartheid, worse than South Africa and Rwanda.[26]

Search for a Stolen Identity

"Until the lion learns to write, every story will always glorify the hunter."
— AFRICAN PROVERB

The issue of a national identity has become deeply ingrained for Palestinian exiles, as it is intertwined with their existential thinking, especially for those who managed to travel to other countries for work or study, remote from their homeland. National identity always involves stories and narratives of the past. The conflict about memory and tradition is very important and complex. There is a belief that identity emanates from the self; from the soul, and its identification is usually based on history and of course the future.

Francis Fukuyama defined how national identity begins:

> But national identity extends into the realm of culture and values. It consists of stories that people tell about themselves: where they came from, what they celebrate, their shared historical memories, and their national language.[27]

The identity experiences of the majority of Palestinians after the 1948 *Nakba* multiplied and underwent a new path of division that unexpectedly invented several contradictory classes of one people.

This includes those who were fortunate enough not to leave their homes in East Jerusalem and the West Bank, and some managed to live with their relatives or fled to the East Bank; but the bulk of the unlucky ones were grouped together like sheep in camps and were given a new abhorrent and shameful description, *"Refugees"*; a strange and unfortunate reality especially as they were displaced to another part inside their own homeland.

A year or so later, the West Bank was annexed to Jordan, and the inhabitants became Jordanians and subsequently lost their previous identity as Palestinians. On the contrary, in the Gaza Strip, the division was limited to two basic categories of *citizens* and *refugees*, living under Egyptian military rule without annexing the Strip to Egypt or giving all of them an Egyptian nationality, preserving the notorious equation that divides the population. But both citizens and refugees were given Egyptian travel documents for Palestinian Refugees.[28]

Upon arrival at London airport for the first time to start my study in engineering, the immigration officer firmly crossed "Palestinian" as my nationality on the entry form and wrote "Uncertain". The following year at the same airport, a young female officer kept my nationality as "Palestinian", probably unaware of certain official instructions. On leaving at the end of the year, a mean officer gave my nationality a new description: "Undefined". And finally on my return a year later, I was given a new and permanent classification, as it was probably the preferred British Government's description, "Stateless".

Nur Masalha commented on the dynamics of memory and stolen identity:

> Since 1948 the Nakba has been central to Palestinian public memory and national identity. Memories of trauma, memory construction and reinvention, remembrance and forgetfulness have also been critical to the struggle in Palestine-Israel.

The Nakba remains a key site of Palestinian collective consciousness and the single most important event that connects all Palestinians to a specific point in time.[29]

For example, the Palestinian flag is very much a part of Palestinian identity as is the kufiyah, humus, falafel, embroidery and dabke dance. The issue of identity for Palestinians living inside Israel was described by Azmi Bishara:

> From both the historical and theoretical perspectives, the Arabs in Israel are part of the Palestinian Arab people. Their definition as 'Israeli Arabs' was formed concurrent with the emergence of the issue of the Palestinian refugees, and the establishment of Israel on the ruins of the Palestinian people… One cannot point at a nationality or national group called 'Israeli Arabs' or 'the Arabs of Israel'. Other terms which are justly used are 'Palestinians of 48' or 'Palestinians inside the Green Line'.[30]

Ilan Pappe similarly writes:

> In the mid-1949, the United Nations stepped in to try to deal with the bitter fruits of its 1947 peace plan. One of the UN's misguided decisions was not to involve the International Refugee Organization (IRO) but to create a special agency for the Palestinian refugees.

He continued:

> It was Israel and the Zionist Jewish organisations abroad that were behind the decision to keep the IRO out of the picture: the IRO was the very same body that

was assisting the Jewish refugees in Europe following the Second World War, and the Zionist organisations were keen to prevent anyone from making any possible association or even comparison between the two cases. Moreover, the IRO always recommended repatriation as the first option to which refugees were entitled. This is how the UN Relief and Work Agency (UNRWA) came into being in 1950. It was not committed to the return of the refugees, but was set simply to provide employment and subsidies...It was also entrusted with building more permanent camps for them, construct-ing schools and opening medical centres. In other words, UNRWA was intended, in general, to look after the refugees' daily concerns. [31]

After the Palestinian Nakba and the attainment of independence by several Arab countries, some of their borders were incredibly established according to the despised Sykes-Picot agreement. There-fore, it became possible for any British, and subsequently any Amer-ican, to cross all the countries of the Arab world without the need for an entry visa. Conversely other Arabs, especially the Palestinians, needed a visa, and sometimes they may not even get one.

General Zinni on the Palestinian nightmare:

The UNHCR, which deals with millions of refugees around the world, has learned one big lesson over better than fifty years of experience: no permanent camps, no permanent refugees. Keeping people refu-gees forever does them no favours, and their presence (whether they are tolerated or despised) is a nightmare for everyone involved-- as Palestinian experience has long demonstrated. [32]

Those who are being killed in Gaza are nothing but "Refugees!"

They are displaced people. They have been kicked out of their homes for decades and despite numerous UN Resolutions nothing has been done to solve their predicament. UN Resolutions are only implemented when it comes to imposing sanctions and or bombing weak countries in the Middle East.

Ghada Karmi reflects on Palestinian identity:

> The *Nakba* had disastrous effects on the Palestinians who were condemned to live in UN-administered camps or went into long-term exile in the various countries of the world. This cataclysmic event was traumatic at every level. One of the most malign consequences has been the fragmentation of their identity. The Israeli project aimed from the start to destroy Palestine's native society, by physical expulsion and, failing that, through breakup of its traditional cohesion to prevent regrouping and resistance.[33]

The young Palestinian poet Haroun Rashid:

> *"Do you think you have obliterated and erased*
> *My identity?*
> *My history?*
> *My beliefs?.*
> *Mistaken who said that I am finished!*
> *I am displaced but my home is there,*
> *beyond those delusional boundaries.*
> *One day, I will return to our neighbourhood."* [34]

John Major's Historic Visit

During the British mandate, "the High Commissioner in 1920 imposed English as an official language and transformed the language of a religious tiny minority group into a second language, Hebrew, parallel to the language of the Arab majority. He also had a major role in redistributing the sectarian composition in order to pass the inclusion of representatives of the new Jewish immigrants in the municipal councils".[35]

The United Kingdom was among the first European states to provide financial aid to the newly born Palestinian Authority. Some diplomats believed it wanted to untie the knot of guilt over its historical and moral (not officially recognised) responsibility for the loss of Palestine.

John Major, who replaced Margaret Thatcher as Prime Minister in November 1990, made an historic visit to Gaza in March 1995, as the first British Prime Minister in office to visit Palestine; even during the thirty-year British mandate, no prime minister had made a similar visit. He was accompanied by a large delegation of ministers and businessmen representing giant British companies. A number of businessmen were invited to attend the meeting, and on my way out, I noticed that electricity poles were decorated with British flags, and for lack of attention, I bumped into a little girl carrying pieces of candy that fell on the pavement. I apologised to her but she too was looking at the flags in amazement and asked, "Who are they for?"

"Britain, I am sorry, but I have to rush to meet its head now."

"Is his wife the queen?" She asked.

"No, he is not a king."

"Please take two pieces of my candy, one for him and one for his no-queen wife."

Unconsciously, I put the pieces in my pocket. During the meeting, John Major announced a package of trade facilities by providing Government guarantees to encourage trade with the Palestinian Authority, he donated 200 Land Rover vehicles for the Palestinian police.

At the invitation of President Arafat, both delegations moved to the Palestine Hotel on the Gaza beach for lunch. While seated between Lord Young, DTI Secretary and Sir Richard Greenbury, Chairman of Marks and Spencer, I told Lord Young the story of the young girl. He insisted that I give John the sweets and told me that his wife's name was Norma.

Indeed, I shook hands with John, and told him the story and gave him the two pieces of candy for him and Norma. To my surprise, he stood up and thanked me warmly and called the UK Consul General, Robin Kealy, and asked him to contact me to thank the girl, then added: "This is the most beautiful gift for me and my wife from a Palestinian girl."

Yasser Arafat was watching with suspicious looks, especially at my long conversation with Prime Minister Major in English, which he didn't fully understand, apparently as it was without his permission.

At the end of that historic visit, both sides decided to form a Palestinian-British committee to follow up and develop future trade between the two countries, of which I was one of its members.

The joint committee held a meeting at Marks and Spencer's (M&S) headquarters in London, in the presence of all the British delegation's members that visited Gaza, and on the Palestinian side: Mohammed Rashid, Zahi Khouri, Khaled Assaily, Mohammed Sabaawi, Walid Najjab, in addition to the committees' coordinators, Oxford based, Ahmed Khalidi and Hussein Agha. The Managing Director of M&S confirmed that his reputable company had placed orders to buy large quantities of oranges and grapefruit from Gaza.

Margaret Thatcher was the first woman to hold the office of prime minister, since 1979. Her victory in the 1982 Falklands War, resulting in her landslide re-election.

Prince El-Hassan bin Talal, whom I met several times in Amman, Prague and London, mentioned his telephone conversation with Mrs Thatcher:

The Israeli Government has declared its intention to annex parts of the West Bank of the river Jordan, ..In 1982, my late brother, King Hussein, asked me to take a call from Margaret Thatcher. She spoke of the United Nations Security Council Resolution 242, which states the inadmissibility of the acquisition of territory by war. Jordan at that time was on the Security Council and she was seeking our support for the British position over the Falklands.

While I assured her of our support, I did ask why the sheep bells of the Falklands rang louder than the church bells of Jerusalem. Her answer was: "You know how it is." [36]

Tony Blair, who defeated John Major in the 1997 election, sadly took Britain into the US-led war on Afghanistan in 2001 and followed that by joining George W. Bush in his war on Iraq in 2003.

It was rumoured that Blair's long-time friend and special envoy, Lord Michael Levy, played a significant role in convincing Ehud Barak to approve the British Gas concession on the Palestinian side on the Mediterranean.

On September 11, 2012, a motion was tabled at the House of Commons that "*supports recognition by the UN of Palestine as a state alongside the state of Israel.*" It was signed by 110 members of all parties, among the signatories were Jack Straw, Sir Gerald Kaufman, Nicholas Soames, Crispin Blunt, Jeremy Corbyn, Glenda Jackson, Charles Kennedy, Lisa Nandy, and David Ward. [37]

Boris Johnson, after becoming prime minister in 2019 said in his speech to the UN:

It is customary…to pledge our values from protecting freedom of navigation in the Gulf to preserving the vital task of achieving a "two-state solution" to the conflict in the Middle East…And added: You may keep secrets from your friends, from your parents, your children…but it takes real effort to conceal your thoughts from Google. [38]

The British mandate approved the establishment of the Hebrew university in Jerusalem, the opening of which was attended by Lord Balfour and General Allenby in 1924. The only school that was authorised by the British army in Palestine was a spy school, teaching Arabic to senior British army officers and diplomats in Jerusalem. "The first Principal instructor of the school was Abba Eban, an officer of South African Jewish origin, educated at Cambridge, an enthusiastic Zionist and an excellent Arabist."

In July 1946 Zionists managed to breach security at the King David Hotel, and to blow up the building with explosives concealed in milk churns. There were scores of deaths and fearful injuries to the survivors. The reaction of the British Commander was to issue a general order banning dealings with Jewish commercial establishments, saying that to hit "these people" in their pockets was the language they would best understand. Abba Eban decided, then and there, to resign from working with the British.

Following the establishment of Israel. The school was moved to Amman then to a suburb of Beirut called Shemlan. Leslie McLoughlin, who wrote about the school, he was the director of, teaching Arabic to British army officers and diplomats since its first location in Jerusalem.[39]

Europeans for Palestine

"Facts do not cease to exist because they are ignored."
— ALDOUS HUXLEY

There is a real and tangible expression on the part of the European peoples in general which remains full of moral sympathy with the oppressed people of Palestine; as well as a popular and continuous demand for firm and serious action to end their suffering and achieve a just and lasting resolution to the conflict.

The extent of their support and sympathy is noticeable by extremely large popular demonstrations in almost all major European cities calling for an end to Israeli occupation, condemning the settlers' crimes and boycotting settlement goods. Unfortunately, their governments repudiated all the aspirations of their people when it came to dealing with Israel, as those governments quickly succumbed to Israeli and sometimes American pressure.

The only exception during the past decade was the decision by a newly elected government of Sweden that responded to the wishes of its people and with extraordinary courage recognised Palestine.

Margot Alstrom, the Swedish Foreign Minister, announced in October 2014, Sweden's full recognition of the State of Palestine, on the borders of June 1967. Sweden was the first member of the European Union to take such a courageous and historic step. Sweden's relationship with Palestine has existed for many years; the United Nations chose Count Folke Bernadotte, cousin of King Gustav, as its special envoy to Palestine in 1947, the year before the British Mandate ended. Bernadotte's task was to mediate and convince the Jewish and Palestinian sides of possible alternatives to the partition resolution, which, the Arabs, Palestinians and Jews also rejected. In September of that year, members of the extremist Zionist Stern Gang led by Menachem Begin assassinated the Count, believing that he was biased towards the Arabs.

It was the Swedish Secretary General of the United Nations, Dag Hammarskjold, who worked diligently to complete Israel's withdrawal from the Sinai and Gaza following the 1956 Suez war. Sweden also participated with a large contingent in the UN peacekeeping force, stationed in Gaza city and lasted for ten years, until June 1967.

During that period, Hanmarsjold visited Gaza twice. Another surprise visit was by the new world boxing champion, Ingemar Johansson, who held an exhibition match with the local boxing champion, Rajab Alyan.

Swedish activist "Ann Linde" who is currently serving as Sweden's foreign minister, participated in a seminar held in London in the summer of 2014 in support of demands by Palestinian prisoners in Israeli jails, in the presence of Ambassador Manuel Hassassian. [40]

Charlotta Sparre, the former Swedish Ambassador to Jordan and Egypt, is the most active diplomat participating in many events calling for the resolution of the Palestine-Israel conflict.

Many activists wonder why all these continuous calls, attempts and interest in reconciliation and peace are not heeded?

A European diplomat offered a historian's answer:

"There are historical facts whose documented authenticity is unquestionable, foremost of which is that 'eternal enmity' is absolutely unrealistic and ephemeral no matter how long it takes. The Romans, who were staunchly hostile to the nascent Christianity, imprisoned and sometimes killed everyone who embraced it, and worse than that, ordered the crucifixion of Christ, according to the circulating narrative.

What happened after that? Rome has become to this day the world centre of Christianity and the seat of the Pope. All warring countries, during their conflicts and their colonial ambitions in the previous world wars which lasted for many years and led to hundreds of millions of victims, and massive and terrifying destruction, was incredibly followed by reconciliation, friendship, and even alliances. Germany now is leading with France the European Union; Japan is a loyal ally of the United States after forgetting Pearl Harbour and

Hiroshima. Thus, is it surprising or unreasonable to call for a joint peace to end the Palestine-Israel conflict, after only one attempt by Yitzhak Rabin? It's a matter of time."[41]

The EU, as a financier of the Palestinian Authority, was once perceived by Palestinians as a counterweight to Washington. European Governments are strong on rhetoric in favour of the Palestinians but this has not been translated into actions that produced any meaningful change either on the ground or in terms of Israeli policy. Pugwash, the conflict resolution organisation, held a meeting in London in support of the Palestinians of Gaza which was attended by Paolo Cotta-Ramusino, Daniel Levy, Nadim Shehadi, Dame Shirley Williams, Chris Doyle, and Dr Rosemary Hollis (we shared the same date of birth) among others. All of its members across the world were urged to contribute to engaging policymakers and politicians in Europe to raise the issue of Palestinian statehood and the rights of its people.[42] The European friends of Palestine crucially exposed the immorality of Israel's military occupation, which was also opposed by many Jewish public figures and Israelis.

The vigorous and peaceful campaigns within Europe against South African apartheid in universities, churches, parliaments, and in the media, highlighted South Africa's discrimination against non-whites, and became a moral cause for many. There was a similar hope for a groundswell of European support and determined action to elevate the Palestinian cause.

A group of European activists placed 4,500 pairs of shoes in the courtyard of the European Union's headquarters in Brussels in an amazing and heart-wrenching scene, to remind the politicians of the number of Palestinians killed in the past decade at the hands of Israeli forces.

Several ships organised by European activists made several attempts to break the Israeli blockade imposed on Gaza. The first, a small boat coming from the Cypriot port of Larnaca, managed to reach its destination followed by four other boats loaded with medical and in-kind aid. On board these boats were some politicians from several Western countries. Then came the Turkish ships, the *Freedom Flotilla,* that was attacked by the Israeli army, which left ten dead and many injured on the main ship Mavi Marmara.

The EU Secretary General, Javier Solana, had a positive role in extending the EU's aid and funding to vital projects in Palestine. In a meeting with members of the Council on Foreign Relations in Gaza, after visiting Jerusalem, he criticised the building of the segregation walls. He pledged to maintain European observers at the Rafah crossing to facilitate the movement of Palestinian travellers. His moderate professional style was complemented by his successor, the Italian politician Frederica Mogherini, who announced that embassies of all EU countries will remain in Tel Aviv and will not be moved to Jerusalem, in clear defiance of Benjamin Netanyahu and Donald Trump's requests.

Marc Otte, the EU special representative for over eight years, has signed a statement with other EU politicians calling for:

> The European governments should not shy away from pushing for a just and secure future for Israelis and Palestinians. The bottom line is that Europeans cannot be bystanders to a conflict that continues to reverberate through their southern neighbourhood. But Gaza's problems are, above all, the product of years of Israeli restrictions and closures. There can be no future for Gaza while Israel's blockade remains.

Harvard, Fighting Corruption!

"Sometimes we only see the shortcomings of others!"
— ANONYMOUS

The "anti-corruption" phenomenon, and ways to combat both political and administrative mismanagement, has been used as a weapon by donor countries in order to restrict its financial support for aid-receiving governments. Some countries prefer to deal with NGOs as they observe high standards of transparency in their transactions.

The Palestinian Authority, and its almost total dependence on external financial support, was not excluded from such demands to take substantial and clear steps to combat corruption. Enron's management in Houston, which became the only American corporation with a substantial investment in the private sector in Palestine, were calling on the directors of the Palestine Electric company - their partners in the Gaza power plant - to combat financial and administrative corruption; they called for strict adherence to legal standards and transparency in dealing with the government, to the extent that they rejected the decision for purchasing a plot of land by the sea in Gaza as a proposed site for the construction of the plant, on the pretext that one of the landowners of that land served as a minister in the Palestinian Authority.

A close political relationship and generous financial aid were still flourishing at the time, between the American Administration of President Bill Clinton and the Palestinian Authority, and through these understandings, PA officials were encouraged to participate in the "Good Governance" program organized by the John F. Kennedy School of Politics at Harvard University in Boston.

Dr. Andrew Parasiliti, the program director, whose name indicates that he is an American of Greek descent, arrived in Gaza, after spending a few days in Ramallah, to help in the selection of participants from ministries, municipalities, NGOs and the Legislative Council.

He provided an overview of the program, highlighting that it includes the prevention, international cooperation and asset recovery aspects of corruption.

As many related institutional cultures and structures influence the levels and types of corruption. The high-level Palestinian delegation of twenty-five senior officials included eight deputy ministers, two judges, one governor, one Legislative Council member, one President's office staff and one university professor. Among them Ibrahim Al-Daghma, Muhammad Qidwa, Osama Al-Farra, Maan Erekat, Hassan Khreshi, Salah Abdel Shafi, Marwan Abdel Hamid, Jamal Zakout and Mohammed Samhouri. The two women participants were Nabila Nashashibi, the daughter of the Minister of Finance and Sulafa Hajawi, a history professor and an aide to President Arafat.

All delegates arrived at the Harvard University entrance on a very cold February day, with over one foot of snow covering the landscape. Those leading participants in the program were eager to be awarded a Harvard University Certificate that would certainly benefit them in improving their status and careers, and they could brag in front of their peers by placing a Harvard University-framed certificate on their desks to prove that they had passed the prestigious Harvard Examination.

Unfortunately, there was a firm belief that over the fifteen-day condensed course, most participants did not benefit in gaining new methods in management and combating corruption. Some thought it was a waste of time while others enjoyed the vacation in Boston, a cultural American city. The lectures focused on several examples and case studies of corruption by officials in the public sector and government departments, mainly in South American countries, unfamiliar to Arab officials in the Middle East.

As a matter fact, most participants were heavy smokers, and since the majority were from the Gaza Strip, which was subjected to almost daily rocket attacks by Israeli *Apache* helicopters, they found smoking as a way out to calm their tense nerves.

Of course, lecture classes and the entire John F. Kennedy School building, like other universities and public places, strictly forbid smoking. On the fourth day of the program, a smoke detector fire alarm rang out in the building, followed by the evacuation of students and lecturers out to the snow-covered courtyard. It was disclosed later that day that behind the evacuation was a cigarette smoker from one of the Palestinian groups. No one recognised the guilty person. However, the group was placed under close surveillance to avoid the recurrence of a similar incident.

The program did not address corruption in the Middle East or even the private and public sectors in North America or any European country. One happy participant repeated a saying in Arabic:

> *"If you can convince the fly that flowers*
> *are better than garbage, then you can*
> *convince the corrupt that the homeland*
> *is worth more than money!"*

On the last day of the program, Nabil Shaath, Minister of Planning and International Cooperation, and his assistant at the time, Majdi Al-Khaldi, joined the group. Framed certificates were presented by the Dean of the Kennedy School, Andrew Parasiliti, and Nabil Shaath. Some participants rejoiced at obtaining a certificate resembling a degree from the most famous university in the world. Sulafa, who used to teach history in Al-Fateh University in Tripoli, gave the group a lesson in Arab history about Haroun al-Rashid, the eighth century Caliph who took Baghdad to great heights in advancement and scientific development; Sulafa explained how all the numbers being used at Harvard are Arabic numbers - no one uses the Roman numerals I, II, III, IV, V. Of course the most important addition was the Zero. Our land was the heart of human scientific progress, centuries before the discovery of America.

A few years, after their auspicious return from Harvard, most participants won and occupied higher positions in the PA. For example, Al-Daghma became Minister of Justice, Maher Ghneim, Minister of Public Works, Qidwa was appointed Governor of Gaza, similarly, Al-Farra, Governor of Khan Yunis, Marwan Abdel Hamid, ambassador to Greece, Maan Erekat, ambassador to the USA, Salah Abdel Shafi, ambassador to Sweden, and Hassan Khresha, was voted deputy speaker to the newly elected Legislative Council.

And of course, not all these appointments to such high positions were necessarily the result of the framed Harvard certificates.

There was no mention of the Enron bankruptcy scandal that would have been an appropriate case study due to the fact that almost all the participants knew about Enron's involvement and ownership in the construction of the Gaza power plant. Enron's chronic corrupt activities had yet to be fully uncovered. It was later discovered that Enron lawyers had established over 3,500 different offshore companies in the Cayman Islands.

Senator Bernie Sanders recently commented on corrupt US companies:

"In the Cayman Islands, there is a modest five-story building that is home to 18,857 companies. Either this is one very crowded building, or it is a phoney address, used by 18,760 corporations for one purpose: To avoid paying taxes to the USA." [43]

Obama's Cairo Speech

"Hard times will always reveal true friends.
Your words mean nothing when your
actions are the opposite."

—ANONYMOUS

On that historic night in November 2008, we stayed up all alone waiting for the official announcement confirming newly elected Barack Obama's victory, and after the congratulations from his rival, Senator John McCain, Obama appeared with his wife Michelle and his two daughters on the screen.

Tears of joy streamed from the eyes of my two cousins who were watching, who graduated from Texas A&M University. They were jumping and cheering as millions more who were excited to realize that dream, the election of the first person of African descent and with a Muslim father to the most powerful position in the world.

Signs of astonishment appeared on their faces when they noticed that I was laughing out loudly. Incredibly, what made me laugh at that special moment in history was that a single and unique sight came to my mind, a strange and amazing scene from a 1961 movie called *"Guess Who's Coming to Dinner"*: about a young woman bringing her fiancé, a handsome African American doctor she had just met in Hawaii (Sidney Poitier), to meet her parents, who had to come to terms with the racial prejudices they still harboured. When her father (Spencer Tracey) asked about the problems that their children would face, the doctor laughed and said: "Actually, your daughter thinks that our child will become the first black president of America!" [44]

A black father, a white mother, Hawaii! What a 1961 coincidence? As a matter of fact, I have read a few deeply intelligent and artfully constructed novels based on true stories, but for the first time that night, I witnessed an amazingly true story unfolding based on a movie!

> Delegates announcing the establishment of the All-Palestine Government at a school in Gaza on 30 September, 1948, headed by Ahmed Hilmy Abdelbaqi.

< Palestinian women at Qalandia refugee camp enjoying a game of basketball. Jerusalem, 1951

v Talaat Al-Ghussein, the first Palestinian to meet with president John F Kennedy at the White House, as the ambassador of Kuwait, 1962.

Members of the 'Women's Renaissance Society' delivering in-kind assistance to the refugee patients of Al-Bureij Hospital, 1952.

>
Actor Yul Brynner talking to Palestinian admirers as UN ambassador during his memorable visit to Gaza, 1960.

<
Jean-Paul Sartre and Simone De Beauvoir visiting a refugee camp in Gaza, with Director of Education Magdi Abu Ramadan, March 1960.

> Ghassan Kanafani with his 2 children, was a man of many talents; novelist, journalist, politician, painter and most of all deeply committed to the cause of Palestine - martyred July 1972.

< Khalil Sakakin, a liberal and secular educator and intellectual, who was born in Jerusalem and founded the Nahda college in 1938, which became a prominent nationalist and educational institution in Palestine.

< Emile Habibi, the highly accomplished writer and politician, who won several literary prizes; famously known as the 'Pessoptimist' and for his symbolic tombstone 'I stayed in Haifa'.

^
Wijdan, vice-chairperson of the
General Union of Palestinian
Women and founder of Wijdan
Shawa Centre for the care of
Palestinian Refugee families in
Egypt, Cairo 1971.

^
Born in Jerusalem, Armenian
photographer Kegham Djeghalian
extensively documented generations
of the Nakba. Gaza, 1959.

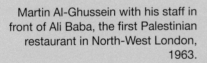

>
Martin Al-Ghussein with his staff in
front of Ali Baba, the first Palestinian
restaurant in North-West London,
1963.

<
A photo of a family
outing taken by master
of photography,
Kegham Djeghalian, in
Gaza beach, 1953.

Edward Said and Ibrahim Abu Lughod speak to reporters at the US State Department after meeting with then Secretary George Shultz, both being members of the Palestine National Council. Washington DC, March 26, 1988.

^
Hisham Sharabi, a Palestinian scholar born in Jaffa and AUB graduate, taught history at Georgetown University where he held the Omar Mukhtar Chair of Arab Culture.

^
Nur Masalha, the historian who devoted most of his time writing articles and books that refute Zionist narratives. Author of the acclaimed book "Palestine, A Four Thousand Year History".

Nelson Mandela and Yasser Arafat waving to the crowds upon Mandela's historic landing at Gaza International Airport - 19 October 1999.

Hasib Sabbagh's first private plane carrying Palestinian entrepeneurs, landing at Gaza airport for the first time in November 1998. (1st plane ever to land in Gaza).

Gaza Marine, September 2000

Gaza Marine September 2021

<
After 21 years, the gas field is still stagnant without commercial exploitation as a result of the Israeli instransigence in preventing the two giant oil and gas companies BG and Shell to develop it.

^
Wail Khoury was credited for lobbying quietly and successfully for Palestinian major projects including the Gaza power plant and the Gas field.

> Father Manuel Musallam from Zababdeh said "God chose me to resist all evil against my people" and "If they demolish your mosque, raise the call to prayer from our church".

<
Nazih Khalil and his daily dream of building a promising future for his hometown, Zababdeh. He calls for co-existence among his countrymen in Palestine.

>
Palm Sunday celebration at "Saint Prophyrios" orthodox church, Gaza, 1996.

With Prince El Hassan bin Talal, the then Crown Prince of Jordan, discussing Palestinian and Jordanian cultural relations - London, 1991. >

^
Dr Zuhair Alami, born in Gaza, obtained a PhD in civil engineering from the University of Texas, was an AUB professor and a member of PLO's Executive Committee. He was also a co-founder of the prominent Khatib & Alami engineering consulting company. Beirut, 2018.

^
Palestinian historian and scholar, Walid Khalidi (left) with Hasib Sabbagh. Beirut, 1994.

<
Mahdi Abdul Hadi, born in Nablus, the founder of PASSIA, a forum for free expression and analysis. He is an active member in many educational organisations including the Arab Thought Forum in Amman.

Kuwaiti General Ali El-Momen former Army Chief of Staff. London, 2018.

Marzouq Al-Ghanim, the speaker of the Kuwait National Assembly, a passionate supporter of Palestine.

Abdel Karim Shawwa, an early leader of the Palestinian community in Kuwait since 1949.

>

Dr Shafeeq Ghabra, a Palestinian-Kuwaiti professor teaching at the Kuwait University, 1999.

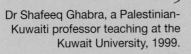

> Two refugees from the same city of Safad. The one on the right, Said Khoury, founded CCC, the largest contracting company in the Middle East.

The one on the left joined Fatah and was elected president of Palestine in 2005.

< First visit to Chariman Arafat in his office (the Muntada) in Gaza. October, 1994

^
Fatenn Mostafa Kanafani, Founder of
ArtTalksEgypt and a committed lobbyist
for Palestine through her exhibitions.

^
Internationally renowned Egyptian
artist and cartoonist, George Bahgory,
holding a watermelon as a symbol for
Palestinian Artists Resistance.
Cairo, 2021.

^
Daniel Barenboim, UN Messenger of Peace, conducts the
Orchestra of Gaza, during a concert at the Al Mathaf in Gaza City,
May 3, 2011 "In solidarity with its Palestinian residents".

The destroyed house of Gaza Mayor Aoun Shawa and his
wife Rawya (a member of the Legislative Council) sitting
on its rubble a day after it was destroyed by Israeli missiles
during the third war on Gaza in July 2014.

"Can a person in the midst of this devastation live
without memory?"

US Secretary of Commerce, Ron Brown, with US ambassador
Edward Djerejian addressing Palestinian businessmen at the'Diana
Tamari Sabbagh Library' during a visit to Gaza, January 1994.

Palestinian Businessmen meeting with Deputy Secretary of Defense
Paul Wolfowitz at the Pentagon - Washington, February 2004

Pugwash conference group photo at Nagasaki on the 70th anniversary
of the Hiroshima and Nagasaki nuclear bombing. Japan, 2015.

Armless artist Karipbek Kuyakov in his
gallery. Astana, August 2017

Professor Athem Alsabti, founder of
the Iraqi Pugwash Group.
Astana, August 2017

> French President Jacques Chirac joins President Arafat and Mayor Aoun Shawa at the inauguration of Charles de Gaulle Sreet in Gaza, 1996.

< Ghada Tarazi Sarraf, a Palestinian activist in Kuwait. Cairo, 1989

Hillary Clinton shakes hands with Marwan Kanafani, Suha Arafat is next to her while Presidents Clinton and Arafat gaze at them. Gaza, December 1998.

An American presence appeared for the first time on the popular level in the Arab world, when President Dwight Eisenhower ordered the British, French and Israeli forces to immediately cease hostilities, in the 1956 Suez War and withdraw their forces from Egypt.

This unprecedented American intervention led to the demise of British and French colonies in Africa and Asia. Secretary of State John Foster Dulles led America's new policy to fill the void left by the European colonial powers. The Dulles plan was also aimed at keeping the Soviet Union out of filling any part of that vacuum, therefore establishing America's monopoly over emerging countries of the Middle East, especially the oil-rich Gulf Arab States.

The one ideological issue uniting Arab views was the emergence of Israel as a sovereign state. Arab resistance to that prospect led to four wars: 1948, 1956, 1967, and 1973. During each, Israeli arms prevailed.

During the 1967 Six-Day war, the Egyptians repeated their accusations that the US had provided Israel with planes, pilots and valuable military information obtained through its spy battleship "Liberty" during the fighting.

It was amazing that Israel tried to destroy the Liberty by firing rockets at it which resulted in dozens of American soldiers killed and over two hundred wounded. Despite this disgraceful, complicated and incomprehensible act, Israel's relations were strengthened under President Lyndon Johnson's administration. During Jimmy Carter's extensive efforts to conclude a peace deal in 1978 between Israel and Egypt, the US ambassador to the United Nations, Andrew Young was sacked because he had a brief meeting with the UN representative of the PLO Zuhdi Tarazi at the house of the Kuwaiti ambassador. The meeting was considered controversial, Israel objected, and Young was dismissed.[45]

When the Reagan administration refused to grant Yasser Arafat an entry visa to address the United Nations General Assembly in New York on the Palestinian issue, in a bold and unprecedented move, the General Assembly took a decision to move its entirety to its European headquarters in Geneva to discuss the Palestine issue and listen to Arafat's speech, who was greeted with an unprecedented welcome.

Secretary of State George Shultz, who previously held a high managerial position at Bechtel Corporation and was closely acquainted with Hasib Sabbagh, had stipulated that in order to begin a serious American dialogue with the PLO, Arafat should announce, in clear and unambiguous language, his condemnation of terrorism, combating it and renouncing all violence. Arafat tried to circumvent that condition by changing the required format and its wording.

The most serious attempt was made when President George H. Bush called for the Madrid Peace Conference. The eight long years of George W Bush's presidency witnessed the worst period in American-Palestinian relations. Indeed, it was full of dreadful events of unrest; the siege of Arafat, and Bush's public demand to exclude Arafat and elect a new leadership, and the Israeli attacks that systematically destroyed the infrastructure of the Palestinian Authority areas. Then the war on Iraq, the hanging of Saddam Hussein, and the 2008 economic crisis that afflicted the entire world, along with its extremely severe impact on the Palestinians.

All these events gave impetus to the dreams of the Palestinians and their constant prayers that Barack Obama would win the next election. The aspiration was that he would sympathise more with oppressed peoples. Will his speech in Cairo give them hope for the realisation of their dreams? As he stated at various parts of his Cairo speech:

> I came to Cairo to seek a new beginning between the United States and Muslims around the world, as the Holy Qur'an tells us 'Be conscious of God and always speak the truth' ... Islam has always been a part of America's story. The first nation to recognise my country was Morocco.
> I have unequivocally prohibited the use of torture by the United States, and I have ordered the prison at Guantanamo be closed by early next year. [46]

...it is also undeniable that the Palestinian people — Muslims and Christians — has suffered in pursuit of a homeland. Many wait in refugee camps in the West Bank, Gaza and neighbouring lands for a life of peace and security. They endure the daily humiliations that come with occupation.. The situation for the Palestinian people is intolerable. America will not turn our backs on the legitimate Palestinian aspiration for dignity, opportunity, and a state of their own.

...Israelis must acknowledge that just as Israel's right to exist cannot be denied, neither can Palestine's. The United States does not accept the legitimacy of continued settlements. This construction violates previous agreements and undermines efforts to achieve peace. It is time for these settlements to stop."

And Israel must also live up to its obligation to ensure that Palestinians can live and work and develop their society. Just as it devastates Palestinian families, the continuing humanitarian crisis in Gaza does not serve Israel's security; neither does the continuing lack of opportunity in the West Bank. Progress in the daily lives of the Palestinians must be a crucial part of a road to peace, and Israel must take concrete steps to enable such progress.[47]

It is no surprise that Palestinian illusory expectations quickly evaporated and conditions worsened.

CHAPTER 3

Palestinian Art & Culture

A nation's culture resides in the hearts and in the soul of its people.

— MAHATMA GANDHI

Culture of Hope

"The greater the torment, the greater the awareness."

— FYODOR DOSTOEVSKY

In the world's battles between the 'power of culture' and the 'culture of power', most of the time, the former manages to survive. Fate had decided that those exiled men and women were to roam around the world chasing their dreams, ones that eluded most of their parents at home. All great successful work begins with a simple idea, and no idea comes to be without imagination and a beautiful dream, possibly through a daydream that brings fascinating results. Each with their individual ambition, they were leading the way.

Life was simpler in the past, as society began to mature with its tendency to give art a wider space to express the development of the people who were eagerly looking to catch up with civilization, after centuries of darkness under Ottoman rule. The Palestinians' ambition was for an open society and free civil life. There was an agreement amongst all sectors that education, industry, opening of high schools and development of agricultural methods were the only way forward in order to demolish the walls of backwardness and combat ignorance and illiteracy. Literature offers a mirror into the lives of individuals and an honest expression of its writers' thoughts, feelings, and understanding of events: to deeply express our people's concerns, and worries about their meaningful fight against time, which pressed hard and violently on their beings, for miserable and long decades; to arouse the souls of generational leaders and future pioneers, who could illuminate the paths through the darkness of an era burdened with worries and setbacks; to cultivate hope in their souls, so that they would finally triumph over the wearied slumber that afflicted them, and over the terrible despair, and to heal the wounds of wandering, loss, and confusion. However, the most difficult pain is the one we cannot talk about ostensibly: it is the most severe pain, that which rests upon the human soul. Kareem Iraqi reflects on the need to heal our wounds.[1]

> *Don't complain to people about your pain.*
> *The wound only hurts the wounded.*
> *If you complain to the one who cares not,*
> *you add wounds to your wounds that is called re-*
> *morse.*
> *Has sympathy liberated a stolen homeland?*
> *Are condolences an alternative to the fallen flag?*
> *Neither despair is my robe nor sorrow breaks my*
> *resolve.*

We write to restore hearts, heal the soul, and build minds in order to give ourselves strength, tranquillity, and a positive outlook away from fear and defeatism.

Upon the establishment of Israel; the prevailing belief by Golda Meir, and many leaders of the Zionist movement including David Ben-Gurion, was that time (and only time) will end the aspirations and demands by the refugees to return back to Palestine; and so with their children with the passage of time, would forget the places of birth of their parents and grandparents.

A powerful example to refute this false, oppressor narrative, was the publication in London of a wonderful book, *"Palestine + 100 stories from a century after the Nakba,"* which contained stories by thirteen young novelists, the children and grandchildren of those who were forcibly expelled from their lands. Edited by Basma Ghalayini who wrote:

> Four generations on, any Palestinian child can tell you all about their great-grandfather's back garden in Haifa, Yaffa or Majdal... Indeed, wherever Palestinian refugees are, one thing unites them: their undoubted belief in their right to return.

In reviewing one of the novels by Mazen Maarouf *"The Curse of the Mud Ball Kid"*, translated by Jonathan Wright, it tells the amazing story of a young boy who lives with his grandmother in her small and only house that remains in their destroyed village due to its location near a kibbutz fence, built on the edge of the village:

> In a primary school in the kibbutz, Ze'ev puts me on display in front of the schoolkids in the playground. None of them have ever seen a Palestinian before. Some of the kids ask, 'Are you the last Palestinian?' or 'Are you the guy who killed Ezer Banana?' Shortly after I was put in the cube, they injected me with a liquid that made me lose all control of my body. It focused my memory on one scene, so much that it made me shiver constantly. The whole process turned my teeth into a soft, bendy material, like the rubber in erasers, making my teeth loosen in their gums painlessly and drop out into my mouth. When I lost my teeth, I lost all sense of myself. The next day, Ze'ev said: 'I'll show you something that will ease your pain.' A footage of a toothpaste advert I had taken part in, though it was

never broadcast…As soon as I saw the footage, I remembered that I once had a sister. She was more than five years older than me, but she always seemed like a little sister. The afternoon before she died, an NGO van arrived to take me to film the advert for the toothpaste, which was called '*Hope*'. The aim wasn't to promote the toothpaste so much as to inspire people with the knowledge that there was one Palestinian child out there who was still in good health. [2]

Widad Kawar, born in Tulkarm, is best known for her passion in collecting Palestinian ethnic and cultural arts, preserving its costumes and heritage. In her book, *Threads of Identity*, she writes that "'Each *thobe* brings to mind an individual or a place: a wife, a mother, a daughter, a family, a house, a village, a town. Each dress was worn on special occasions, happy and sad, that marked the owner's life." [3]

The talented young painter, Ismail Shamout, arrived with his family to Khan Yunis a few days after the loss of their home in Jaffa to the Zionist militias. Jaffa was famous for its orange groves, one of its renowned golden brands was called the Shamouti orange, possibly related to his family name. Cultivation of that species was tried in Gaza but failed to match the flavour, taste, and size of the "*Yafawi Shamouti*". Ismail gained fame at a young age for his distinctive drawings of exiles and in particular women wearing their colourful traditional dresses. A few years after the *Nakba*, he was able to find employment as a teacher in Kuwait, where he created dozens of paintings of exiled women in his favourite colours of Gold and Blue. One of his creations was a wonderful painting of cousin Abeer in Kuwait dressed in her Palestinian "*Thobe*" dress embroidered with the names of dozens of Palestinian cities and villages.

Sliman Mansour, the contemporary painter and the artist of intifada, talks about his iconic painting "*Jamal al-Mahamel*" (Camel of Heavy Burdens), as named by Emile Habibi:

"In 1976, I participated in an exhibition in London. The painting was bought by the Libyan ambassador there, who asked me to write a dedication on the face of the painting in order to give it to Muammar Gaddafi for his birthday. I only signed it on the back. In the year 2000, we contacted the embassy to check on the fate of that original painting; unfortunately, we were told that it might have been destroyed during the American bombings of Gaddafi's home in Tripoli that were ordered by President Reagan in 1986." [4]

Artists For Palestine

In an unremitting search for justice, an elite group of artists from different nationalities, with their incredibly noble ideas and actions, inspired many diverse people around the world, celebrating their tremendous achievements; they embraced great and fair ideas, and contributed emotionally and practically in lobbying for Palestine. As the actor and activist, Richard Gere, once stated on Remembrance Day, "We know that more hate and more anger will never lead us out of this. Israelis won't have a home until the Palestinians have one." [5]

From identifiable murals on the segregation wall in the West Bank and the destroyed homes in Gaza, the great British street artist Banksy's work highlights Israeli military oppression. Banksy questioned: "How illegal is it to vandalise a wall if the wall itself has been deemed unlawful by the International Court of Justice?" This suggests that a better landscape could emerge if the barrier were destroyed. He included children in most of his pieces of art to emphasise the terrible toll that local conflict inflicts on the innocent children.

In his "Welcome to Gaza" murals, he felt the wall essentially turns Palestine into the world's largest prison. His biggest landmark is the "*Walled Off*" hotel in Bethlehem, located just metres away from the segregation wall. Each room looks out on the illegal barrier. Banksy boasts it is "the worst view of any hotel in the world". [6]

The Greek musician and composer Mikis Theodorakis co-authored and composed the Palestinian Anthem, following the Algiers' declaration of Palestinian Independence in 1988, in a gesture of support for the Palestinian cause. He is also remembered for composing the music of the film "*Zorba the Greek*" based on a novel by Nikos Kazantzakis, and his famous dance with Anthony Quinn. His favourite dialogue in the film:

> *I don't see you praying, Zorba.*
> *He who prays, you will not see.*
> *Does that mean you are praying?*
> *Yes. A drop of the sea can only*
> *be in the depths of the waves.*

Mikis wore the Palestinian Kufiyah in his shows and public events, as an expression of solidarity and pride. He once commented that: "Israel has become like *Sparta* — you are fighting a million Palestinian children — you are now *Goliath* and Palestine is David, and I am with David." [7]

Michael Moore pointed out how "a documentary filmmaker, Yaser Murtaja, was shot dead by Israeli soldiers on Friday while wearing helmet and vest with "PRESS" marked on them. He was filming a nurse, a doctor and a 12-year-old student who were protesting. I ask the documentary community to please speak about this travesty." [8]

Fatenn Mostafa Kanafani, the founder of ArtTalk Egypt, is extremely passionate about fine arts and philanthropy. She took the initiative to organize an exhibition to raise funds for the children of Palestine, and to raise awareness of the chronic oppression of existence of the Palestinian people under Israeli occupation. Amazingly, sixty Egyptian artists donated their artistic works to the exhibition which had the title "Doko al-Jidran," based on a phrase from Ghassan Kanafani's iconic novel, Men In The Sun: "Why didn't you knock on the tank's wall?" Fatenn, in her book "Modern Art in Egypt, Identity and Independence, 1850-1936", embodied the historical, artistic and political relations in the works of Egyptian artists and similar artists of the Levant and Palestine, the cradle of Christianity, especially in the works of Marguerite Nakhla about Christ and Jerusalem. Also, the exhibition of works by artist George Bahgory who demonstrated his solidarity with Palestinian artists through his photo carrying a watermelon.

Celtic fans never gave up to show their support for Palestine. They are the most faithful fans in the world. They fly Palestinian flags every week during games in order to show solidarity with the people of Palestine.

Vanessa Redgrave, in her 1978 Oscar acceptance speech, stood firm in support of *The Palestinian,* a documentary about the Palestinian struggle which she narrated herself, and despite threats from an Israeli lobby group, she courageously continued: "You have refused to be intimidated by a small bunch of Zionist hoodlums, whose behaviour is an insult to the stature of Jews all over the world and to their great and heroic record of struggle against fascism and oppression."

Pink Floyd's legendary Roger Waters waves the Palestinian flag on stage during his concerts and has condemned Israeli violence against the Palestinians. He led a campaign against the eviction of Palestinians from their homes in the Sheikh Jarrah neighbourhood in East Jerusalem.

Diego Maradona said "I am the number one fan of the Palestinian people."

The Hollywood actor Mark Ruffalo is a known defender of Palestinian human rights against Israeli repression.

Eric Cantona recited in public Mahmoud Darwish's Poem:

> As you prepare your breakfast, think of others,
> As you conduct your wars, think of others,
> As you return home, to your home, think of others,
> As you liberate yourself in metaphor, think of others.[9]

Sally Rooney, the young Irish author, rejected a bid by an Israeli publisher to translate her latest novel "*Beautiful World, Where Are*

You" into Hebrew in a show of solidarity with the Palestinians. In her 2018 novel, *Normal People,* the hero of the novel "Connell" is redolent of a citizen of Gaza in terms of pessimism, homelessness and loss of future:

> *I feel my future is hopeless and will only get worse.*
> *I have lost confidence in myself.*
> *I would kill myself if I had the chance.*

Rooney quotes a passage from the last novel of George Eliot, *Daniel Deronda,* written at the end of the nineteenth century, although some strongly believed that the latter was related to Zionism; Edward Said persuasively wrote: "The crucial thing about the way Zionism is presented in the novel is that a backdrop is a generalised condition of homelessness. Not only the Jews, but even well-born Englishmen and women in the novel are portrayed as wandering and alienated beings." [10]

Sarah Graham-Brown echoes this sentiment when she states that the "Palestinians have tenaciously through photography art preserved the memory of their past, which acts as a form of reinforcement in an unenviable present and a strong assertion of national and personal identity." [11]

Palestine used to attract most Arab poets, artists, and singers for its historical and religious status. The famous Iraqi singer, Nazem Al-Ghazali, made a visit in 1948 to support and entertain the Iraqi army fighting in the Palestine war, where he met Colonel Abdul Salam Aref, who later became president of Iraq. Among Iraqi poets who were racing with great desire to visit Jerusalem were Marouf Al-Rasafi and Jamil Al-Zahawi who met with violinist Sami Shawa, nicknamed the *Prince of Violin* in Jerusalem in 1932.

Almost all Arab artists sang for Palestine with dedication and sincere sympathy: Fairouz's songs for Jerusalem were very popular, as was Umm Kalthoum's song "Take me to Palestine", and Abdel Wahab composed and sang one of the early songs for Palestine in 1947 "*Akhy*

Jawaz al-Zalimoun Al-Mada," with lyrics by Ali Mahmoud Taha.

Lutfi Bushnaq, the popular Tunisian singer / musician, is a very passionate voice in lobbying for Jerusalem and Palestine. He performed the most-anthologized poems and composed the greatest patriotic works in the Arabic song repertoire. His repeats: *"Jerusalem runs in my veins".* [12]

Muhammad Assaf's winning of the title *"Arab Idol"* has enabled him, with inspiring solidarity, to convey the voice of Palestine to the world, as evidenced by the way his song *Ally El-Keffieh* rose to the level of becoming a beloved symbol of Palestinian identity.

Palestine, An Inescapable Duty

"In My Heart, I'm Palestinian."

— DIEGO MARADONA

Culture, and the impact it has on the nation from which it is born, is a significantly diverse entity giving strength, identity, and purpose to its people. Every country, every community is tied together by an intricate tapestry of values, customs, and history. Societies in our countries are united by the Arabic language with its deep sounds, modulation, rhythm, and beautiful vocabulary. At a time when London, amazingly, appeared as the cultural capital of the Arab World, it came to serve as a major centre for Arabic publications of daily newspapers, weekly magazines, books, periodicals and followed by the launch of Radio and TV stations especially, MBC and Al-Jazeera news channels. The growth of Arab presence in Europe spread further through sports and the popularity of players in European teams of Arab origin; and beyond that, the Arab ownership of several famous football clubs.

The launch of *Dar Al-Hani was* the first Palestinian publishing company in Britain. Al-Hani's office became bustling with journalists, media men and women of Arab and foreign press — mostly associates and contributors, among them: Abdel Ghani Mroueh, Ahmad Zikra, Riad El-Rayyes, Salim Nassar, Rana Qabbani, Patrick Seale, Basil Akl and Nassir El-Din Nashashibi. The first book published in English was *Palestine, an Inescapable Duty* by David Watkins, MP and Director of CAABU, who wrote:

> In the Venice Declaration of June 1980, the Palestinian right of self-determination was confirmed and the PLO must be involved in negotiations. Those who oppose the national liberation of oppressed people always describe national liberation movements as "terrorist organizations" because that automatically stops most people from thinking about the real issues of national liberation. Above all, the technique is used by the Israelis. Yet they themselves, every day, are terrorizing the civilian population of the occupied territories.[13]

Jabra Ibrahim Jabra's first visit brought pleasure and a lot of attention from everyone in Al-Hani. Jabra was the most prolific Palestinian novelist, poet, painter and critic. Al-Hani's patrons raced to welcome him, eagerly hoping to hear the story of his meetings with the famous novelist "Agatha Christie." He would answer, laughing and coy, "Agatha died and I forgot!". After the *nakba,* he left Bethlehem and went to Baghdad, and was appointed as a lecturer in English at the Preparatory College. There he excelled in writing many of his novels, including the acclaimed *"The Search for Walid Masoud".*

Eduard Shevardnadze, the last foreign minister of the Soviet Union, had the rights for his book, *The Future Belongs To Freedom,* purchased by Al-Hani, with potential plans for the author attending a book launch in London, in addition to a proposed meeting with Douglas Hurd, the then British Foreign Secretary.

Issa Khalil Sabbagh, director of the Voice of America Arabic and BBC Arabic radio stations, before moving to the White House as the official translator for Presidents Nixon, Ford and Carter, and Secretary of State Henry Kissinger, travelled extensively with all of them to the Middle East on their official visits.6 His book, "*As the Arabs Say!*", contained over fifty Arabic quotes and proverbs translated into English.

Hala Espanioli, an author, born in Nazareth, has collected hundreds of proverbs that help in preserving the Palestinian cultural heritage.[14]

Many scholars who translated Arabic novels into English were friends, among them Jonathan Wright, Maher Othman, Mohammed Ayoubi and Leslie McLoughlin.

Al-Hani published Samir Attalah's book "People and Cities",

Mustafa Ben-Halim, the ex-Prime Minister of Libya, and one of the fiercest opponents of President Gaddafi, pleaded with Al-Hani to publish his memoirs that harshly attacked Gaddafi. He had miraculously survived an attempt to kidnap him in Beirut, by a Lebanese gang hired by Gaddafi.[15]

Riad Aboushi, a close friend of Emile Habibi, who worked for the Saudi newspaper "Asharq Al-Awsat," came with a script to publish a book entitled, "From River to the Sea," in which he recalls that immediately after the establishment of Israel in 1948 and for many years after that, a strategic slogan was aggressively used by the Israelis and their allies throughout the world, "The Arabs will throw the Jews into the sea".

Then came the 1967 war. The war that ended before it began! It was believed that Henry Kissinger advised Israeli leaders to refrain from using this slogan, which became discredited and illogical after Israel had defeated the three most powerful Arab armies in six days.

Ibrahim Abu-Lughod expresses the historical links between Europe and Arabic literature, stating that:

> The modern revival of Arabic literature, the purification and simplification which made it a new medium of thought and communication, cannot be entirely

explained without reference to the impact of the nine-teenth-century translation movement. This movement which Muhammad Ali initiated outlived him, but to him and to the early generations of Arabs who worked in this field must go much of the credit.[16]

Nasir Nashashibi encouraged my intention to return: "Samir, the publishing business does not suit you, your home is Gaza, you belong there.. Remember Tariq bin Ziyad entering Spain with his small army, ordering the troops to burn their ships: "*Now, the enemy is in front of you and the sea behind you. Either you will be victorious or martyred. There is no third choice*". Your clear mission is to use your tremendous engineering experience in building Palestine, the country and the people need brilliant engineers like you."

Iraqi poet Buland Haidari's advice was to remember that, "when you are stopped at a checkpoint, then subjected to a thorough search by some young Israeli soldiers - most of whom are either Russians or Ethiopians, who cannot speak neither Arabic nor English - if you are happy, you smile. But during humiliating searches, smiles become a powerful weapon, an act of resistance and standing proud in such awful moments. I am confident that young Palestinians have more patience as they grow older."

Iraq and Buland bring us back to "Baghdad Memories" by Jabra, where he told his story at length:

"I was invited to meet a British archaeologist Max Mallowan who introduced me to Mrs. Mallowan, a lady in her late fifties, and she asked me 'What brought you to Baghdad?'

'An old love,' I said briefly, 'and our tragedy in Palestine.'

'Oh, yes, yes... Come and tell us. At least you're an eyewitness... Yes, what exactly happened to our Jerusalem?'

"Our conversation about Palestine was quite long, and I concentrated on the Zionist acts of killing, eviction, and land expropriation; the fine lady said 'All this must be known to the world...And in detail... Writers must write about these atrocities, about this inhumanity.'

"I later saw Max Mallowan and his wife once or twice, then we attended a play in English. During the intermission, our mutual friend Stewart asked me, 'Have you found a solution to the crime?'

'What crime?'

'The crime invented by the lady, whom I saw you talking to. Have you not been talking to Agatha Christie? I thought you knew! Mrs Mallowan is the mystery writer Agatha Christie.'

I went to her and asked her directly,

'Are you really Agatha Christie?'

The fine lady laughed and simply answered, 'Yes.'"

The historian Mustafa Murad Al-Dabbagh, born in Jaffa in 1898, during his work as educational inspector roaming through schools all over Palestine in the Mandate years, published numerous books, the most important of which is the encyclopaedia *"Biladuna Falastin"* (Our Country Palestine).

Naturally, the past has a sufficient stock of knowledge and experiences that serves as a motive for developments. Any society or country who ignores the importance of education as the gateway to the future, will never progress. Our diaspora leaders and inspiring achievers provided significant intellectual materials and scientific impetus that elevated the Palestinian cause to do better at the global level.

Some thinkers were concerned with the issue of intellectual heritage and the need to employ it in preserving the distinct and insoluble Palestinian identity.

This expresses that one generation fades into another, and the sun will continue to rise, while each generation passes on.

Trees Die Standing

*"Can a tree rise, if it does not rely on
its roots embedded in the ground?"*

— AUGUSTINE

History has never witnessed the emergence of a thinker or reformer without being hounded and distrusted by envious opponents of reform in his life, catalysing schemers to get rid of him and his ideas, as they curse him after his death. Ibn Sina, Ibn Rushd, Jaber Ibn Hayyan, Al-Farabi, Al-Razi and many others fall into this category. In spite of this, the names of these great thinkers have remained a shining beacon in the records of human civilization.

The beauty and splendour of old tales, such as the one who spreads flowers of joy from the quiver of pain, to draw a smile and awaken warm memories at a time when we are in distant countries; we fear losing them, especially, from the crowding and darkening of thoughts in our minds.

Writing is the mirror of the soul, reflecting the significant images of our past, our memories and our deepest thoughts. Our scholars chose to answer the call, within the context of their vocations, to address the needs of Palestinians who are suffering, exploited, dehumanised and oppressed. Their collective strategies founded upon revolt and protest for freedom became their agenda for involvement, leadership and writing. They had an absolute faith that the most precious thing that people possess is their national memory, the issues they embraced, the battles they fought and the mistakes they made so as not to be repeated.

During the post-*Nakba* years and departure from long periods of sadness, monotony, stagnation and harshness of feelings, a new generation of poets, authors, artists and musicians emerged, enjoying fertile imaginations and a vast vocabulary from the dictionary of the absent homeland.

Muin Bseiso, author of the collection of poems under the title "*Trees Die Standing*," and a prominent member of the Palestinian Communist Party, regularly repeated a phrase that he believes is a communist principle: "The *aims justify the means*". Ramzi Baroud, editor of the Palestine Chronicle, recalls that Resistance in all its forms featured prominently in almost everything Muin wrote:

> *If I fall, comrade, in the struggle, take my place,*
> *And gaze at my lips as they halt the madness*
> *of the wind. I have not died…*
> *I am still calling you from beyond my wounds.*
> *Sound your drums, so that the whole people*
> *may heed your call and fight.* [17]

Muin was a celebrated poet in Moscow with awards for his advocation to the communist ideology. He was fortunate to die before seeing Mikhail Gorbachev leave the Kremlin and lower the Soviet red flag decorated with the hammer and sickle for the last time in December 1991.

He couldn't welcome Che Guevara during his visit to Gaza in April 1959, as he was jailed in an Egyptian prison. Che said:

> Resisting oppression is not determined by belonging
> to a religion, race or sect, but rather by the nature of
> the human soul that refuses enslavement and seeks
> freedom. The Palestinians must continue the struggle
> and your country will be liberated.[18]

A local poet, Ahmed Dahbour, expressed his pity for those exiles who read books with deep understanding, but when they emerged from the world of books and their own rich experiences to real life, they are shocked by the shallowness of people's ideas, which do correspond to such books that are filled with sources of wisdom and culture.

Now, in real life, words are useless because they have lost their meaning. We don't know each other's value until it's too late.

It is a struggle over historical narrative and heritage. Ghassan Kanafani wrote: "When the defenders of the cause fail, we must change the defenders, not the cause."

Muin's greatest and distinguished comrade in communism, inside the Green Line, Emile Habibi, criticized the communists in one of his novels after the defeat of 1967.

> Who are the communists? — People who disbelieve in grace. They claim the ability to change the written.
>
> Pain flares up in the writer's chest for nine months, nine years, his whole life, until the pain of labour hits him, and his story is born! If it breathed the air of our earth, it would live, but if it descends on us from another planet, in which they do not breathe our air, it will suffocate and be born dead.
>
> How is it difficult to create imagination in a story that lives? Even more difficult is the birth of the truth in a story wrapped in imagination to protect it from the cold ? [19]

Muin and his most communist colleagues were indefinitely rejecting the policy of refugee subsidies, without specifying a period that ends with their guaranteed return to their stolen homes. But, Muien Badri, the history and philosophy teacher, had other ideas:

> Refugees' statehood is perpetuated by the absence of a political solution, they are only accepting aid for their survival. Not only in Palestine, in our renewed world, not many nations actually control their destiny. In every country that was seized by colonialism, states

were created, and at the same time ethnic and national identities were invented within those states. In ancient Roman religion, there was a Greek God named *Janus*, is the god of all beginnings, usually depicted as having two faces, likewise is the identity of many of these newly created states, a face that they make themselves and the other that is made for them by invaders, occupiers, imperialists or dictatorial leaders. The face they create represents their longing for freedom, and when others create it, it becomes a painful source of domination. What appears to be external conspiracies, as some leaders claim, is in fact an internal weakness.[20]

Adania Shibli, the Palestinian Bedouin, writes in her novel:

I open the map which depicts Palestine until 1948 and let my eyes wander over it, moving between the names of the many Palestinian villages that were destroyed after the expulsion of their inhabitants that year. I recognize several of them; some of my colleagues and acquaintances originate from there, from the villages of Lifta, al-Qastal, Ein Karem, al-Mallha, Abu Shusha, Siris, Innaba, Jimzu and Deir Tarif…I look at the Israeli map again. A very large park called Canada Park now extends over the area where all these villages used to be. [21]

Sheikh Kholousi Bseiso always quoted Imam Shafi'i, "Don't destroy the bridges that you built and crossed, you may need them to return someday. How can you convince the new generation that higher education is the key to success and the only way to a bright future? As long as we are surrounded by many poor and unemployed university graduates, unfortunately, thieves and the illiterate are very wealthy?"

"The spirit of all religions and worship is the glorification and veneration of God." I could draw only one logical conclusion. Creating life ... requires God." [22]

The men who waited for Godot.

The Agency Cafe *"Wikala Cafe"*

"No man is hurt but by himself"
— DIOGENES

Kamal Barbari was a prominent Palestinian lawyer who studied International Law at Cambridge University in the 1930s, and defended Palestinian prisoners of the resistance before the British military courts in English. He was, among others, very critical of the creation of a special agency for the Palestinian refugees called the United Nation Relief and Works Agency (UNRWA), that aroused suspicion of a conspiracy against the refugees, instead of involving the already established UN agency, the International Refugee Organization (IRO). Ilan Pappe explained:

"It was a well-known practice by the IRO to recommend repatriation as being the first option to which the refugees were entitled. It seemed that by avoiding the involvement of the IRO, the main purpose was to deprive the Palestinian refugees from that option, and by feeding them and helping to find them jobs in an attempt to silence them and keep them away from demanding the return to their homes and towns." [23]

By issuing cards to the refugees, causing a national and social rift and unwanted division between two factions of the inhabitants of the same country, they were branded with new descriptions: Citizens and Refugees.

Relying on outside aid became pervasive and entrenched among refugees in their camps; this was probably the hidden objective of those who created and supported UNRWA. Barbari, the most vocal critic of that organisation, used to mention the tale that when Indira Gandhi came to power in India, she immediately blocked international relief aid. Her ministers objected that the people would starve to death. She replied, "*Let them die with honour instead of becoming defenceless, beggars without dignity.*" Barbari continues: "Continuous humanitarian aid undoubtedly kills capabilities and peoples' potential, turning them into beggary society, waiting in long lines to get a handful of wheat or a drop of oil dipped in an insult of dignity, destroys the virility of man and turns the free and proud people into a lazy pet cat waiting for his share of aid. If only our people would realise that?" [24]

But, of course, the poor refugees welcomed the arrival of the Agency's first aid crews who started to distribute in-kind aid followed by building semi-permanent houses. The owner of Samara Cafe changed its name to Agency Cafe as none of the refugees was familiar with the name UNRWA or understood what that peculiar acronym actually meant. It was easy for everyone to memorise the name "*Wikala*" *(Agency)*, which is being used until today. The Wikala Cafe has become a favourite place for teachers, writers, poets, refugees and citizens alike, as it was the only cafe that had a radio. The cafe has become a pilgrimage site for most visiting high-ranking United Nations officials or international celebrities.

Subhi Alhashwa, the optimist, arrived in Gaza in April 1948, accompanied by his family of four, after the fall of Haifa to Jewish militias. Three years later, he managed to work for UNRWA in the capacity of public relations officer; an essential part of his duties was preparing schedules for UN diplomats and other dignitaries' visits to Gaza, that included Dag Hammarskjold, the UN Secretary General, Jawaharlal Nehru, Prime Minister of India, Hollywood actor Yul Brynner and the Swedish World Boxing Champion Johansson. Other visitors were the legendary revolutionary figure, Che Guevara, who came to Gaza on his own from Cairo after meeting President Gamal Abdel Nasser, and Jean-Paul Sartre who visited Gaza on 1st March 1960, accompanied by his long-time friend and author Simone de

Beauvoir. After visiting the Beach refugees camp, and condemning the occupiers for the pain they have inflicted on the Palestinians, he said: "One could only damage oneself through the harm one did to others. One could never get directly at oneself."

He also met with a Palestinian doctor, a psychiatrist, and gave him a copy of a small book he wrote in which he underlined the following paragraph as translated by Magdi Abu Ramadan:

> The significance of a fact of consciousness, it always pointed to the whole human reality, which was making itself emotional, attentive, perceptive, willing, etc. What it signifies indeed, in effect, is the totality of the relations of the human-reality to the world. [25]

Alhashwa's son, Saad, was attached to his father's hobby of collecting stamps and postcards that they received from those famous personalities.

One of the first American public figures to visit Palestine, during that stable period in 1964, was the political activist, and companion of Martin Luther King, Malcolm X, who met Ahmed al-Shuqairi in Cairo, but insisted on visiting the refugee camps in Gaza. He said after meeting with religious leaders, among them Sheikh Kholousi Bseiso: "Your cause is just, if you are not ready to die for it, take the word 'freedom' out of your vocabulary. If you're not careful, they will have you hating the people who are being oppressed, and loving the people who are doing the oppressing." [26]

Tragically he was assassinated the following year.

One of the worst misfortunes of the establishment of the Palestinian Authority in 1994, and thus the national struggle turned to the practice of beggary from donor countries. In the eyes of some, the Authority had joined the refugee queues for monthly aid, and Israel renounced, with glee and great satisfaction, its responsibilities towards the people under its complicit occupation. Many prominent cafe-goers were the new PA officials, surprisingly all of them were accomplished backgammon players. It seemed that it was their only amusement during the days and nights of struggle and the long siege, as happened in Amman and Beirut. The most skilled among them was Ziad Abdel Fattah, a close aide to Arafat and the head of Palestine News Agency (WAFA), a writer and a long-life friend of Mahmoud Darwish. His nick-name was "*Al-Kumayt al-Abjar*", name of the famous horse of the poet Imru' Al-Qays who was invincible. After living through the last three wars in Gaza, Ziad finally decided to go to Cairo, where he could have Shisha and play backgammon in the Fishawi cafe, and look for the ghost of Naguib Mahfouz, the only Arab to win the Nobel prize for Literature.

After President Trump decided to stop US funding to UNRWA, which caused its biggest financial crisis since its creation, its Commissioner General Philippe Lazzarini stated:

"It is not UNRWA that is perpetuating refugee statehood. Refugee statehood is perpetuated by the absence of a political solution, and there is no Palestinian that wants to remain a refugee after such a long time".[27]

With no political solution to the problem over the past seven decades, its mandate is being challenged by Israel and exploited by its foreign donors. The rebellious teacher, Yasser Shihab, a philosopher, a refugee living in the Jabalia camp and a regular customer of the cafe, complained bitterly:

> What is required in our deteriorating situation is some serious writings that reveal the truth which spares us from loitering in the narrow streets of this unpleasant camp and strolling on the long beach of Jabalia. The truth is about such words that aged in the tongues of many world leaders and their absolute silence in telling the truth.
> Where is Diogenes?
> We need a glimmer of light from his luminous lantern in broad daylight. All doors are closed, and our places are shrouded in complete darkness."

Tears at the Heart of Things

Is human freedom different in different societies? What does this freedom mean when society is forever changing and becoming more complex? Does this freedom change with the changes of the social and cultural context?

Advanced societies and nations are characterised by a high level of cooperation and concerted efforts. When a behaviour is characterised by collective cooperation, the achievement is much greater, and it can also be noted that the absence of the institution or cooperation, no matter how distinctive the efforts of the individual, does not achieve the desired results.

The second, and most dangerous, war was against knowledge and higher education in particular, to prevent the Palestinians from keeping pace with global scientific progress.

In Mandate Palestine, education abruptly stopped in the penultimate year of high school, which was called "Matriculation".

Why has no missionary or Christian church or any Western Government funded the construction of a single university in Jerusalem, Bethlehem or Nazareth, the cradle of Christ?

Despite the misery they have experienced, hope stirs their hearts by jumping outside the high wall of the largest open prison in the world, through reading, education and perseverance. They endured to realise their dreams to shine in their homes the sun of freedom, the sun of the beautiful existence made by the great Creator, that will open the world of knowledge and humanity.

Fortunately, some of the displaced Palestinians and those who lost their homes did not surrender to defeat, they enrolled their children to Arab and foreign universities, which resulted in academics having graduated from unique universities.

Salman Abu Sitta, who is credited for publishing the Atlas of Palestine, commented on education for refugees: "Education was the only battlefield in which I was soldiering. My tanks and planes were my pen, paper, and school records. Like the thousands of refugees from Gaza, I discovered that education was the mission of our silent army and was filling Egyptian universities." [28]

Notable academics and historians in exile have emerged, who excelled through their writings in portraying an objective narrative and comprehensive explanation of the Palestine cause.

Among these scholars who became globally recognised as the most distinguished references to our core issues, are Walid Khalidi, Edward Said, Ibrahim Abu-Loghud, Hisham Sharabi, Rashid Khalidi, Nur Masalha, Elia Zureik and many others.

Their greatness lies in their control of their abilities, which they harness lucidly to explain the national issues clearly to the world. They were able to advance the pursuit of knowledge and science and literature, and significantly, exceeded that goal by becoming professors and scholars, teaching students in the most prestigious universities in the western world, especially in the United States, Britain, Canada and other European countries.

Khalil Sakakini, born in Jerusalem, a revolutionary Palestinian in the field of education, formed the Wataniyya School and An-Nahda College in 1938. While working as head of the Education Department, he was credited for many of his patriotic positions, especially writing his famous books on teaching Arabic for beginners; generations learned to read and write through his well-known books for primary grades. A centre bearing his name was founded in Ramallah to preserve and continue his legacy through the promotion of arts, culture and education.

Until 1993, the people of Gaza did not have access to information. A group of academics had a desire to establish a high quality and useful library that could be expanded to become a modern science and technology library in all fields. A committee was formed, chaired by Antoine Zahlan, with Khalil Hindi, Rosemarie Said, Samir Shawa, Flora Hindi, Mashour Abudaka, and Shukri Nabulsi. Professors Abdus Salam, Sir Eric Ash, H. Rosenbrock, and Sir Michael Atiyah became sponsors of the project. Yazid Sayegh in Oxford, Mike Reed

in Cambridge and Ross Campbell in Scotland were the main col-
lectors of books. The project received a generous donation of one
million dollars by the Palestinian businessman and philanthropist
Hasib Sabbagh. The committee decided unanimously to rename
the library in recognition of the spirit of Sabbagh's late wife "*Diana
Tamari Sabbagh*".

Remarkably, the first public event held at the newly fitted library
was a meeting in January 1994, of local businessmen with the visiting
American Secretary of Commerce, Ron Brown, who was the first
African American holding such a high position in any American
Administration; he was accompanied by the American ambassador
to Israel, Edward P. Djerejian.

Very sadly, Secretary Brown was killed in an air crash in Africa three years later. The library still operates under that name in
Gaza to this day. Edward Said wrote about Hasib's distinctive and
unique personality:

> My strongest impression about Hasib, however, is
> based on what I have interpreted as an abidingly sad
> expression on his face. He can be silent in company,
> of course, but generally he is affable and engaging.
> He never speaks of his tremendous achievements,
> nor does he remind people of how he helped or con-
> tributed generously. Yet something about his look of
> composed reflectiveness reveals a kind of sorrow, not
> at the specific suffering he has so stoically endured
> along with his people, but a more general kind, rather
> like Virgil's *sunt lacrimae rerum* [there are tears in
> things.] [29]

Jimmy Carter also wrote in his introduction:

> If there be any truth in the contention of the English
> writer *Thomas Carlyle* that all history is but biography,

then this small volume may also help our understanding of history, for Hasib Sabbagh's life spans most of
the twentieth century and teaches us much about one
of the world's most vexing conflicts. His story also
shows how, ultimately, strife must be overcome in the
human heart. [30]

Many of us see mistakes and love criticism, but no one offers any
solution. The leaders are happy to lead a nation that is well versed in
criticism, and has failed in taking the decisions to initiate the necessary solutions and much needed reforms.

In culture, societies flourish and thrive in openness to other
cultures. So when a society closes in on itself, it condemns itself to
isolation from the rest of the world. In Palestine, everyone, especially
intellectuals and creators, is looking forward — they dream of and
aspire to a free society that confronts mistakes and demands reform.

Someone, somewhere is badly needed to pursue the role of mediator among our contending parties; in the quest for a free Palestinian
people, we need a conciliator among the Palestinians themselves and
between the Palestinians and the rest of the Arab nations.

Many who mistook Hasib's propensity to reconcile for a willingness
to compromise eventually realised that their assessment needed urgent
revision in light of the recent development with the Abraham Accords.

The Pessoptimists

"Humans are like books:
there are those who deceive us with the cover,
and there are those who amaze us with content."

— UNKNOWN

Reality is the reflection of a continuous history and recurring events; it is also the basis for the formation of our present with all its ramifications and the generator of the future with all its possibilities.

The Palestinians must know their reality, accept it and carefully manage its affairs, they must never lose sight of the reality, as slogans about achieving aspirations and beliefs are not enough to save them from the shameful reality. In culture, society thrives in openness to other cultures so that it does not close in on itself and becomes isolated from the rest of the world.

As a matter of fact, the Arabic language's influence over English, Spanish, Farsi and even Hindi is well documented. The unique Mediterranean culture that was free from restrictions and religious or racial fanaticism, and its diverse composition resulted in the emergence of writers and philosophers who enriched life with all that is beautiful and sublime.

Ghassan Kanafani was not only a novelist and journalist, but also a fighter and a politician who devoted his life to his Palestinian cause. Indeed, it was reported in the Arab press that when Golda Myer made a list targeting a number of Palestinian leaders and intellectuals to be assassinated, Ghassan was top of that list.

Mossad agents planted a bomb under his car that killed him with his young niece, Lamis Njeim. During his early life in Damascus, he was full of resolve. He used to carry an old *Olivetti* typewriter to earn some money to help his parents by typing letters to the court for many illiterate citizens.

"It is not important for a person to die before he achieves his noble idea, but rather what is important is to find for himself a noble idea before he dies." [31]

Al-Hani declined to publish Abboushi's book, *From River to the Sea*. He came again accompanied by Emile Habibi, Abu Salam, wearing his blue French beret. I gave him the choice to pick a restaurant for lunch, either a Lebanese, Swedish or Irish pub that is famous for Salt Beef sandwiches. Emile chose the pub that was owned by two Irish brothers. Once seated inside, suddenly the two owners rushed to us and shook Emile's hands with a warm and exciting welcome that surprised me. I asked him: "It seems that you are also famous in Ireland, right?" He replied, laughingly, "I have never been to Ireland, but I've been a member of the Knesset for a long time, and well known to the Israeli public, didn't you know that the two brothers are Israelis?" Abboushi added, emphasising, "The Israelis are everywhere. Did you know that "Abu Salam" was awarded the Palestinian Prize 'Jerusalem Medal' and the Israel Prize for Literature for his novel *The Pessoptimist?*"

We discussed my intention to go back home, so what was the advice of a veteran with long experience in dealing with Jewish and Arab politicians? He answered in a serious tone, "Actually I served in the Knesset for over twenty years, but, how can I oppose the return of a Gazan to his hometown, Ghazzat Hashem? As for the Oslo agreement, you can consider it as a step forward, but as for optimism about its future, I am a Pessoptimist as you know." We all laughed.

He invited me to visit him in Nazareth, upon my return to Gaza. I promised him that certainly I would also come to visit my friends in Haifa. He said: "I am from Haifa, and I will accompany you there." Emile Habibi sadly died a year after my return, and I was unable to visit Nazareth. [32]

Habibi recalled the extremely difficult early years of the Nakba and the sad disappearance of almost all intellectuals, writers, artists and teachers.

Ian Black reaffirmed "Israel's government was dealing with a traumatised community. The people who remained were like 'a headless

body'. It was the same story in West Jerusalem.. The near total departure of the more affluent and educated urban population meant the
loss of the intellectual core of the Palestinian society." [33]

Palestine is also the greatest literary experience. Its tragedies and
the pain of its people in exile have turned into the pain of human
exile in this brutal neoliberal era.

Of course, there is sadness in the Palestinian journey, but, there
is also joy. We must keep putting one foot in front of the other even
when we are hurt. For we will never know what is waiting for us
around the bend.

Without romanticising a painful and miserable situation of
Palestinians living under occupation, struggle will always breed
defiance. The people in Palestine used to celebrate their joyous
occasions and feasts with songs, Dabke dancers, and brass bands
roaming the streets followed by large crowds of fans. National songs
and anthems dominated their lives in the post-Nakba years, where
many poets, musicians and singers produced great works of art and
immortal songs.

Amazingly, the modest town of Zababdeh has produced many
distinguished personalities, including Nazih al-Khalil who is funding
several health and social projects and is sponsor of Zababdeh Art and
Dabke Troupe; also, the patriotic Catholic Father Manuel Mussallam,
who said "God chose me to resist all-evil against my people" and "
If they demolish your mosques, raise the call to prayer from our
churches," and the martyred ambassador Naim Khader, Professor
Bishara Khader, Ministers Khloud Daibes and Asma Khader all came
from Zababdeh. [34]

The growing role of women in public life through creativity became evident in the work of many artists, writers, activists and academics. Young and glamorous Palestinian fashion model Gigi Hadid
declared "*You will Not erase Palestine,*" and her sister Bella Hadid
echoed "*I stand with Palestine,*" in addition to singers and musicians
performing their patriotic acts, singing for love and hope; Dalal Abu
Amneh, born in Nazareth, was a neuroscientist and best known for

her songs for Palestine. The list goes on with artists, painters and sculptors whose works adorn several international museums, and some aspiring film directors such as Farah Nabulsi and Mai Masri, whose short films have won acclaim and international recognitions - including awards and nominations for the Oscars. Huzama Habayeb, describing the life of a Palestinian woman in a refugee camp, stated: "This amazing capacity for imagination was forged from experience of limited possessions, of life measured in droplets, of many accumulating deprivations, as well as the experience of days of extreme drudgery and of nights drained by sorrows." [35]

There are dozens of "Rosa Parks" among Palestinian women who have resisted the Israeli apartheid occupation, arbitrary arrests and brutal attacks on unarmed women, and almost all of them have never heard of Rosa Parks, the civil rights activist who refused to give up her seat on a bus to a white man, and became an icon of the resistance against racial segregation.

Emphasizing the role of women, Nora Shawa is the first recognised Palestinian publisher to establish Rimal Books in Nicosia in 1993, and to publish dozens of books celebrating Palestine and the preservation of its culture and heritage.

The Edward Said National Conservatory of Music was established in 1993 as a national institution with a clear mission to strengthen Palestinian identity through music. Daniel Barenboim, a friend of Edward Said, conducted the orchestra in Gaza in 2011. On its performances in Europe, Nai Barghouti was its principal voice.

> *Take me back to my country with the morning breeze,*
> *With a sunbeam lost between shore and vale,*
> *Take me back to my country.* [36]

CHAPTER 4

A Thorny Path of Struggle

*"Our journey oscillated between incessant
pessimism and a little bit of optimism."*

PLO-Fatah, Politics of Survival

*"But man is not made for defeat...
A man can be destroyed
but not defeated."*

— ERNEST HEMINGWAY

The Palestinian diaspora, especially in areas far from the homeland, helped to protect the existence and identity of the Palestinians after being uprooted from their land.

Kuwait was the main incubator for healing the wounds of the *Nakba*, and it became the Arab pioneer in nurturing the depth and economic status of the Palestinian national movement for more than forty years. Kuwait was blessed with rulers, '*Sheikhs*', who had absolute open-mindedness and a national pan-Arab vision. Significantly, even under British protection, Kuwait had a Legislative Assembly in 1938: "Many of its members were largely motivated by their political ideals. One was their work in obtaining money and arms for the campaign of 1936 to halt the Zionist colonisation of Palestine" as Alan Rush noted.[1]

The Kuwaiti elites in the forties and fifties were clinging to their Arab national affiliation and cautiously preparing for their upcoming independence from Britain. They very much welcomed the coming Palestinian professors, doctors, engineers and ex-officers to benefit from their scientific and practical experiences for a temporary period, until their expected return to their homeland within a few years. Palestinians' arrival in Kuwait was mainly to look for work, not to seek refuge, housing and protection from Zionist attacks and massacres that befell most refugees in other neighbouring countries. Thus, the Palestinians in Kuwait became the third largest community among refugees.

Abdel Mohsin Al-Qattan arrived in 1951 and worked as a teacher, then became Director General of the Ministry of Electricity until he resigned his post in 1963 to start his own contracting company. As did Hani Al-Qaddumi, Khaled al-Hassan and many high-ranking officials, in order to give way to the rising Kuwaiti graduates.

Abdul Karim Al-Shawwa, a member of the old and leading families of Gaza, arrived in 1949, took a leading position in the Public Security Department under the leadership of Sheikh Jaber Al-Sabah. He also took a leading position in the Oil Ministry, but what distinguished him was his support for hundreds of Palestinian families who sought to build a new life and future in Kuwait after their devastating catastrophe. His ability to support families was essential in the expression of his adherence to the Palestinian cause. He also managed to establish a group of private companies.[2]

Said Khoury viewed his father's ordeal as a result of the *Nakba* as the driving motivation to bear the hardship of working in extreme desert conditions to relieve his father, who suffered poverty. He had been turned into a refugee after being a distinguished rich merchant in Safed. He managed to build the largest contracting company in the Arab world.[3]

Yasser Arafat arrived in Kuwait in 1958 and worked as an engineer for the Ministry of Works in Kuwait; his good relations with local and Palestinian contractors was strengthened quickly. He met many Gazans working in Kuwait, in particular two teachers: Khalil al-Wazir and Salah Khalaf. The three formed the first nucleus of the resistance movement and called it *"Hareket Tahrir Falastin"* Fatah. They were joined later on by Farouk Qaddoumi, Khaled al-Hassan, Salim Zanoun and others. Three years later, Mahmoud Abbas, arriving from Qatar, joined the movement. The blessed and humble birth of Fatah was in that great and hospitable country of Kuwait. [4]

Subsequently, it became the largest Palestinian resistance movement that took the lead in all future struggles. "During the 1967 and 1973 wars, Kuwait provided diplomatic and financial backing and Kuwaitis fought alongside Egyptians, Palestinians and Syrians. They also extended massive support for the economies of the confrontation states," [5] said Chief of Staff, General Ali Al-Moamen, who remembers his role in the wars that one third of the Kuwaiti forces were ordered to engage on the Arab-Israeli fronts, from 1967 to 1974 and during the war of attrition. He was in charge of training Palestinian volunteers in Kuwait military camps in coordination with the PLO representative Khairi Abu el-Jebain, who incidentally was his teacher in secondary school.

Following the defeat of the six Arab armies in the 1948 Palestine War, the slogan of the "Liberation of Palestine" remained firmly stuck in the Arab conscience, and it was kept as a mantra in the political programs, agendas and manifestos of the progressive and nationalist parties.

The painful and humiliating 1967 defeat was also the final blow to the slogan of liberation, as it was promptly replaced by a new and urgent collective cry of "Removing the Traces of Aggression" *[Izalet Athar Al-Idwan]*. The use of such popular slogans that inspired the enthusiasm of the Arab masses did not last long, until the 1973 war had ended all previous slogans. The official Egyptian demand became clearly a peaceful settlement based on the June 4, 1967 borders, which ironically are the same Rhodes Armistice borders of 1949 negotiated and agreed by the Egyptian military. The young Sheikh Fahad al-Ahmad served as a commando in the Sinai campaign of the 1967 war. Shortly afterwards he unofficially joined the *"Asifa"*, a fighting unit of Fatah. He was wounded in the Jordan valley in 1968 and again in southern Lebanon." [6]

General Giap, the legendary Vietnamese military Commander, gave advice to a visiting Palestinian revolutionary cadres headed by Khalil al-Wazir:

> Revolution and wealth don't meet. A revolution that is not led by awareness and consciousness turns into terrorism. A revolution that is showered with money, turns its leaders into thieves, if you see someone claiming to lead a revolution while living in a villa, eats the most delicious dishes, lives in luxury and complete comfort, while the rest of his people live in camps and receive international aid to survive, regrettably, it is clear that this leadership does not wish to change the unjust reality. How can a revolution triumph, while its leadership does not want her to win? [7]

Upon their return to Gaza after an absence of thirty years, many Fatah members and supporters found that a large majority of young students had joined Hamas. They wondered about the reasons for their sudden swing towards religion, remembering that most of their parents were purely secular; their newly religious convictions were incongruent with the secular atmosphere in which they grew up in Gaza and Palestine in general.

The new officials sensed that their passive response showed, with great determination, their faith in the absolute ability of Hamas, rather than Fatah, to continue the resistance and force Israel to end the occupation. The youngsters expressed deep anger at the unprecedented suffering of insults, humiliation and even beatings by the Israeli soldiers who often forced them in the middle of the night to go down to the street, ordering them to erase the slogans supporting the Intifada from outside the walls of their houses. During the past hundred years, the Palestinian people have established and supported several institutions to lead their struggle: the Supreme Islamic Council during the Mandate years, headed by Haj Amin Husseini, the All-Palestine Government two weeks after the establishment of Israel and headed by Ahmed Abdel Baki, the Palestine Liberation Organization initially headed by Ahmed Shuqairi and replaced by Yasser Arafat, the Palestine National Council headed by Abdel Mohsen Qattan, Khaled Al-Fahoum, Abdel Hameed Al-Sayeh; and for the past twenty five years by Salim Zaanoon, the Palestinian National Authority headed by Yasser Arafat who was succeeded by Mahmoud Abbas.

The Legislative Council was initially headed by Haidar Abdel Shafi for a few months, before he was replaced by Ahmed Qurei, and a short-lived National Unity Government headed by Ismail Haniyeh, before it was dissolved. In addition to two dozen, or more, smaller liberation fronts and resistance movements that became known as Palestinian Factions, residing in many places and allied to several liberal and ideological parties.

All these national entities that were supposed to work diligently in the interest of their people, preserve their unity and fulfil their hopes and aspirations, ultimately failed and were significantly ineffective, mostly destroyed by their stupid and factional leaders. Slogans of victory, socialism and freedom flew high in the sky of Arab and Palestinian dreams, then suddenly crashed on the ground of reality. It was like a violent earthquake that destroyed all hopes of liberation and victory.

The setback and defeat of June 1967 planted the seeds of despair in Arab societies, but especially among the Palestinians, who woke up on a pitch-black morning and found the rest of their historical land, including East Jerusalem, had suddenly and unbelievably fallen under the control of the Israeli army. This caused the dissolution of that official illusion that rode their minds for over twenty years, of formulating the principles and constants of many factions and parties to free the people and the cause from the delirium of ideologies and the manipulation of Arab leaders and politicians. The confrontation between Ahmed Shuqairi and most Arab leaders in the Khartoum Summit after the 1967 setback, ended his presidency of the PLO, and the Arab leaders supported Arafat to take his place.[8]

Unfortunately, they increased the rhetoric of illusion in their statements and public programs. Hope is the height of despair, when aches and calamities befall us, and it was very painful when we had nothing left but hope itself.

The unified resolution by the Arab League's summit in Morocco's capital, Rabat, in 1974, which stated that the PLO is the sole and legitimate representative of the Palestinian people, was a fundamental turning point of the beginning of the transformation of Palestine from a national issue for all the Arabs to a purely Palestinian cause.

The loss of Beirut, and the expulsion of the resistance forces and its leaders to Tunisia, was a severe blow that some believed was the final straw that broke the camel's back; this despite many attempts by Arafat to go back or at least to send a small contingent in order to protect the defenceless refugees from upcoming massacres similar to Sabra and Shatila.

In the first precedent of its kind, Israel agreed to the largest prisoner exchange deal, with the help from the International Red Cross, in November 1983: 4,700 Palestinian and Arab prisoners were released from camps in southern Lebanon and Israeli prisons, including resistance leader Salah al-Taamari, a Fatah leader, who later married *Sharifa Dina*, the first wife of King Hussein.[9]

In Tunisia, Arafat found himself and the PLO in a desperate and unenviable situation, and was excluded by several Gulf Arab governments following his declared support to Saddam Hussein's invasion of Kuwait in 1990. It was undoubtedly a major mistake for which hundreds of thousands of Palestinian families, living and working in Kuwait, who lost their jobs, have paid a heavy price.

In the face of that critical situation, while he witnessed the assassination of a number of Fatah figures, including his lieutenants Salah Khalaf, Khalil Al-Wazir, Hayel Abdel Hamid and others, Arafat found in the Oslo Accords a lifeline. [10]

As Rashid Khalidi put it:

> When we first saw the text of what had been agreed in
> Oslo, those of us with twenty-one months' experience
> in Madrid and Washington grasped immediately that
> the Palestinian negotiators had failed to understand
> what Israel meant by autonomy. What they had signed
> on to was a highly restricted form of self-rule in a frag-
> ment of the Occupied Territories, and without control
> of land, water, borders, or much else. Israel retained
> all such prerogatives, indeed amounting to virtually
> complete control over land and people, together with
> most of the attributes of sovereignty. [11]

In politics, there are no shocks, no constants or principles. Interests come first, and every state views it from its own perspective,
not from the perspective of its enemies or even its allies. Politics, as
they say, is the art of the possible. As Khalidi further explains about:

> ..the deep tensions running between the PLO in Tunis
> and the official delegation. We were aware of this ten-
> sion, and we saw it flare into open dispute on occasion.
> Many of us were present in Faysal Husayni's Wash-
> ington hotel suite during furious phone exchanges
> between him and Arafat. [12]

In 2005, after Abu Mazen assumed the helm of leadership, the
PLO was relegated and no longer operated in a major way in his daily
administration. Rather, he preferred dealing with the Arab and International official bodies as the President of Palestine, or sometimes
the Palestinian National Authority.

Following the failure to resolve the old and continuing dispute
between Fatah, which controlled the PLO, and other factions such
as Hamas and Islamic Jihad, who were not originally members since

its formation, all sides were demanding reforming the structure of the PLO and changing the membership conditions to allow for their inclusion according to the proportion of their enormous public and popular standings. Of course, Abu Mazen aimed with this pressure card that he held through his presidency of the PLO to keep these factions away from its membership, in order to maintain his dealings with international governments - especially the Americans who still considered it a terrorist organization - and the Europeans who provided important financial aid to the Palestinian Authority. Marzooq Al-Ghanem, the Kuwaiti Parliamentary speaker, shone regularly in international parliamentary conferences in defending the rights of the Palestinian people and reprimanding Israeli delegations.

Many observers believed that the PLO was going through a state of severe and painful decline, and had been suffering a slow decline, and possibly terminal death. The word *"Liberation"* had become incompatible with its current composition, and it was an empty word in content and meaning in that humiliating state. It was an absolutely ineffective and failed experiment that had no legitimacy or respect from its enemies, nor sympathy from its supporters; and no commitment from its leaders. Fraih Abu Middain, a former Minister of Justice, claimed that the U.S. refused to withdraw its designation of the PLO as a "terrorist" organisation despite hosting the ceremony of the Oslo Accords in the courtyard of the White House. All visits by Arafat and his delegations were given a one-time *"waiver"* visa". [13]

A Provoked Intifada?

Despite the unforgettable failure of the Camp David peace talks between Yasser Arafat and Ehud Barak under the auspices of Bill Clinton, which lasted for twenty days, Arafat's return to Gaza was astonishingly marked by a huge welcoming crowd, cheering him for his ability not to forfeit a single inch of the 1967 occupied lands (which was less than 22% of the historic lands of Palestine).

A few weeks later, Ariel Sharon paid his planned and provocative visit to the Al-Aqsa Mosque in Jerusalem, which immediately sparked a second Intifada, later named the "*Al-Aqsa Intifada*". As a result, Palestinian casualties of deaths and serious injuries accelerated for several months until then prime minter Ehud Barak's defeat in the elections, which brought Sharon to power. Israeli air attacks continued on selected targets, but surprisingly, the Gaza Power plant was a unique and unexpected one, given the fact that the American company "Enron " owned a third of its equity.

The picture was quite rosy in the beginning for Arafat, with the election of the first legislative council and remarkable achievements in the housing sector, health and social services; the building of the first independent power-generating plant; work began for the construction of a sea port; and operating of the Gaza airport, which, for the first time, linked Gaza to several Arab capitals, and Palestinian pilgrims were able to fly directly to Mecca.

The 27th of September 2000 was a memorable day in the history of the nascent Palestinian Authority, as this day witnessed Arafat's boat heading to light the gas torch for "Gaza Marine 1", the first well in a gas field, west of Gaza, thus declaring Palestine's accession as one of the few gas exporting countries in the Eastern Mediterranean. Unfortunately, the joy was squandered the following morning by Ariel Sharon's provocative visit to the Al-Aqsa Mosque in Jerusalem, which ignited the second intifada.

Observers were unable to analyse this strange and incomprehensible event, namely that Arafat did not prevent it from the beginning, and in some way even blessed and supported it. Incredibly, this was shortly after the conclusion of the Camp David talks with Ehud Barak, who appeared on television screens as he jokingly wrestled with Arafat, pushing him to enter the hall in front of him as a gesture of respect to that Palestinian leader, or perhaps out of respect for Arafat's old age!

The daily conditions began to recede, the Israeli attacks targeting government buildings (and security forces quarters) became a daily occurrence, infrastructure projects were destroyed including the seaport, and with great sadness and astonishment, the airport was completely demolished.

With the intifada entering its second year, Gaza was subjected to an organised campaign by groups that sowed hatred with the aim of causing strife among the citizens. Disagreements in beliefs that were taken for granted in the past surfaced, including the attack on a house selling alcoholic drinks, and the burning of a hotel lobby that served beer. Suffering increased due to the daily rocket attacks on Gaza and other cities of the West Bank, during which people shared condolences with dozens of families for the loss of their martyred youth in the mourning tents, which became an almost daily occurrence.

What saddened observers most was watching innocent children being pulled from under the rubble of their destroyed homes as a result of the indiscriminate bombing. The daily funeral processions were so numerous, our eyes filled with petrified tears. "Martyrdom is at the heart of all religion, the Shahid in Islam, Christ on the cross for the Christians and The Kedoshim of Judaism," one must be prepared to suffer for one's beliefs and holy cause. One had a crazy, desperate, hidden and tempting feeling of becoming a martyr.

It has long been falsely assumed that Palestinians living inside the Gaza and West Bank under the occupation have an inherently weaker capacity to mobilise their unified action.

Abu Ali Mustafa (Mustafa Zabri), the newly appointed PFLP leader replacing its founder George Habash, was allowed to return and was then assassinated by a guided missile through the window of his Ramallah apartment. Ahmed Sa'adat was elected a new leader, but a few weeks after his election, he was arrested by the Israeli army and sentenced to life imprisonment.

The security chaos intensified when a group of Hamas fighters kidnapped Brigadier General Rajeh Abu Lahia, commander of the Rapid Intervention Forces in the Gaza Strip, in broad daylight, heralding the beginning of the fall of the National Authority in Gaza.

House fires became a regular occurrence due to the burning of candles that Gazan families began using to light their homes; such as the tragedy of the Al-Hindi family and the burning of their home in the Shati refugee camp, which resulted in the death of their three children. That incident was not the only one to take place in the Gaza Strip; dozens of children suffered similar fates as a result of power cuts. There were many faces of daily and horrific sufferings; the siege, closure of land borders, blockade on fishing boats and bombardment of the only airport. Deaths were reported daily, but this time remarkably by a strange and a new enemy: electricity blackouts, the frequent cuts which occurred daily, reaching twenty hours.

The communities in Palestine had always been united for decades, and neither the forces of the British Mandate nor the Israeli occupation army were able to break their solid ranks, as they resisted enormous attempts. Unfortunately, some groups with religious facades and subversive esoteric purposes, succeeded in transforming science into religious myths, and culture into tales of hell, fire and the torment of the graves. They managed to spread fear in the minds of the young generation.

The United Nations established a committee in 1975, with a mandate to advise the General Assembly on a program to enable Palestinian people to exercise their inalienable rights, including the right of self-determination, without external interference, and the right to national independence and sovereignty; as well as the right of return to their homes and land from which they had been displaced. This mandate has been renewed on an annual basis since.

Nizar Qabbani wrote his famous poem, *Children Bearing Rocks*, in 1987. He died 3 years before the second intifada:

> *With mere rocks in their hands,*
> *They stun the world...*
> *Ah, generation of betrayal,*
> *of surrogate and indecent men,*
> *generation of leftovers, we'll be*

swept away — never mind the slow
pace of history —
by children bearing rocks."

Edward Said, who strongly opposed the Oslo Accords, described it as "the final trap for the complete elimination of the Palestinian Liberation movements." [14]

Amin's Good Friday!

"The evil that men do lives after them,
The good is often interred with their bones."
— SHAKESPEARE

At every stage of history, we find a group of people who are conservatives or reactionary, and another revolutionary and calling for change. The strife between these two groups is neither quenching nor interrupted as long as society remains dynamic. In the eyes of the conservatives, the revolutionaries are heretics and foreign agents. As for the conservatives, they are in the eyes of the innovators, tyrants and oppressors.

In the cradle of Christianity, people describe the Friday of Christ's crucifixion as "Friday of Pain", "The Holy Friday", and "The Great Friday", in contrast to the current description by Christians living in the west, who, at odds with other Christians, describe it as "Good Friday".

Gaza is quite possibly the only city where one of its Christian citizens, Kamal Tarazi, leads his blind Muslim neighbour to the mosque every day to perform his prayers. His older brother, Khader Tarazi, was the first Christian martyr in 1987 during the first intifada, his body was displayed on top of a military tank near Jabalia, to frighten people of a similar fate. His daughter mourned him with an expression of sadness resembling the martyrdom of her father to the crucifixion of Christ. She proudly adds: "Of course Jesus Christ was the first Palestinian

Martyr of Nazareth, who was born in Bethlehem." [15]

On a rainy Friday in late November1994, gunfire erupted near the *Falastin* Mosque in the Rimal neighbourhood, immediately after the midday prayer; as dozens of police and other security services set out towards the mosque, some people gathered in the streets, where there were violent confrontations between the security men and the crowds of worshipers leaving the mosque. People could clearly hear the screams of the injured, residents ran to the streets to find out what was happening, or check on the fate of their relatives.

Old men begged the policemen to stop firing at their fellow worshipers, but to no avail, as they were obeying their commanders' orders and were not aware that they were killing members of their own families. Skirmishes and sporadic gunfire continued until sunset. Early in the evening, Muhammad Qidwa, Arafat's cousin, who became the first Governor of Gaza, came to our house, carrying an invitation for me to meet the President urgently to discuss with others the critical situation. [16]

Arafat was sullen and showing signs of anger mixed with amazement. Sitting in front of a small group of local leaders, Amin al-Hindi was standing next to Arafat. I recognized Dr. Haidar Abdel Shafi, Fayez Abu Rahmeh and Aoun Shawa among them. The discussion revolved around what the newly formed authority should do to solve this critical and unforeseen crisis, as it was the first time that Palestinian-Palestinian fighting had occurred in Gaza. There were two options: either the police struck with an iron fist against members of Hamas and those who violated the law and imposed the authority of the state, or to negotiate with Hamas' leadership and end this crisis through dialogue.

Riad Al-Zanoun, the Minister of Health, suddenly entered and informed the President that the number of dead until now was 17 and the wounded were 98. These numbers were shocking to everyone. Silence reigned in the room for a while. Finally, Arafat agreed to form a committee headed by Dr Haidar to mediate with Hamas leaders. I was one of those calling for peaceful dialogue and avoiding the use of violence. The next day, it was announced that the number of dead was 13 and the wounded were 212.

This was a painful and sad beginning that forced me to wake up from my beautiful dream of participating in building civil institutions for our next state. It became clearer to me that things on the ground were much more difficult than all expectations. A few months after the 9/11 attacks, I was having dinner at the home of Omar Sarraj, with our mutual friend and neighbour since childhood, General Amin al-Hindi, head of the Palestinian General Intelligence. His sadness and regret of what happened in New York's twin towers were apparent, but he expressed surprise at the inability of the extremely powerful American intelligence and its great advanced technological capabilities to identify and thwart this evil operation before it occurred? He also expressed bewilderment mixed with astonishment at the ability of Osama bin Laden, and his group, living in the remote caves and mountains of Afghanistan to plan and implement a daring and dangerous operation with the utmost precision in execution.

For the first time, he revealed that fifteen of his men were secretly planted in the ranks of the Mujahideen and Al-Qaeda, to the extent that two of them served among bin Laden's escorts. His main interest was to identify any Palestinian's affiliation there who might be joining with a Palestinian Muslim Brotherhood leader named Abdullah Azzam.

Of course, Amin 'Abu Fawzi' had good working relations with the CIA director George Tenet and his successors, they cooperated fully in the fight against Islamic extremists and the so-called 'war on terror'. He quietly admitted, according to confirmed information, the presence in Afghanistan of some Israeli intelligence operatives who spoke Arabic fluently.[17]

Following the massive devastation suffered by Shejaiya and its residents, the moderate history teacher, Wael Ayyad, a Christian, who lost his sister in that recent attack, spoke with a strangely soft tone:

History testifies in the past few centuries that the Christians of Europe, being kings, princes or soldiers had hearts of extreme cruelty, and increasingly fossilised, in uncharacteristic ways among other civilised peoples. They brutally participated in the colonisation of other poor and weak countries during that period.

The ugliness and horror of their cruelty reached many high levels that ignited several wars among themselves and culminated in their initiation of the most dangerous wars mankind has witnessed in the last century, the first and second World Wars which resulted in nearly a hundred million people dead in addition to unprecedented destruction.

We, the Palestinian Christians were affected by the shocking news of the mass Nazi Holocaust of Jews and others that were among the cruellest crimes committed with their hearts devoid of any mercy or compassion.

In Jerusalem, on Great Friday (or Painful Friday, as initially described by Eastern Christians before being changed to Good Friday by the Western churches), Muslim children used to walk happily behind the cross on "*Via Dolorosa Street*," the path of suffering that Jesus walked carrying the cross on the way to his crucifixion. [18]

Today we remember the words of that esteemed teacher who explained on another occasion:

It is really unfortunate that some descendants of those Europeans still live in our world and occupy sensitive positions of power.

A hateful example was the deliberate strangulation by the US police officer of the African American citizen George Floyd; his gruesome death ignited the global popular movement of "Black Lives Matter". That was clear evidence of cruelty, hatred and racial superiority that the world suffered from in the past.

Taawon…Welfare

The British Mandate administration rigorously and treacherously did not allow the establishment of a university for the Palestinian Arabs, despite their encouragement and blessing for Jews to build the Hebrew University in Jerusalem in 1924. The closest university geographically to the Palestinians was the American University of Beirut, which was founded by Bliss, the American Christian missionary in 1866 under the name "The Syrian Protestant College."[19]

Fortunately, the university had produced many Palestinian graduates who had succeeded in achieving great innovations in their various fields of science, medicine, engineering and economics, and beyond that, some of them had excelled in teaching at that unique institute. Amongst its graduates were Ibrahim Touqan, Haidar Abdel Shafi, Hasib Sabbagh, Fuad Hijazi (the martyr), Abdel Mohsin Qattan, George Habash and Hanan Ashrawi. Some of those who had the honour of teaching there included Walid Khalidi, Zuhair Alami, Mohammed Nagem, Issam Ashour, Nabil Shaath, Antoine Zahlan and Rashid Khalidi. The first Arab president of the AUB was Professor Constantin Zureiq in 1957.

Lebanon, like Palestine, was blessed with a moderate and beautiful climate, and in the 1950s enjoyed an economic and social renaissance. It became a focal point for Arab culture, arts, paintings, songs, theatres and music; an inspiring and fabulous place for the privileged and a favourite destination for an important segment of many Arabs, especially those from the Gulf states, and other nationalities. Hence Lebanon earned the moniker *the Switzerland of the East*. In this environment, some Palestinian exiles who succeeded in establishing flourishing businesses which expanded quickly to other countries, suddenly began to feel that they were embarking on a new phase of their lives, and quickly realised that there would be a humbling and daunting responsibility waiting for them in the future.

Years later, sadly, they were shocked by the incomprehensible and strange social interactions which began to unfold in Lebanon, and unthinkable behaviours began surfacing whereby people began to deal with each other on a sectarian basis: Maronite, Orthodox, Druze, Sunnis, Shiites, etc.. Such terms were unheard of and definitely unpalatable by their parents in Palestine, as their social fabrics did not differentiate between people on the basis of their religious beliefs. As a matter of fact, in many Palestinian cities and town landscapes, we can see a mosque adjacent to a Latin Monastery.

Several educational and cultural institutions were formed to improve the conditions of the Palestinian refugees in Lebanon, who numbered around 300,000. Walid Khalidi noted that on the establishment of the Institute for Palestine Studies, "Clearly the most hospitable country would have been Lebanon, because of its open political environment and lifestyle... Constantin Zureik, Burhan Dajani, Antoine Zahlan, Ramzi Dalloul, and myself were actively involved in two projects that included the Royal Scientific Society as well as the already founded, inter-Arab Institute for Palestine Studies in 1963. Zahlan was appointed director." [20]

One of the darkest, and painful, days that will never fade away from Palestinians' recent memory, took place during the summer of 1982, when on the 16th of September people around the world watched the horrific, bloody and harrowing images of the innocent victims of the Sabra and Shatila camps' massacre of children, women, and elderly Palestinians. The young men had been already deported on ships signalling the great resistance's final exit from Lebanon, and the beginning of another chapter of Palestinian resistance alienation. A few days earlier that month, thousands of fedayeen headed by Yasser Arafat, his Fatah comrades and other factions' leaders boarded three ships as arranged by the American envoy Philip Habib, and sailed away to Athens and then to Tunisia.

Hasib Sabbagh, who was very distressed and terrified by that horrific and criminal event, called for a meeting of Palestinian businessmen to be held in London in an effort to help the besieged and destitute refugees in the Beirut camps. That first meeting led to the establishment of the non-political, non-profit Taawon ['Welfare Association'], followed by its first constituent meeting which was launched in Geneva exactly six months later. Dr. George Abed became the first Director General of the association, a senior International Monetary Fund official, he later assumed the prestigious financial position of Governor of the Palestinian Monetary Authority, of which I was also an unpaid member of its Board of Directors. The meeting was chaired by Abdel Majid Shoman, chairman of the Arab Bank, and was attended by over forty participants, who were committed to contributing to its immediate relief work. [21]

The highlight of that meeting was focused on having intellectual conversations with Palestinian academics, scholars and cultural figures who were invited to present their thoughts and ideas and to find a way out of the crisis and predicament that the PLO had fallen into. Edward Said, Hisham Sharabi, Ibrahim Abu Lughod, Mohamed Negm, Issam Ashour and Yusef Sayegh were some of the many names of such distinguished Palestinian historians, thinkers and intellectuals attending. Shoman announced that donations had reached twenty million dollars, which exceeded all expectations, and then asked Edward Said to speak in that inaugural meeting:

Said's opening remarks were as follows:

> To the best of my knowledge, it was the first time in the modern history of the Arab World that individuals, many of whom had never actually met each other before, came together on their own and on such a scale expressly to contribute money, time, and intellectual effort to what in effect was a moral cause.

That purpose involved neither the taking of power nor the expectation of victory, as that word normally understood, added to the remarkable quality of the occasion.

All of us knew that there was no real way of stopping Israeli tanks and planes as they poured their rockets and bombs on an essentially undefended small country that contained a large Palestinian refugee population driven from their land by Zionist forces in 1948. We knew that not as an abstraction, but as part of our own life history - each of us with a family uprooted, years of travail, decades of frustrating work behind us - and we also knew that we had to gather together to act in resistance to this devastating fate we all shared. [22]

During the final day's dinner, sharp and muted discussions took place on our table between Said Khoury, Abdul Karim Shawwa and Jaweed Ghussein, the three being active members and directors of the Palestine National Fund. Jaweed believed that the association project would definitely fail in the very near future, due to traditional competition between businessmen, and their lack of agreement on any collective work in the past — especially in the field of public services; this despite their amazing individual successes.

Said Khoury raged in disagreement and said angrily: "Oh Jaweed! This new association will succeed and live for a long time, I am sure that its life will be longer than yours."

Said Khoury, one of the founders, had been a driving force behind its success, an advocate for entrepreneurs across the Arab world. As the founder of CCC, he had been a prolific and unrelenting motivator, a position made all the more unique by the fact that he was also a Palestinian refugee, who understood all too well what losing a home means. One month later, Jaweed Ghussein, who resigned from the Welfare Association, was appointed chairman of the Palestine National Fund in Tunis by Yasser Arafat.[23]

In another meeting while in the presence of Walid Khaldi, Basil Akl, Issam Ashour and, of course, Edward Said, a heated discussion broke out between Hasib Sabbagh, a devout catholic, and Edward over Salman Rushdie's book *"The Satanic Verses"*. The book had aroused great indignation and objection from many religious and political parties; loud demonstrations took place in several Islamic and Arab cities, condemning the author and protesting its publication.

Imam Khomeini issued a *"fatwa"* dissolving Rushdie's blood.

Edward had written an article strongly objecting to Khomeini's unacceptable *fatwa*, which probably implied that Edward endorsed Rushdie's book. Hasib, on the other hand, reprimanded him for interfering in the affairs of the monotheistic religions, especially the Islamic. "Edward, it is necessary for us, the Palestinians, to exercise extreme caution in dealing with such sensitive issues, and try to avoid siding with a writer at the expense of our brotherly relations with our Arab Muslim partners."

Edward, with his characteristic resolve, affirmed his commitment to freedom of religion as well as freedom of expression, and reiterated his rejection of the "fatwa". "It is not permissible for Khomeini or any other religious or political leader to order the killing of a writer because of his ideas or opinions that do not appeal to that ruler. Dear Abu Suhail, all religions started with an idea!" The debate dragged on without a tangible result. The discussions reminded me of an amazing phrase: "No one can kill the idea." Despite my great admiration for Edward Said's progressive ideals, in that meeting I thought that we should not delve into Satan's troubles.

Annual meetings continued to be held in Geneva for several years, then it was decided to transfer the association's offices to Amman, and later to Ramallah. One of its founders, Abdel Mohsin Qattan, born in Jaffa, was a member of the PNC until resigning — along with Edward Said and Ibrahim Abu Lughod — in 1990, in protest at Arafat's support of Saddam Hussein's invasion of Kuwait. His foundation built in 1998 a Centre for the Child in Gaza city, which encourages young artists through prizes, awards and training programs, and is currently run by Omar al-Qattan.

Taawon's Board of Trustees, headed by Nabil Qaddoumi, and succeeded by Faisal Alami, was able to attract several Arab and International donors to support many reconstruction projects and oversee the implementation of several humanitarian and community programs in Gaza, the West Bank and refugee camps in Lebanon. Indeed, the Welfare Association "Taawon" will soon be celebrating its Fortieth year of proudly serving people in Palestine and the refugees in Lebanon.

Martyrs of Creativity

*"I bear many scars, but I also carry with me moments
that would not have happened if I had not dared
to go beyond my limits"*
— PAULO COELHO

In the past, Arabs have expressed their appreciation for the creators, especially poets and scholars. The poet was considered a shield who protects the tribe, and a gallant defender of their high position among other tribes. One of the most famous gatherings of intellectual dialogues in pre-Islamic days was Souk Okaz, where oratory competitions and recitation of poems and novels were held.

Since the beginning of the Palestinian revolt in the 1920s, with considerably limited resources and weapons, against the British Mandate forces and the increased militant Jewish immigration, there was an unspoken and inhumane policy by the British in targeting the educated leaders of the resistance. Their despicable goal was to get rid of as many creators and university graduates or scientists, as possible.

The targeted executions of Palestinian creators began in the wake of the Al-Buraq revolution in 1929, when the Mandate forces arrested hundreds of Palestinian youths and quickly sentenced 26 of them to death; the sentence was reduced to 23 in life imprisonment and upheld the death penalty for the remaining three.

The three consisted of Fuad Hijazi, who was born in Safed, a graduate of the American University in Beirut and his two colleagues, Muhammad Jamjoum of Hebron and Atta al-Zier. The three were hanged in front of the main gate of the notorious Acre prison on June 17th 1930.

A young popular poet, singer and composer, Noah Ibrahim, was targeted and killed during the longest Arab strike in 1936.. Born in Haifa, he had resisted the British occupation and the growing Zionist Settlement activities through his national chants and music.

By the end of the Mandate, Israel adopted a more violent, cruel and bloody policy in fighting the prominent Palestinians, and entrusted the operations of eliminating creators, academics, thinkers and scientists to its intelligence agency called the Mossad.

They invented new and complex means of assassinations that the Arabs never knew. The Egyptian Colonel Mustafa Hafez was assassinated in his office in Gaza in July 1956 by a letter bomb, delivered by a Bedouin who was recruited by the Mossad. Wadie Haddad, a senior member of the PFLP, was also assassinated in Baghdad by a box of poisoned chocolate sent by the Mossad. The killing of engineer Yahya Ayyash in Jabalia camp in 1995 from a distance, by means of an explosive charge planted in his mobile phone; this technical feat had not been used before in similar operations conducted by the Mossad.

The young American activist, Rachel Corrie, was killed by an Israeli military bulldozer while standing in front of a Palestinian home that she was helping to protect, in the Rafah refugee camp.

At a regional conference at the Italian city of Bari, a strong presence of Palestinian officials including Nabil Shaath were in attendance and, on the other side, among the Israeli delegation, was Ephraim Halevy, the former head of Mossad. [24]

During lunch break, it happened by chance that Halevy sat next to me, and I took that opportunity to ask him a question that had been in my mind for several years: "Why does the Mossad assassinate Palestinian intellectuals and writers, such as Ghassan Kanafani,

Kamal Nasser, Naji al-Ali and other non-combatant individuals?" He denied any knowledge about those assassinations! In the closing session, as we were leaving the hall, he stopped me and said: "I think it is not necessary for Israel to assassinate anyone. The Arabs are killing each other."

The martyrdom of Ghassan Kanafani in Beirut in July 1972 was a cowardly operation, the first of its kind against one of the intellectuals and creators of the Palestinian youth in Lebanon. Mossad agents placed an explosive device under his car, which exploded as soon as he started the engine, and as a result of this criminal act, another innocent victim in the prime of her life was killed: Lamis Njeim, his niece, the daughter of his sister Faiza.

I have had a long friendship with the Kanafani family, especially with his younger brother Marwan, who used to talk about their exile and the harsh life of refugees in Damascus, Ghassan's activities, his national ambitions and the need for a unified front to liberate Palestine. Ghassan warned against the failure of some leaders: "If we are unsuccessful defenders of the cause, it is better for us to change the defenders, not to change the cause." Also: "When you betray the homeland, you will not find dust that longs for you on the day of your death, you will feel cold even when you are dead." Among his most popular novels are "*Men under the Sun*" and "*Returning to Haifa*", a small part of Ghassan's incomparable literary and patriotic legacy.

Said Hamami, the first representative of Palestine to the UK, won the admiration of many MPs in the British Parliament through his good relations with the media, with a distinctive and candid manner in presenting his just cause, which made him an obvious target by the enemies of Palestine. Sadly, he was assassinated in January 1978 in his London office.[25]

Naim Khader, who was assassinated by Mossad agents in June 1981, was the first Palestinian representative to the European Union; he succeeded with courage and diplomacy, in establishing professional and personal relations with many important figures in the EU presidency in Brussels. He also played a prominent role in advancing the European-Arab-Palestinian dialogue that culminated in the historic Venice Declaration in June 1980. His younger brother, Professor Bishara Khader, contributed to lobbying for Palestine through his teaching at the university of Louvain in Belgium.[26]

Naji al-Ali, the famous cartoonist, was born in the town of Al-Shajara, and has kinship and friendship with my wife's family in the Upper Galilee. His arrival to London with his friend, the Iraqi poet Ahmed Matar (both were expelled from their work in the Kuwaiti *Al-Qabas* newspaper) was an opportunity to get to know him and his family. He laughed about the reason for their dismissal being their demand for their share of Gulf oil, based on a popular slogan "Arab oil is for all Arabs".

His soul and life-long friend was undisputedly *Handala*, the character he created who symbolised the patience of the Palestinians over their catastrophe. Naji was very critical of the policies of all the Arab regimes, without exception, and their failure to solve their national issues, at the forefront of which was the issue of Palestine. He smoked heavily, and the psychological scars that had befallen him on his complex journey of asylum and life as a refugee in Lebanon and exile in Kuwait, and the fact that he lost his Palestinian nationality and identity, were clearly visible on his face. He was assassinated by an unknown killer in July 1987 in broad daylight on the street where the offices of his newspaper were located. He was kept in hospital on life support for a month and then died on August 29th, 1987. Many experts agreed that the assassination was carried out by professional Mossad agents.[27]

Kamal Nasser, a poet born in Birzeit, studied political science at the American University in Beirut. He was famous for his mastery of poetry about love for the homeland and was one the distinguished writers and the editor-in-chief of the "Palestine Revolution" magazine in Beirut. He was assassinated in April 1973 during a massive Israeli operation that killed other PLO leaders, Kamal Adwan and Abu Yusef al-Najar, along with other Lebanese citizens. It was widely reported that the mission was led by Ehud Barak, dressed as a woman, who later became the Prime Minister of Israel. Hillary Clinton confirmed his involvement in the attack: *"Barak was also one of the most decorated war heroes. As lore has it, he even dressed in drag during a daring commando assault into Beirut in the 1980s. We got along famously."* [28]

In the event of his death, Kamal Nasser had bequeathed to be buried in a grave next to his friend Ghassan Kanafani, who was also assassinated a year earlier. Indeed, this sensitive poet and Protestant Christian fighter was buried in the Muslim cemetery of martyrs, near the grave of his friend.

A wave of anger prevailed in Lebanese streets, which prompted the Prime Minister Saeb Salam to demand the dismissal of the army chief, as he bore full responsibility for the failure of his forces to confront the attackers.

The then President, Suleiman Franjieh, did not agree, which also led the prime minister to resign. Palestinian Christians have played an historical and effective role in all areas of life, and they still do. Significantly, they are maintaining the patriotic model of safe co-existence and social cohesion with each other despite all external challenges.

Archbishop of Sebastian, Atallah Hanna expressed: "I am a Palestinian Christian. We also say *"Allahu Akbar"*, as well as *"InshaAllah"* and *"Alhamdulillah."* This is simply because Arabic is our language, and the Arabic word for "God" is *"Allah"* whether you are a Christian or a Muslim." [29]

When searching for people who truly supported justice and fought the oppressors, injustice, fanaticism and extremist ideology, two figures shone in particular: Dr. Ghassan Al-Rifai, who joined the World bank in 1972 and served as its vice-president for the Middle East until 1998 -a leading economist and former Minister of Finance in the first Syrian Government of Bashar Al-Assad in 2000, and a long-time supporter and lobbyist for Palestine; there was also a man of science and culture, a member of the Omani Shura Council, Muhammad al-Mahrouqi.

Two powerful advocates for Palestinian legitimate rights through their participation in international forums and conferences, both were regular speakers in the Doha Forum, Pugwash conferences and CMED (Center for Middle East) meetings as organized by Steven Spiegel and his assistant Mani Jad of UCLA. Incredibly, Mohammad Al-Mahrouqi used to append all his correspondence with an amazing quote by the American author Ernest Hemingway:

> The best people possess a feeling for beauty,
> The courage to take risks,
> The discipline to tell the truth,
> The capacity for sacrifice.
> Ironically, their virtues make them vulnerable;
> They are often wounded,
> Sometimes destroyed.

The Palestinian "*Creative Martyrs*" are the best people. Mohammad Mahrouqi really wished to emphasise this fact.[30]

Fragments of Division

> "*Nothing proves that I am alive,*
> *nothing proves that I am dead!*"
> — MAHMOUD DARWISH

Historically, the Palestinians have encountered repeated plots, conspiracies, the loss of their homeland, destruction of houses, the torment of asylum to neighbouring countries, the humiliation of criminal occupation forces, the indignity and ceaseless arrests, torture, death and hundreds of thousands of prisoners during the post-Nakba years.

Palestinian society was firmly united; neither the British Mandate administration nor the Israeli settler occupation were able to split their unbreakable unity. The 1967 setback planted the seeds of despair in the Arab world in general, and the Palestinians in particular. The enthusiastic crowds of people who were once flying high in a sky of dreams had tumbled unconscious within six days, upon the ground of a new and painful reality.

Generations of Palestinians who had witnessed and experienced this disastrous transition remained attached to their culture and heritage, despite poverty, social deprivation, and miserable lives in refugee camps. They would never have dreamt of expropriating or accepting an alternative homeland. Even those who migrated outside the homeland to very far places had consciously and honestly preserved the love of Palestine, forever engraved deeply in their hearts. They carried it on their backs as well.

Nur Masalha blamed Israel: "Since 1967 Israel has fostered further Palestinian splits: between East Jerusalem and the West Bank; between the West Bank and Gaza." [31]

Years went by until the fighters and some of the displaced finally returned to a small part of their country, which was so dear to their hearts, and a glimmer of hope appeared on the horizon that they harboured since the early years of the *Nakba*, the "right of return".

During the seven years of hope since the establishment of the National Authority, these parts were subjected to organised campaigns by groups very alien to the vast majority, who sowed hatred to cause strife among the masses, and deepened the differences in beliefs that were forbidden in the past. Unfortunately, they succeeded in transforming science into religious myths and culture into tales of hell, fire, and torment of the graves, then they spread fear in the minds of the young, and fratricide that led to the hateful division.

There is a fine line between demanding the right and confiscating the right of the other, and a fine line between demanding the right and heading towards chaos, between shouting and self-expression. A people represented by groups steeped in political ignorance cannot suddenly awaken to awareness. Wisdom does not awaken in a short period of time, because wisdom is a long process of awareness.

When analysing the mistakes of the liberation movements, there were many; the last of which was undoubtedly Oslo, which did not aim to liberate the land, but instead led to the termination and sabotage of the counter-revolution that was in the making. They forgot about the tens of thousands of martyrs who fell under the command of an unreliable leadership. Some grieving families ask with a clear sorrow:

"Why us? Who is responsible for this?

"Where is the Divine Providence for what happens to us?"

The truth is, there is no one left under colonialism except the Palestinian people, who are still plagued by the harshest and most brutal occupation known to the peoples of the region. Nur Masalha argues that the *Nakba* led to the dispersal and fragmentation of the Palestinian people and produced a major division between the minority who remained inside Israel and the refugees forced outside its borders.[32]

Franz Fanon also urged the colonised to continue their struggle:

"If a man is known for his acts, then we will say that the most urgent thing for intellectuals is to build their nation."[33]

Whoever visited Gaza one year after Hamas seized power would be stunned by the incredible scenes of destruction close to Beit Hanoon or the Erez crossing; the new wasteland whose fruitful trees of oranges, olives, figs and apples were uprooted, houses and buildings completely demolished and the Industrial Zone adjacent to the border vanished.

A small group of businessmen sat at a table in a hotel and cafe called *Al Mat-haf* (the Museum) — this was a bold venture by the Gazan contractor Jawdat al-Khudari, who transformed part of the restaurant into a small museum, in which he displayed some of the visual pieces of ancient heritage from the *Al-Blakhiya* area, which was close to the hotel.

The group was joined by Ibrahim Abul Naja, a former minister of agriculture, who then served as Governor of Gaza. Suddenly three Hamas officers in civilian clothes appeared, moving between tables and staring at the customers. Abul Naja sighed saying: "These are Hamas intelligence men; the tall person was the senior prison official during my recent arrest. I shared the same cell with my friend Mohammed Qidwa, the former Governor of Gaza and a cousin of Yasser Arafat. We were in *Al-Mashtal* prison. I am free now, but it is possible for them to arrest me or any member of Fatah at any moment". [34]

Upon the completion of the Palestinian General Intelligence building in the Al-Mashtal neighbourhood, which was funded by the United States, the Director of the CIA, George Tenet, visited Gaza for its inauguration ceremony along with General Amin al-Hindi, Director General of Palestinian Intelligence.

The large building housed a secure and modern prison, fully equipped with clean rooms and furnishings. It seemed that the prison rooms were intended for Hamas leaders and their activists, but all its inmates were Fatah leaders and officials from Gaza.

The question that arose, and always, was: Why do Hamas leaders in Gaza and Fatah leaders in the West Bank fail to recognise the bitter truth that the first and last beneficiary of this odious division was the Israeli Occupation?

Obviously, the solution is not easy to overcome, nor is it easy to reframe the concepts of division, as they had been entrenched in certain segments, without stopping to assess their disastrous results. There is no place for ideal values in this hellish world. Many started to lament the progress in cultural heritage made by the great men of science and knowledge in recent times. How to get out of this predicament, rise from complete darkness? Historically states had been either too weak to protect individuals, or too strong for people to protect themselves from despotism. How can this new situation be resolved? When will the Authority wake up from its deep slumber and realise that protecting its national project is an absolute priority? When would they bridge the divide and fight this dangerous spiral? That is, fight everyone who oppresses Palestinians, as well as everyone who sows discord and incites killing and vilifying the other.

In light of these incredible divisions and the unprecedented intensity of their internal hatred and the absurd classification among these factions, the occupier became the last thing on their minds! An enemy had been imposed upon us, an enemy who knew all our faults and could see us quite clearly, from where we could not see him or his soldiers.

Memory preserved disasters and their perpetrators as well. What we were experiencing was most probably the outcome of what our grandfathers did; we could not blame them entirely for the mistakes they made due to ignorance and naivety. Unfortunately, these mistakes left us desperate, destitute and not expecting a better tomorrow. We became a people making crazy leaps in the void, with a common failure shared by everyone.

The inexplicable behaviour of our opportunistic leaders perpetuated this disaster, and they were absolutely determined to stay in power. A group of local intellectuals, in their continued attempts to create a new framework for serious dialogue between the factions without upsetting anyone — as they strived to avoid anything which could provoke a painful experience — were resisted by one side as an attempt to exclude any form of conflict, stifling innovative solutions and open debate. Despite the fact that people are more willing to respond to harm than they are to reward kindness and favour; gratitude is a heavy burden, while revenge sadly generates pleasure.

Pope Francis, who visited Palestine, had followed with concern about what had been happening in Gaza, and was always sad about the conditions of the Palestinians; he called for their support in achieving their long-deserved independence:

> Self-accusation" is a simple notion set down by a sixth-century desert monk, *Dorotheus of Gaza,* drawing on the wisdom of the desert fathers who showed how God never leaves us alone. In accusing ourselves, we "lower" ourselves, making room for the action of God to unite us.[35]

Time kept fluctuating during the years of political decline and the sharp and shameful division between the two parts of the homeland that had lasted for an unbelievably long time. Most observers agreed that Palestinian leadership barely existed, stagnant and ossified. Would Gaza permanently separate from the West Bank and East Jerusalem? Would Gaza remain under the control of Hamas and the Israeli siege forever?

The ideal description that *Ibn Khaldun* gave centuries ago to the corrupt rulers applied literally and sadly to the factional leaders who controlled the components and future of the Palestinian people over the previous two decades:

> They commit injustice and deliberately humiliate the innocent and honourable citizens, due to their constant inferiority complex that accompanies them and refuses to leave their souls.

We must stay away from the so-called "factional quotas" that make the two main factions dominate and monopolise the decision-making process.

Fatah appeared to have learned nothing from the backlash following the fall of Gaza to Hamas in 2007; on the contrary, on the 55th anniversary of its launch, "Abu Sa'ab", one of its leaders, stated:

"Until today, we are still reproducing all the causes of our misery. The laughable thing is that in any case, we claim that we are absolutely right in everything we do."

This division was a painful deprivation to millions of Palestinians, and reminded us at every moment of the tragedies that had continued to pursue us like a crazy fate.

One of the most pressing demands of the Palestinian people was to have a leadership that has sufficient maturity to admit their mistakes, smart enough to learn from them, and a solid will to correct them.

There was no intention to charge the Palestinian Authority in Ramallah, and no intention to focus on the failure of the governing authority of Hamas in Gaza. But this book is also a documented testimony to their responsibility in the disaster that the people in Gaza and the West Bank had endured for so long, and still do.

Everyone failed…Everyone is guilty.

Prisoners of Freedom

"Faith is seeing light with your heart
when all your eyes see is darkness."
— BARBARA JOHNSON

A person's life is measured by the extent of their ability to find their freedom and to which they are able to enjoy it and be creative in life.

Freedom is the most gracious gift that God has given to us. What hurts a nation in a dire life situation is a time of perplexity, the rule of doubt and the annihilation of certainty. This may be because the hidden intentions of human beings towards each other are unhealthy and treacherous.

The Palestinian strike of 1936 during the British Mandate rule, the longest in modern history, lasted for more than six months, and throughout the duration of the strike, civil disobedience was declared, which included the complete closure of several Palestinian towns. The Mandate forces arbitrarily arrested thousands of young men and imprisoned most of them without trial.

During the second meeting between Rabin and Arafat at the Erez crossing in northern Gaza, the debate raged over Arafat's demands for the release of thousands of Palestinian prisoners; the number offered by Rabin was too little and unacceptable.

Rabin responded calmly: "Abu Ammar, there are thousands of your comrades in Arab jails, much more than we have in ours at the moment, for example, in Syria over three thousand Palestinian prisoners without trial languish in prisons. Why don't you negotiate with Hafez Al-Assad for their release?"

Arafat fell silent and didn't answer. Later that day, one of his advisors admitted that there were over two thousand Palestinian prisoners in Syria. He added angrily: "Were it not for his fear of an angry and deplorable popular reaction, Hafez Al-Assad intended to arrest Chairman Arafat as well, due to the overwhelming personal hatred for each other." [36]

To verify the validity of Rabin's claim about our prisoners in Syria, I called my friend Abdullah al-Hourani, who was born in the town of Masmiya, part of the Gaza District at the time of the Mandate. He was a prominent member of the Baath party from the 1950s, and held an important position being an independent member of the Executive Committee of the PLO, as well as being a writer and he held several media and cultural positions, including the director of the official Syrian Radio and Television stations in Damascus.

Prior to the historic visit of President Clinton to Gaza, where he was to address the National Council — who voted to delete the "armed struggle" from its charter — Arafat formed a new Executive Committee of the PLO; Al-Hourani resigned or was excluded from its membership due to his rejection, alongside three other members, to Clinton's demands. In a remote suburb of Damascus, there was a notorious prison called "El-Mezzeh", a typical residence for political prisoners, or as they became known, the "Prisoners of Opinion". As a gesture of goodwill, the prison's administration added a small library to the compound; the inmates, most of them being intellectuals, could borrow one book at a time to read in their cells, and of course the choice of books was limited and subject to censorship. One day a prisoner who searched for a specific book which he couldn't find, politely and respectfully asked the prison's officer about the possibility of obtaining that book; to his surprise, the officer answered laughing: "The book is forbidden.. But you can meet its author, you will find him in the fourth cell to the left of yours." Hourani laughed and shook his head in the affirmative.

My friend, Dr Ghassan Al-Rifai also laughed, he was a fierce defender of the Palestinian cause,, a leading Syrian economist who worked for the World Bank as vice president to James Wolfensohn, in charge of the Bank's operations in the Middle East. He was later appointed by President Bashar al-Assad as Minister of Finance in his first cabinet of 2000.

During the second intifada, Abdullah invited me to dinner at one of his Gaza beach restaurants. He was sitting with a tall and big man, and introduced him:

"This is brother Mahmoud, my comrade "Abu Al-Abbas," incidentally, he is the one who can help with the fuel."

"Are you Abu Abbas? The Italian ship? *Achille Lauro*?"

He burst into laughter and said, "Yes my friend. I am him exactly, it seems that you are quick to note, and your historical information is quite accurate."

"Are you not being chased or wanted by Israel?"

"Yes I was, Abu Ammar was called the most wanted terrorist by Israel, my brother Hourani was forbidden from returning to Palestine. What is the problem then?" He then added, "I actually live in Baghdad, the most beautiful place despite the unjust US sanctions, our love for Iraq because of our leader President Saddam Hussein, he is admired by every Palestinian, don't forget he was the only leader to fire scuds at Israel." I felt anxious being in that restaurant, with the power failure, which is usually a sign that precedes an Israeli bombardment, and I was afraid of a surprise Israeli raid or drone attack.

Hourani noticed my clear anxiety and said, "Abu Abbas has an excellent relationship with President Saddam Hussein, who promised to supply quantities of Iraqi oil for Gaza's needs" then added, "Abu Ammar warmly welcomes Abu Abbas, he requested his help in another matter, which might interest you as I know you have many Kuwaiti relatives, he wants him to verify the fate of hundreds of missing Kuwaiti prisoners in Iraq, after its withdrawal from Kuwait in 1991. It seems that Arafat has been working seriously for some time on reconciliation with the State of Kuwait." [37]

At this moment, Abu Abbas wiped his hands on his face, as if he was reciting *Surat Al-Fatiha*, usually said on the spirit of a deceased, and said, "Unfortunately, my sources confirmed that there were no Kuwaitis alive in Iraq. I will return the day after tomorrow to Baghdad and will be meeting the great President Saddam, God willing. When you need oil from Iraq in the future, please inform comrade Abdullah, and I will oblige."

When I was about to leave, Abu Abbas got up, shook hands and said, "Is Menahem better than me?"

"Who is this Menahem?

"Menachem Begin, the most wanted terrorist by the British for his responsibility in killing hundreds in the King David hotel massacre, and the killing of Count Bernadotte. By the power of God, he became the Prime Minister of Israel, received at the White House, and a close friend of Anwar Sadat. I also want security and peace for my people."

That was the first and last meeting with Abu Abbas.

A year later, Al-Hourani informed me of Abu Abbas' death in a detention centre belonging to the American forces after the occupation of Baghdad, where the US military had arrested him on his way to the Syrian border. Abu Abbas was not the only prisoner who fell into the hands of the American army, his beloved and great leader, Saddam Hussein was arrested, imprisoned and executed by hanging on the first day of the blessed Eid al-Adha, despite its sanctity for Muslims. Great Prisoners of Time? [38]

Yasser Arafat remained hostage to two rooms in what was left of his destroyed headquarters in the Muqata'a building in Ramallah for more than two years after being besieged by the Israeli army forces. He was a political prisoner, but some Europeans called it "under house arrest".

President Hosni Mubarak, who was trying to mediate his release, claimed that Ariel Sharon would allow Arafat to leave Ramallah as long as he did not return to Palestine.

Arafat rejected this solution and shouted his famous phrase: "*They want me expelled, and I want to become a martyr*".

In late October 2004, Sharon allowed Arafat to travel to France for treatment after receiving intelligence information confirming that Arafat had only a few days left before his death.

Another great prisoner of time? Not a year has passed since the beginning of the *Nakba* in 1948, without the Israeli occupation forces arresting hundreds of innocent citizens, including children, women and the elderly. Their alleged crime is seeking freedom in their country and ending the brutal occupation.

Nael Al-Barghouti, the longest serving Palestinian prisoner on his 43rd year in several Israeli prisons, had been dreaming since his capture that the next year he would be released, through a prisoner exchange deal, and would start his first day of freedom by kissing the hands of his mother and father. But, sadly, his mother died, followed by his father, then his uncle. His younger brother was imprisoned too, his older nephew was martyred, the younger one carried out a commando operation and was sentenced to life imprisonment.

No one is exempt from arrest and pursuit. Among these prisoners were the Legislative Council's members, Palestinian Authority ministers, high ranking police officers, Fatah, Popular Front and Hamas members.

Some high-level prisoners, supposedly intellectuals, were subjected to torture by brain-washing, leading the prisoner to play a game of collaboration, invited to lead a double life: a person well-known for their patriotism, imprisoned for preventative reasons.

The task undertaken was to attack from the inside those elements which represent national consciousness. Not only was the intellectual in question expected to collaborate, but he was given orders to discuss matters "freely" with those opposed to his viewpoint. This was an elegant way of bringing him to focus attention on other patriots, and thus serve as an informer.

Every year, a number of prisoners would go on hunger strike to protest against ill-treatment and the infamous "administrative detention" that is Internationally condemned.

It allows Israel to imprison Palestinians without charge or trial; the detainee does not have free access to a lawyer, and detention can be extended indefinitely.

Dr. Iyad Sarraj confirmed many psychiatric symptoms encountered among the survivors of the Israeli interrogation included stomach ulcers, nephritic colic, menstruation trouble in women prisoners, intense sleeplessness caused by idiopathic tremors, hair turning white early, cardiac rhythm acceleration, and muscular stiffness.

Issa Qaraqie, the Minister of Prisoners' Affairs, was at an event in London, attended by many European public figures — among them Ann Linde, who then served as the Foreign Minister of Sweden, and made a wonderful speech in support of the release of Palestinian prisoners who were suffering from hunger strikes.

Issa told a true story about an old man who lived with his son, on his land in a village near the West Bank city of Jenin, which he cultivated with tomatoes and potatoes. The settlers came and took over half of his land and his only son who helped him was arrested, and sentenced to three years imprisonment. When the planting season arrived, the man was unable to plant anything due to his old age, and other villagers were not allowed onto his land. From the severity of his sadness he sent a letter via the Red Cross to his son in the nearby notorious Ofer prison in which he said, "I wished, my beloved son, that you would be here to help me grow the potatoes as usual; unfortunately, no one can come to help me for fear of attack by the settlers."

A reply letter arrived: "My beloved father, please never plough the land, because I hid something precious and important in it. When I get out of prison, I will tell you about it."

On the next day, a military force arrived and surrounded his house and dug its entire land with great care; when they found nothing, they left.

A few weeks later a second letter arrived:

"My dear father, I hope that the land has been well ploughed, this is what I was able to help you with, you can plant your potatoes. Forgive me for any shortcomings. Your son, Talal."

President Abbas abolished the Ministry of Prisoners and established an independent body that performed similar duties, in response to the enormous pressure exerted on him by the US. This resulted in the loss of Qaraqie's position.

Khalida Jarrar, a politician and elected member of the 2006 Legislative Council, and Head of the Legislative Council's Prisoners Committee, an active member of the PFLP, was also the Palestinian representative on the Council of Europe. She had been subjected to multiple arrests by the Israel army. Sadly for Khalida, her daughter, Suha, died, two months before her intended release; the Israelis refused to allow her to attend the funeral of Suha, her 31-year-old daughter, despite many appeals from various European and Israeli organisations.

Khalida sent a message from her cell:

> When Suha came to the world, her father was incarcerated. And she is leaving it now while her mother is behind bars. This is a condensed example of human life for Palestinians who love freedom despite the cruelty of occupation and colonialism which rob us of the oxygen we breathe. [39]

All these heroic tales of prisoners of time and their loved ones immediately resonate within anyone who has warm blood in their veins.

This is from the story of a Kurdish revolutionary woman prisoner "*SARA*" who spent years in Turkish prisons:

> I had become acquainted with the prison in Azmir. Above all we had to try to understand what prison meant for the enemy. They want to exploit our weaknesses by individualising us, they'll use all the time it takes. [40]

According to International Human right groups' statistics, one out of every five Palestinians is imprisoned or detained by Israeli forces.

There has not been in modern history a nation with a fifth of its population suffering varying periods in the dark prisons of the occupier, but still standing tall, steadfast and valiantly resisting, and smiling at the failure of the power of injustice and predatory Israeli arrogance. Palestinians have become one of the stoics of the world, the silencer of pain and the inhabitant of silence during a time when depths have been polluted with fear and carelessness. Yes, they survive, despite the darkness that surrounds them, and despite their losses and heartbreaks, they endure in a very strange, unusual and abstract way.

The two million people of Gaza live in the largest open prison in the history of mankind, and the (not so) funny thing about it is that the prisoners have to provide their own food, drink, and medical treatment for themselves.

CHAPTER FIVE

Lobbying Adventure

*"The reality of the other person lies not in what he
reveals to you, but what he cannot reveal to you.
Therefore, if you would understand him, listen not
to what he says, but rather to what he does not say."*

— KHALIL GIBRAN

Unofficial Diplomats

Palestine. Its memory, legacy and identity were at the core of many
young exiles, believing that every opportunity should be explored,
every door knocked upon, irrespective of the adverse political circumstances of the moment. Many people see flaws in everything.

But unfortunately, reformers are rare, and thus were the
majority of our people at home and in the diaspora. Most political
analysts did not formulate creative ideas, to counter the empowered
Israeli lobby in the western world. Regrettably, almost all parties and
factions at home never accepted advice or guidance, as transparency
was completely alien to their awareness and discourse. As long as
criticism was forbidden and condemned, and as long as acknowledgement of wrongdoing was eliminated from the dictionary of their
shoddy experiences, nothing could be reformed. Unfortunately, some
minds and insights were completely closed off.

From this standpoint, the idea of participating in a serious way that contributed, even in a small part, to rectify errors
at home and improve the image abroad, was deemed necessary

to find appropriate solutions that could be actioned to help the Palestinian Authority in reforming the economic and social environment in the homeland.

The Palestinian Businessmen Committee for Peace and Reform was born, headed by Samer Khoury, the chairman of CCC with their offices in Athens. A group of twenty businessmen, most of whom were born, lived, and worked outside Palestine, agreed to join the committee to follow up on economic, commercial and scientific relations with international donors. They also believed in the necessity of taking the initiative and seizing the available opportunities.

The American aid programs to Palestine were negatively affected during the period of the second intifada and the violent and mostly brutal reactions of the Israeli army. The siege imposed on President Arafat in Ramallah also confirmed the failure of previous negotiations and the apparent lack of contact between the Palestinian Authority and the American Administration.

The committee's prime goal in Washington was to seek the resumption of the suspended US aid, especially for the badly needed infrastructure projects in the Gaza Strip. This was in addition to endeavouring for the return of the situation in Palestine to what it was before September 2000, the end of which witnessed an unprecedented escalation of violence.

Its first meeting in Washington DC included two former US diplomats who ran a PR business. Rick Burt, the fun and smart partner, was famous for his role as US Ambassador to Germany in receiving Anatoly Shcharansky across the bridge in Berlin; he served as chief negotiator for the START treaty. He started with his remarkable notes: "You don't need to lobby your friends and supporters, but those who oppose you." Then he continued to state, "and, of course, you are embarking on a difficult task especially for the great influence on the policy makers in Washington by those who oppose you."

The serious and quiet partner was Ed Rogers, a Republican diplomat, who served in The White House under both Presidents Reagan and Bush senior, and was a life member of the Council on Foreign

Relations. In addition to the two veteran diplomats, there was a young and tall lady, Ihsana Sadr, of Iranian origin, who was admired for her self-confidence and sincere sympathy for the Palestinian cause. At a later stage, the energetic lawyer Randa Fahmy of Egyptian descent also participated in scheduling and attending the committee's meetings with American officials.[1]

Rick Burt, explaining the plan of action, stated:

> As you all know, the American system, whether political or social, is based on capitalism, our field of work here is dedicated to serving successful people, it seems that your group is made up mostly of successful young businessmen, you will be well received by most officials who would of course prefer to listen to financially successful men rather than poor politicians from your countries and their boring requests. Our plan for you is to have a series of meetings with influential and important personalities in Washington during your current and upcoming visits.

The projects that the committee presented on an ongoing basis were the Gaza seaport, water desalination plants and the Jenin power plant in the West Bank which would provide half the amount of electricity supplied by Israel. This was in addition to the continuous search for external financing and encouraging banking institutions to participate in the projects of the Palestine Investment Fund.

The activities were not limited to meeting American officials, but also included getting to know other activists and members of Palestinian and Arab communities, to inform them of the conditions in Palestine and encourage them to invest there.

A distinguished Palestinian-American lawyer, George Salem, a Washington resident and an active member of the Republican Party, joined and became a permanent member, attending most of the committee's meetings in Washington.[2]

Many leaders and activists of the Palestinian community in the US, who met with members of PBCPR, were stressing the necessity for the restoration of our national unity; that was a major and critical demand in order to form a powerful and united front that interacted with the popular Arab environment and allied itself with the growing supporters for our just cause, in America and other parts of the world.

In order to gain sympathy and respect from others, we needed to respect ourselves by demanding that the PA respected the rights of all citizens and applied the law fairly for all. During all the visits made to Washington, the committee members stayed at one of the oldest landmarks in the city, The Willard hotel, on Pennsylvania Avenue, near the White House. There was a widespread belief that the verb "to lobby" originated from The Willard, as people used to meet a congressman requesting favours for their own business or their communities in the lobby of that hotel; thus their actions were called lobbying!

Some community leaders who met with committee members at The Willard's lobby reacted with welcome and admiration to the members' bold steps and their efforts for the restoration of good relations between America and Palestine. They gave the committee a proper and appropriate description: "Palestinian Lobby in the United States." [3]

Knowing that some members of the group were critical of the PLO-Israeli agreements, the advice by a truly wise businessman conciliator — who had said "getting upset will never sort out any issue," being aware of the growing importance of the role of the United States in the Middle East — was that prejudice should not deter persuasion; adversity sometimes can be removed.

The committee group was generously invited to dinner at the residence of the Egyptian Ambassador in Washington, Nabil Fahmy, who was following and supporting pro-Palestine initiatives that could help in resolving the issue in accordance with international legitimacy resolutions. He was later appointed Minister of Foreign Affairs for Egypt.

At another event, the Jordanian Ambassador Karim Qawar had a meeting with the group, expressing his willingness to assist in any future activities of the group. The committee had an important role in the development of career education in Palestine; Shibli Tallhami, a media activist, arranged several meetings with Ron Bruder, president and the founder of EFE Organisation, which established a program called "Education for Employment". Indeed, two branches were opened in Gaza and Ramallah headed by Yasmin Nahas and managed by Mohammad Naja. Samer Khoury pledged that CCC would employ fifty of their Palestinian graduates annually. [4]

Palestinian ambassadors, officially known as the "PLO Represen- tatives" in Washington, always welcomed the members and partici- pated in some of the relevant meetings at The Willard; amongst them were Hassan Abdel Rahman, and Afif Safieh — a veteran diplomat, who spent several years as ambassador in London and to the Vatican.

Maan Erekat, who was a participant in the Harvard program a few years earlier, had an active role in meetings with members of the community and other organisations. At the end of his term, Husam Zomlot was appointed in his place.

Unfortunately, Zomlot did not last long in his new post as Donald Trump ordered the closure of the PLO offices in Washington DC, and thus the prompt departure of Zomlot and his family. He was then appointed by President Abbas a few months later as the PLO ambassador in London. [5]

The chairman of Aspen, William Meyer, hosted a dinner in Washing- ton attended by the committee members, Secretary Madeleine Albright, the president of the World Bank and Dr. Salam Fayyad, who became the PA's Prime Minister a year later. It was emphasised that "economic peace" would not be a substitute for the stalled political negotiations.

The committee's goal was to work hard for the return of the situ- ation to what it was before September 2000. In most of the meetings that followed, the committee adopted Salam Fayyad's vision for the economic future of Palestine, based on *"Ending the Occupation.. Building the State."* [6]

In addition to meeting politicians, the committee recognised the need to respond to the fact that many Americans had been deliberately misinformed about the conflict. The predominant narrative was about Israel's right to defend itself. We needed to answer questions, build bridges and promote understanding.

The importance of education — in particular, keeping the next generation in Gaza exposed to the world, despite the closures — was top of the list in discussing the need for initiatives seeking the support of the international community as well as USAid, noting that "people are the product of their environment."

Remarkably, most committee members had never been confronted with a hostile reception from Israel's supporters in Congress or other Departments; on the contrary, surprisingly they were welcomed by many who expressed their commitment to ensuring a better life for the Palestinians.

After more than twelve years of the committee's diligent activities, and its success in strengthening the bonds of actual friendship with many politicians, diplomats, financiers, businessmen and aid organisations in the American capital — in addition to its practical and professional input in concluding agreements to finance the activities of Palestinian local banks — the committee's chairman and members who attended regularly were given the title "Unofficial Diplomats." [7]

Aspen Wye River

One of the first scheduled appointments of the PBCPR was a visit to the Washington Offices of the Aspen Institute and a meeting with its CEO, Walter Isaacson, a writer on American history who worked as president of CNN.

It was a pleasant meeting with general discussions about the possibility of helping the members to meet some influential people who were interested in the situation in the Middle East, especially the two-state solution. Isaacson agreed that Aspen could provide opportunities for members of the Palestinian private sector, who themselves were leaders in their own communities, to engage with leading thinkers and advocates of the Middle East.

Isaacson stressed the role of the Institute in hosting the Wye River talks between Netanyahu and Arafat under the auspices of President Clinton, as the venue was owned by the Aspen Institute; he then surprisingly suggested that all members of the committee be invited to spend a day or two there.

Three months later, a Palestinian group headed by Samer Khoury and including Nassar, a famous Palestinian Marble maker, and Walid Najjab, a businessman based in Ramallah, were heading to Maryland's Wye River.

The Aspen Institute Centre overlooked the river, in the middle of a dense plantation, on approximately one thousand acres. Looking at those tall and old trees, Clark Gable's scenes in *"Gone with the Wind"* and *"Band of Angels,"* manifestations of slavery, and the long-time oppression and racism against African-Americans, appeared before my eyes. Sheikh Mustafa's words rang in my ears: "The initial struggle for emancipation from slavery culminated in its abolition by the prophet Mohammed in early Islam." [8]

A beautiful picture of Nelson Mandela stuck in my mind as I watched his plane arriving at Gaza airport a few years previously, which gave us a dose of hope that freedom for peoples will be achieved no matter how long it took, and that our own apartheid will inevitably end.

Once inside the Centre, members were shown bedrooms: one which Arafat slept in, another for Abu Mazen on one side, the opposite side had Netanyahu and the Israeli delegation. Also President Clinton and Secretary Albright were in attendance, and King Hussein made a surprise visit to the Centre during the negotiations. During the evening, the group was met by Walter who introduced the group members to Martin Indyk and Dennis Ross. Discussions centred on the stalled negotiations between the Israelis and the Palestinians. Indyk gave a detailed account of America's attempts to find a permanent peace solution, based on the two-state initiative. He touched on his own experience in the region, serving as the US ambassador to Israel for two separate terms under two different presidents, and emphasised his continued personal demand for a settlement freeze as a vital and necessary step to achieve some progress in any future negotiations.

Then it was Dennis Ross' turn, who made dozens of trips to Palestine, Israel, Egypt and Syria, meeting their presidents in an effort to reach a peace deal, being the US Peace envoy to the Middle East. His position was well known to the Palestinians. Ross said that he accompanied President Clinton to Gaza later that year for the fulfilment of a vital clause in the accord, related to the PLO charter that was confirmed during Clinton's address to the Palestinian National Council meeting. He also explained in detail the great difficulties that faced direct and indirect talks between the parties during the week-long negotiations. He stressed that the wisdom, patience and determination by President Clinton were what made the conference successful and led to the final announcement of the Agreement.[9]

There was a huge collection of photos of the event: a picture of King Hussein, who came to help achieve an agreement despite the obvious illness he was suffering from; and another photo of Arafat and my friend Kanafani walking among the trees, followed by his bodyguards.

Neither Indyk nor Ross mentioned that Netanyahu intended not to sign the Accord at the last moment, as he demanded the release of the American spy Pollard; but Madeleine Albright mentioned the incident about reaching agreement on the Wye River Accord:

> We began planning for a ceremony at the White House, then noticed Bibi sitting alone on a sofa, glowering. That couldn't be good. The President came up to say that Netanyahu was threatening to back out of the agreement unless the United States released Jonathan Pollard.

I told the President, "This is blackmail… we can't go along."

Jonathan Pollard had been jailed for spying on the US, and was finally released by Donald Trump nearly twenty years after the Wye River agreement.[10]

Hillary Clinton stated:

> On that earlier visit, we had also gone to Bethlehem, now returned there with Yasser Arafat to visit the Church of the Nativity, where we sang Christmas carols with Christian Palestinians, still holding out hope for the peace process.
>
> Bill was scheduled to make a ground-breaking address to the Palestinian National Council and hold other meetings with the Palestinians, and we landed at the brand-new Gaza International Airport. This was a momentous event because the opening of the airport had been one of the tenets of the recent Wye Peace Accords that Bill had brokered between Arafat and Netanyahu to help advance economic opportunity for the Palestinians.[11]

After that pleasant visit to Wye and its huge plantation, a new idea emerged to develop a joint committee on Middle East Peace, that eventually led to the establishment of a strategy group with the task of helping both Palestinians and Israelis achieve a peaceful end to the conflict. It was given the name the "Middle East Strategy Group."

MESG Honorary Chairs were Henry Kissinger, Madeleine Albright, Dianne Feinstein (the veteran Democrat Senator from California), Chuck Hagel (the Republican Senator of Nebraska), Samer Khoury (president of CCC) and Idan Ofer (Israeli businessman), who was interested in buying electricity from Gaza. Its members included Queen Noor, Ephraim Sneh (a retired army general who had many dealings with the PA), Dennis Ross (former Middle East peace envoy,) Martin Indyk (former ambassador to Israel), Edward Walker (former ambassador to Israel), Samir Shawa (Palestinian businessman), Tarek Aggad (chairman of Apec), Daniel Abraham, Rick Burt, William Rogers, Jane Harman (congresswoman from California) and Walter Isaacson.[12]

Palestinian expectations were so high that President Bush, during his second term, imposed a satisfactory solution to the two-state initiative, especially after the election of President Abbas, who won the approval of many world leaders.

Sadly, in the summer of that year, all eyes were on Louisiana as it was tragically hit by Hurricane Katrina, causing an unprecedented environmental disaster, massive floods and a large number of victims. The widespread compassion and support for those affected by the hurricane reached most parts of the world, including Palestine and Gaza, where a group of young students collected their pocket money and handed a sum over to Al-Hani Library, whose owners doubled the amount. A cheque was issued by the Bank of Palestine and delivered to the Aspen Institute later that year.

After presenting the students' donation letter and cheque to Walter Isaacson, Jane Harman, the congresswoman, insisted on bringing it to the attention of other members of Congress; it was also printed in Aspen magazine.[13]

Walter invited me to his office to write a thank you note. He gave congresswoman Harman a photocopy of the letter and the cheque to be deposited in the Library of Congress.

Suddenly, Albright entered the office, to the annoyance of Isaacson who, surprisingly, picked a copy of his latest book, *Benjamin Franklin: An American Life*, signed it quickly and gave it to me![14]

The idea of collecting donations for the Katrina victims was initiated by a young student who kept a photo of his grandfather, a policeman, with Malcolm X during his visit to Gaza in the 1960s. He also loved the legendary Muhammad Ali. He approached the Al-Hani bookshop manager and gave her 30 Shekels, as he saw on TV that the majority of victims were poor African Americans, and he had persuaded his friends and other students to donate. The bookshop was located next to five schools in El-Rimal district, where thousands of children attended their schools which operated in two shifts, morning and evening, due to lack of space. One wonders what future awaits them? Would they find suitable or available jobs in future, or would they join the long unemployment lines?[15]

During another meeting at Aspen in Washington DC, Dr. Iyad Sarraj, founder of the Gaza Mental Health Program, who was my classmate at Palestine High School, was invited to present and explain some of his activities in Gaza in order to secure financial aid for some of his projects. He successfully gave a detailed presentation about the services his Program provided to a large number of mental health patients who suffered acute illnesses as a result of the cruel attacks and the extremely harsh treatment of Palestinian prisoners by the Israeli army upon their arrest from their homes, mainly in front of their children, which caused additional psychological disorders.

A member of the delegation who lived in Dubai was clearly touched and promised to donate a substantial sum; he asked Iyad about a hormone found in all humans responsible for giving us the feeling of happiness when we do good deeds to others, especially when expecting nothing in return. Iyad replied: "Yes my friend, it's actually called Oxytocin, which binds human beings and makes people feel good upon doing acts of kindness or generosity. This hormone exists in abundance in the bodies of normal people in the world, but it is certainly and unfortunately absent from the blood of Israelis in general, and particularly in the hearts of their soldiers and settlers." He then added, "It is true that a person should not go to sleep immediately after hearing bad news! The memory stores that abhorrent news, which may negatively affect a person's psychological, physical and mental health; fortunately, people in Gaza have a divine immunity against it. They hear the worst news day and night." [16]

During a meeting of the Middle East Strategy Group at Aspen's offices, which was attended by almost all its members including Henry Kissinger who made a short speech, I found myself sitting next to Kissinger during one lunch. He asked me "Which city are you from?" When I told him from Gaza, he said: "It's a hard place to live in at the moment."

I heard a lot of talk about Sadat's offer to Arafat, that Begin was willing to give Gaza back as part of the peace deal, so I asked him: "Was Gaza really dropped by Sadat during the peace talks with Begin? Was it mentioned as part of the deal at all?"

He kept eating from his plate, then said: "The peace treaty was concluded by the parties with the help of President Carter. Gaza was not mentioned to me."

In his book, *World Order,* Kissinger mentioned his last meeting with Sadat in Washington. [17]

It was noted that all MESG meetings at the Aspen Institute's Washington offices were attended by Queen Noor.

Back in Washington, the Egyptian ambassador, Nabil Fahmy, invited the delegates again to his home and in the presence of Karim Kawar, the Jordanian Ambassador, the Ambassador of Qatar, Walter Isaacson and a representative of RAND Corporation, who gave a video presentation with comprehensive analysis of the Red Sea-Dead Sea Water Conveyance Project (Red-Dead). The Arc project was also discussed for a unified Palestinian transportation, infrastructure, and development corridor, with focus on how such a corridor could be linked to trade and transportation routes into neighbouring Egypt, Jordan and Israel.

The possibility of using Rafah as a transit point for goods, not just for people, out of Gaza through Egypt was also discussed. Ambassador Fahmy indicated that Egypt was prepared to allow safe passage of goods through Rafah to the airport of El Arish, so long as it did not have to compromise its sovereignty in any way.

A few months later, Jordan, Israel and the PA signed an agreement to go ahead with a study in order to proceed with this vital project, which was followed by another agreement signed by Bob Zoelick, President of the World Bank, for financial support to a project that was called "*The Peace Conduit*" which would benefit the three countries involved.

Several years later, Toni Verstandig, who worked under Secretary Albright at the State Department, became responsible and Chair for Aspen's Middle East Programs, as MESG had been dissolved. She invited a group of Palestinian businessmen from the West Bank to a luncheon in Washington with participation of Hady Amr, who was senior advisor to Secretary John Kerry on Israel-Palestinian Affairs, Bashar Masri, Samir Zraiq, Michael Ratney, the Consul General in Jerusalem, and Nafez Husseini.[18]

Finally, the special relationship between the Aspen Institute's management and some members of the PBCPR contributed significantly to consolidating friendship ties with quite a few officials and diplomats that helped in opening channels with various Departments of the American Administration.

However, despite all these efforts by members of the Aspen group and the apparent sincerity of some, and the constant optimism of the Palestinian members, the peace process had come to a complete halt, and the Netanyahu government had publicly confirmed its indifference to any agreement with the Palestinian Authority, including the Wye River Accord. To make matters worse, the presidency of Donald Trump cut ties with the Palestinians including stopping America's payments to UNRWA and the closure of the PLO office in Washington. Regrettably, it was also clear that the hopeless "two-state solution" had gone with the wind.

The White House, The Capitol and States

"In diplomacy, the golden rule is:
Sometimes honesty is not the best policy."

— UNKNOWN

The simple journey of lobbying began with a visit to the State Department. At the entrance hall on the ground floor, no one could miss the innumerable flags of so many nations. But try to find the flag of Palestine! Ed Rogers' strict advice for the delegation was "try to avoid getting bogged down in interminable discussions."

The delegation was scheduled to meet with David Satterfield, who made visits to Ramallah earlier that year, and a Senior official from the US Consulate General in Jerusalem. The main objective was to urge the US officials to act favourably and quickly on the resumption of US aid to Gaza, especially the water projects. We were absolutely tense and psychologically uncertain of the utility of such a visit. Luckily, we were directed to meet a young woman named Elizabeth who greeted us with a cordial welcome.

We felt comfortable as tension subsided quickly. Mr. Rogers whispered that the woman who greeted us was the daughter of vice-president Dick Cheney. She was responsible for the International Aid Program.

She promptly confirmed that the suspension of aid was not her decision, nor anyone in the State Department, but rather it was blocked by the Department of Defense. She added, "As soon as they lift the embargo, we will immediately inform USAid to resume funding for the stalled projects."

"Is there a possibility to meet with them?" asked Rogers.

With a quick move, she made a phone call and then said, "Yes, Mr. Rodman agreed to meet you tomorrow at nine in his office at the Pentagon."

The meeting with Liz Cheney was so positive that it stuck in our minds, due to her respectful, ethical and professional manner, in addition to her apparent sympathetic attitude towards the poorer nations of the world. She apparently gave the members of the delegation a dose of hope, as they bade her goodbye and thanked her for her great efforts.[19]

There was a brief meeting with David Satterfield who was critical of Arafat's lack of vision, following his meetings with Arafat during his two previous visits to Ramallah. Members of the PBCPR had little or no ambition to visit the White House, as most meetings were taking place at the State Department, the Capitol and other organisations. The morning after several meetings at the Capitol, Rick Burt arrived at the Willard with a smile, "Prepare yourselves to enter the most prestigious building in Washington DC' a meeting has been arranged with President Bush's Senior Director on the National Security Council, Elliot Abrams, who is also tasked with following up on the progress on Israel-Palestine negotiations."

I remembered that Talaat Al-Ghussein, a refugee born in the city of Ramleh, was the first Palestinian to be officially received at the White House by President John F. Kennedy, as the ambassador of the newly independent State of Kuwait. The President, knowing that Al-Ghussain was of Palestinian origin, quoted from a letter he sent to six Arab Leaders in May 1961:

> My thoughts often turn to the Middle East, an area which has contributed so much to the religious and cultural heritage of the world today, and whose potential for further rich contribution to civilization is great…
>
> The American government and people believe that an honourable and humane settlement can be found and are willing to share in the labours and burdens which so difficult an achievement must entail. We are willing to help resolve the tragic Palestine refugee problem.[20]

Al-Ghussain was honoured to meet Jacqueline Kennedy.[21]

Yasser Arafat was believed to have been lavishly received at the White House several times, surpassing any Arab leader in the history of US-Arab relations. In September 1993, the White House courtyard witnessed the signing ceremony of the "Declaration of Principles" and the historic handshake between Yitzhak Rabin and Yasser Arafat, which was the beginning of a remarkable series of visits to the White House, and according to one of Arafat's escorts, amounted to eleven visits.

This was in addition to the one and only special visit by an American president-in-office to Palestine, when Bill Clinton, his wife Hillary and daughter, Chelsea, landed at Gaza airport and met with the Palestine National Council on 14 December 1998.

There was also the three-week long Camp David negotiations with Ehud Barak in 2000, which ended as it began without achieving any significant progress. These somewhat intimate encounters were considered by some Arab critics to be a great privilege presented to the chairman of the PLO, if they could indeed be considered a privilege; yes, an enviable effort by many, a privilege that no Arab president or king in modern history had ever enjoyed! Most members knew of Abrams as he had visited Ramallah on many official visits, one of them accompanying Condoleezza Rice. We were reminded that President George W. Bush a year earlier did use of the word "Palestine" and the two-state solution:

> And when the Palestinian people have new leaders, new institutions and new security arrangements with their neighbours, the United States of America will support the creation of a Palestinian state. Israel also has a large stake in the success of a democratic Palestine. Permanent occupation threatens Israel's identity and democracy. So I challenge Israel to take concrete steps to support the emergence of a viable, credible Palestinian state.[22]

The members' second visit to the White House was rather unexpected, but arranged by Mr. Rogers, we met with Scooter Libby, the Assistant to Vice President Dick Cheney for National Security affairs, and Cheney's Chief of Staff. Libby was smiling and cheerful, completely the opposite of Abrams' personality. He stressed his support for the two-state solution and confirmed that he was, with a White House team, responsible for drawing the "road map" for peace in the Middle East. He expressed support for the resumption of US aid to the Palestinians.

But the general feeling among the members was that he was a strong supporter of Israel. I was fascinated by the beauty of his office decoration and furniture, especially the ceiling that was decorated with ancient Pharaonic golden paintings with utmost beauty. Libby noticed my great admiration for the ceiling, and said laughingly: "I got to know these Pharaohs in Egypt," probably because he wanted to remind us about the story of Moses and the Pharaoh who drowned in the sea.[23]

As we were leaving his office, a member of the delegation reminded us by recalling Cheney's statement the year before, in which he said that there were some justifications for the policy of assassinations pursued by Israel against Palestinian terrorists. It provoked angry reactions from many Authority officials; although White House spokesman Ari Fleischer said that the vice president meant to say that both sides found justifications for their actions and confirmed that Cheney, the President and Secretary Colin Powell agreed on the need to stop the violence.

Members welcomed the day's schedule with enthusiasm, which included a possible meeting in the late afternoon with Secretary Condoleezza Rice at the State Department.

Upon arrival, and to their great disappointment, the meeting was chaired by her deputy, Bob Zoellick. For an unknown reason, the room lights were dimmed, and further to their disappointment, they sat silent throughout the meeting, but were urging Sabri Saidam to speak. Sabri, who was one of Fatah's rising stars, was invited by Samer Khoury to participate, and he became Minister of Education in Rami Hamadallah's government a few years later. On our way back to The Willard, someone suggested that Zoellick probably was sensitive to strong light. He was appointed by President Bush to President of the World Bank, in a similar way to the appointment of Paul Wolfowitz.

Elliot Abrams' sharp and piercing glances at the Palestinian delegates did not suggest sympathy or even respect; most of them felt that he was highly biased towards Israel's unjust positions, and an arrogant diplomat. The committee enjoyed regular meetings with Ziad Asali, who managed the American Task Force for Palestine (ATFP) which had an office close to the White House. John Sununu, the former White House chief of staff, who was of Palestinian-Lebanese origin, had also joined in some meetings at Ziad's office. His son John was also a Senator. After a meeting at the State Department, members were invited to meet the Egyptian Ambassador Nabil Fahmi at his residence, and the Jordanian Ambassador Karim Kawar. Randa Fahmy also joined the group in various meetings as she was also a recognized lobbyist, where another businessman, Jawdat el-Khodary, who travelled from Gaza with Khaled Abdel Shafi, the Head of UNDP in Palestine, were present. Rick declined to attend meetings with Martin Indyk at the Saban Center for Middle East Policy at the Brookings Institution, probably for some personal reasons.

Our visits to the Arab American members of congress started with Democratic Rep. Nick Rahall, who was celebrating his 28th year as a member of Congress for West Virginia; a brilliant achievement and a very pleasant and cheerful personality, and he insisted on having his photo taken with the delegation.

During one of the meetings at the Department of State, discussions revolved around improving living conditions for the besieged people of Gaza. The official replied that there were serious negotiations that would lead to a successful conclusion; once Gilad Shalit was released in a prisoner exchange deal, there would be a gradual improvement. A delegation member complained about the horrific treatment that Palestinian prisoners in Israeli jails faced daily. He added with a smile: "By God Almighty, your treatment of prisoners in the infamous "Abu Ghraib" is considered sweet and gentle compared to the notorious Israeli Ofer prison!" [24]

The dreaded Abu Ghraib prison gained notoriety after the torture and inhumane treatment of Iraqi prisoners by their American military captors was exposed. Incredibly, Samer Khoury informed us that his company had built the prison in Baghdad a few years before the US invasion of Iraq. He continued ironically: "There was an amazing story circulating among our employees that Saddam Hussein ordered the imprisonment of the top three Palestinian engineers who oversaw its construction, for a few days, without food or water, to verify the prison's durability and security against any escape attempt. But, I cannot honestly confirm that story."

The last visit to the White House, happily without meeting Elliot Abrams for a change, was straight to the offices of Dennis Ross, who was appointed by President Obama as his Middle East Senior Advisor, and Dan Shapiro, who later became the US ambassador to Israel. [25]

The discussions centred on the future of talks between Israel and the PLO, following the end of recent talks at the White House between Presidents Abbas and Netanyahu. They confirmed frankly that all that the administration was doing or hoping for at the time was "an exercise in confidence building measures. Netanyahu doesn't trust Abu Mazen and we believe President Abbas shares the same feeling of distrust." They urged the members to encourage Abu Mazen to keep calm as things could change for the better, as President Obama wanted to find a new path in the near future.

At the end of the meeting, I actually struck a joke about both leaders meeting in the Casino at Jericho as part of a confidence-building measure. Dan asked me whether I agreed for him to tell the joke to the President without necessarily mentioning my name! I said, "Please do and you can certainly mention my name." Abu Mazen's last visit to the White House, during the month of

Ramadan, was his last during President Barack Obama's second term. King Abdallah II, President Mubarak and Prime Minister Netanyahu were also invited.

The final conclusion, after all the visits and meetings with officials and others in an attempt to understand how foreign policy decisions were managed in the US administration and Congress, was that it was possible to deal with the Americans comfortably, beneficially and positively with everything that came to mind, except politics related to Israel, Palestine and the Middle East!

"Back in 2009, in the heady days of enthusiasm that accompanied the election of a black man, Barack Obama, to the presidency," a solution for Palestine seemed inevitable.[26]

President Obama said he consulted with Secretary Hillary Clinton and his special envoy for Middle East peace, Senator George Mitchell. We began by calling for a temporary freeze on Israel's construction of new settlements in the West Bank, a significant sticking point between the two parties, so that negotiations might proceed in earnest. Settlement constructions, once limited to small outposts of religious believers, had over time become de facto government policy, and in 2009, there were about three hundred thousand Israeli settlers living outside the country's recognized borders. [27]

President Obama, during his second year in office, stated:

> ...our plans for peace talks went nowhere until late in August 2010, when Abbas finally agreed to direct talks.. We arranged to have Netanyahu, Abbas, Mubarak and Abdullah join me at meetings and an intimate dinner on September 1 to launch the talks. I still have a photograph of the five of us looking at President Mubarak's watch to check that the sun had officially set, since it was the month of Ramadan.[28]

> I imagined them shaking hands afterward, like actors taking off their costumes and makeup backstage, be-

fore returning to the world they knew — a world in which Netanyahu could blame the absence of peace on Abbas's weakness while doing everything he could to keep him weak, and Abbas could publicly accuse Israel of war crimes while quietly negotiating business contracts with the Israelis, and Arab leaders could bemoan the injustices endured by the Palestinians under occupation while their own internal security forces ruthlessly ferreted out dissenters and malcontents who might threaten their grip on power. And I thought of all the children, whether in Gaza or in Israel, on the streets of Cairo and Amman, who would continue to grow up knowing mainly violence, coercion, fear, and the nursing of hatred because, deep down, none of the leaders I'd met with believed anything else was possible. A world without illusions — that's what they'd call it.[29]

As he faced pressure about his relations with Palestinian academies in Colombia University, including Edward Said and Rashid Khalidi, he added:

I'd been on the receiving end during my presidential campaign, as Jewish supporters reported having to beat back assertions in their synagogues that I was insufficiently supportive — or even hostile toward — Israel. They attributed these whisper campaigns not to any particular position I'd taken (my backing of a two-state solution and opposition to Israeli settlements) but rather to my expression of concern for ordinary Palestinians; my friendship with certain critics of Israeli policy, including an activist and Middle East scholar named Rashid Khalidi.

"Whether Netanyahu also inherited his father's un-abashed hostility toward Arabs (The tendency towards conflict is in the essence of the Arab. He is an enemy by essence. His personality won't allow him any compromise or agreement) was harder to say. [30]

Hillary Clinton, who accompanied Obama on his visit to Egypt, wrote:

Vice President Biden was visiting Israel on a goodwill tour, reaffirming the administration's strong support for the country's security and trying to put the un-pleasantness of our row over settlements behind us.

While he was still on the ground, the Israelis announced plans for 1,600 new housing units in East Jerusalem, a move certain to inflame Palestinian sensitivities, Netanyahu said that he had nothing to do with the unfortunate timing of the announcement, but it was taken by many as a snub of the Vice President and the United States. ... Both President Obama and Rahm were furious, and they asked me to make that clear to Bibi. In a long and heated telephone conversation, I told the Prime Minister that President Obama viewed the news about East Jerusalem as a personal insult to him, the Vice President, and the United States.

Strong stuff for a diplomatic conversation. I didn't enjoy playing the bad cop, but it was part of the job.

Let me assure you and the President that the timing was entirely unintentional and unfortunate,' he replied, but he refused to reverse the decision. [31]

It was amazing how President Obama boasted of the increasing popularity of the United States after taking office: "Around the world, public attitudes toward the United States had steadily improved since I'd taken office, demonstrating that our early diplomatic work was paying off."[32]

The Nobel Prize comes with a gold medal and a million dollars paid from the legacy of the Swedish inventor "Alfred Nobel," an engineer, chemist, author and peace lover on the one hand, but also the inventor of the deadly dynamite, which increased the rate of murder and destruction in the world, and brought him great wealth. He died in 1895.

The awarding to Yasser Arafat, Yitzhak Rabin and Shimon Peres of the Nobel Peace Prize in October 1994 was certainly a premature decision; it was unexpected by many, that they received this honourable and unique prize so soon after achieving real peace.

However, awarding President Barack Obama that same prestigious prize a few months into his first year in office, without achieving peace in any part of the world, was an astonishing and unmerited decision; even Obama himself was stunned. Some sceptical journalists in Washington laughingly suggested giving the next prize to Donald Trump after his meeting with the North Korean leader Kim Jong-Un for a second time![33]

The Pentagon and WMD

"If the loser keeps his smile, the winner
will lose the thrill of victory."

— BULAND

It was extremely difficult and almost impossible for any Palestinian to enter the Pentagon due to the stringent security measures, especially after it was attacked on 9/11. There were no direct contacts between the Department of Defense and the Palestinian Authority.

The delegation was headed by Samer Khoury and Jawdat Shawwa, accompanied by Ed Rogers and Randa Fahmy. The main objective for the meeting that had been arranged by Liz Cheney was to explain that the people in Gaza who relied on foreign aid, due to the Israeli occupation-imposed restrictions, were unaware of the reasons behind the decision in stopping American aid; such a decision would be considered by local NGOs as collective punishment.

After completing all security checks, we were received by Peter Rodman, the Assistant Secretary of Defense for International Security Affairs: a tall man, very quiet, who showed us the way to the conference room but kept us waiting at the entrance door for over five minutes, during which he enquired repeatedly about the incident near the northern border of Gaza, where three American security guards were ambushed and killed.

As we stood in the corridors of the Pentagon, the image of screaming women and children after an attack on the first day of the war in Iraq — which left over 600 fatalities, by an American ballistic missile that lost its target — came to my mind.

One was also surprised that this building controlled the movements of the most powerful army in the world, with its fleets roamed the seas and oceans, and its hundreds of air bases scattered around all continents without exception. All of this stemmed and was planned from these rooms in this building. The video of grief moved quickly from the scenes of the destruction of Iraq and Gaza, as well as the twin-towers in New York. Then it stopped, why were we here? Yes, it was a noble initiative and a serious attempt to help our people in Palestine, and alleviate the suffering of the wounded and devastated Gaza.

Suddenly the door was opened and The Deputy Secretary of Defense, Paul Wolfowitz, appeared and shook hands with everyone. He started the meeting by saying: "When informed that a Palestinian delegation is meeting with Peter, I came to see you for a little while. My main message is to inform you that I am not against the Palestinians, as most of your local media claim, and I sincerely support your development to live in peace with Israel. Furthermore, you may be interested to note that the two-state solution policy adopted by President Bush was initiated by me."

We were overwhelmed with such wondrous optimism listening to his opening remarks, and firmly believed that he would agree immediately to the resumption of US aid. Samer thanked him and requested his instructions to lift the restrictions imposed by the Pentagon on the aid for Gaza.

He replied while pointing his finger towards me: "There is one condition. The PA should hand over the terrorists who committed the horrendous killing."

"Sir, we are not sure that the Authority knows the killers, there is an unconfirmed report that they fled to Israel. Besides, Chairman Arafat has been locked inside two rooms in the Muqata'a, and is surrounded by Israeli troops."

"No, we are confident that Arafat knows their whereabouts, you should persuade him to hand them over to us so that they can be put to trial. I may accept an alternative; the Department of Defence has no objection to their trial being held in public in Ramallah. If Arafat is considered to be your true friend, you must persuade him to do that."

The dream of the water plant flew away; what a cruel condition, no one knew the extent of its ramifications. Suddenly, I remembered what my friend Marwan Kanafani, Arafat's advisor, told me about an incident regarding WMD, during the meeting between President Clinton, Netanyahu and Arafat at the Erez crossing on December 15, 1998.

Wolfowitz looked at a paper handed to him by a female aide. "I actually left the Defence Minister of Kazakhstan waiting and came to meet you. I must go."

We felt that we had failed, and while he started to stand up to say goodbye, I remembered that he narrowly escaped an attack on his hotel in Baghdad a few months ago, so, I said jokingly, "Mr. Wolfowitz, we were so happy for your miraculous escape in the Baghdad hotel. We will always pray for your safety, you have been looking for weapons of mass destruction in Iraq, and surely you knew the extent of the special relationship between Arafat and Saddam Hussain. It is possible that some WMDs are probably hidden in Gaza. Would you invade us if we give you the exact location?"

He didn't laugh, nor did he show any sign of exclamation or concern, but as he was leaving the room, said, "I wish you a quick and safe trip back to Gaza."[34]

On our way out, Randa questioned the authenticity of my remark about WMD and nuclear bomb in the Gaza meeting. I told her it was based on a true story that happened five years earlier during a meeting at the Erez crossing. Ariel Sharon was also present, but refused to shake hands with Arafat. Dennis Ross confirmed the incident: "Bibi immediately read a laundry list of Palestinian failings, including the alleged stockpiling of illegal weapons, including heavy weapons — prompting Arafat sarcastically to say, "You left out the nuclear weapons, why haven't you mentioned those?" [35]

A year later, Paul Wolfowitz resigned his post at the Pentagon, and was later appointed President of the World Bank succeeding James Wolfensohn.

Among the provisions of the 1979 Israeli-Egyptian peace treaty, Sinai would consist of three demilitarized zones, and in order to monitor their implementation, a multinational force and observers (MFO) were established in 1981, with most of the members being American and Canadian officers.

The traveller from Gaza to Cairo via the Sinai could clearly notice the presence of MFO observation posts. A Canadian officer said: "The interest of Israel and the United States in keeping Sinai demilitarized is of great importance to maintaining peace in the region, which explains what an American general meant when he described Sinai as the 'Pentagon of the Middle East'. The Egyptian analyst, Muhammad Gabala, attributed the officer's last remark to Sinai's status as "… probably being an historical and strategic military battleground for many years, and in particular the last three wars with Israel. Or he was thinking about protecting one of the most important sea lanes in the world, the Suez Canal. Or possibly due to its natural and geographical expansion for both countries?

"Another simple analysis was that the Sinai Peninsula similarly has exactly five distinct sides: The Mediterranean to the north, the Suez Canal to the west, Israel and Gaza to the east, the Gulf of Suez to the west and Gulf of Aqaba to the south east."

A few years later, an unidentified terrorist group attacked two checkpoints and observation posts belonging to the (MFO) in Sinai, wounding eight soldiers, including four Americans.

Commentators in the US media, as well as the former US ambassador to Egypt, Daniel Kurtzer, demanded the withdrawal of all American troops in that force and the abolition of their outdated mission.

The following day after the failed Pentagon conquest, Randa arranged a meeting with Senator Chuck Hagel, an active member of the Foreign Aid Committee in Congress. The delegation was met by a smart and confident senator, who welcomed the opportunity to meet with Palestinian businessmen: "I am happy to deal with you as I was a businessman like you, but entered politics without prior planning. I have visited Palestine and Israel, and hopefully will make another visit soon."

Samer Khoury briefly explained the miserable conditions of the residents of Gaza, the scarcity of potable water, and the cessation of US aid. Randa added that the delegation met with Wolfowitz the day before at the Pentagon without achieving any positive result. She noticed that Hagel was unhappy with the policy of President George Bush and Dick Cheney in the Middle East. He didn't even comment on Wolfowitz, and his two-state solution initiative.

"I look forward to a just solution to end the suffering of your people. I have seen the horrors of war with my own eyes, as I participated in the Vietnam war. I wish we can stop all wars." [36]

He promised to make every possible effort for the resumption of US aid to the Palestinian Authority, especially for the infrastructure projects in Gaza.

Almost four years later, the second meeting with Senator Chuck Hagel took place at his office on Capitol Hill; he was a strongly fancied candidate to run for the presidency on a Republican Party ticket at the end of George W Bush's second term in office. Two surprises awaited the Palestinians. The first was a familiar figure sitting behind the Senator's reception desk: Dr. Andrew Parasailiti, welcoming the members as the senior staffer of the Senator, and he immediately started recalling his visit to Gaza and Harvard's John Kennedy program in Boston. The second surprise was when I shook hands with Senator Hagel saying that my daughter was excited for us to meet the candidate whom she hoped would be the next president of the United States.

He laughed and said, "I wish to thank your daughter, is she here in DC? Please tell her that I will not be a candidate in the upcoming primaries." He then added, explaining apologetically in a low voice: "Senator John McCain is a close friend of mine and I do not intend to run against him for the presidency. Anyway, how is the situation now in Gaza and Palestine?"

Samer replied that the situation in Palestine had become more complicated with the extremist governments in Israel, the election of Hamas and the Gaza siege.

The Senator looked really worried and moved, and he stated, "I don't agree with our military policies, but situations are bad in many parts of the world. I am not going to stand for re-election this autumn, I hope to see you during your next visit in my private office."

President Obama nominated Hagel for the position of Secretary of Defense, and although his candidacy was met with many objections in Congress, finally he was confirmed.

The Palestinians welcomed his appointment, hoping that they would have an opportunity to visit his new public office to congratulate him. Indeed, when they arrived on their last trip to Washington, Hagel had unfortunately resigned office. They missed the chance to enter the Pentagon again. [37]

AIPAC, Perle and Abraham

"Those who deny freedom to others
deserve not for themselves."
ABRAHAM LINCOLN

The word "lobby" had spread in the Arab world, attributed mainly to the description of the powerful "Jewish lobby" in America. Of course, whenever a Palestinian leader called for taking similar action, such demands were immediately rejected on the grounds that this was a quite impossible task, and ridiculed as a waste of time.

Rick Burt confirmed that the next program would include meetings with Republican members of Congress and an important discussion with a senior official of AIPAC, the largest pro-Israel Zionist group that wields significant influence in Washington.

The outer steel door of its Washington office reminded us of the security caution that exists in Israel. The lone official welcomed us and stressed that he knew our background was purely as businessmen, with no affiliation to any military or political factions. Rick explained that the purpose of the committee was to seek the resumption of the US aid program to the Palestinian Authority. Samer explained that Ariel Sharon also demanded that we build a water treatment facility as part of the power plant. He also explained that we also needed stability to ensure the progress of the stalled economy, and look forward to reaching a just solution to the two-states that President Bush called for. As he put it, "We are not opposed to improving the economic conditions of the Palestinians at all, what matters to AIPAC is maintaining and developing the US partnership with Israel by providing financial and military assistance to maintain Israel's military domination and strategic advantage in the most volatile region by ensuring its technological superiority."

"In your opinion, how will it end? This ongoing bloody conflict between us and the Israelis" was my innocent question.

His response puzzled us. "Usually wars end with a decisive victory of one party over the other, so that the loser will submit to the conditions of the victor. As for the foreseeable future, this is a very long struggle, much longer than some observers imagine!" At the end of the meeting, the advice was as follows: "I believe you are a bunch of successful contractors, and of course you bid for projects in which you expect to make profit, so I advise you not to waste your money on a losing project."

Possibly it was a veiled message. On our way back to the hotel, I kept thinking about the decisive victory and somehow started humming an Abba song, *The Winner Takes It All . . . And The loser has to fall.*

President Obama wrote:

> But as Israeli politics had moved to the right, so had AIPAC's policy position. Its leaders increasingly argued that there should be "no daylight" between the U.S. and Israeli governments, even when Israel took actions that were contrary to U.S. policy. Those who criticized Israeli policy too loudly risked being tagged "anti-Israel" and possibly (anti-Semitic) and confronted with a well-funded opponent in the next election. [38]

Our next meeting in a nearby cafe for afternoon tea, with Mr. Richard Perle. We had no idea who Perle was at the time, or the purpose or benefit of a meeting with him, but were told he was the senior defence advisor to President Bush, and most probably, he was behind the invasion of Iraq, as he was also adviser to Donald Rumsfeld. He was also involved with Israeli-Palestinian conflict.

On our way to meet Perle, we were advised by Rick to buy copies of Perle's new book, *An End to Evil: How to Win the War on Terror*, from a bookshop next to the Willard hotel. We bought three copies. During the discussion, he answered our questions in a clear manner; when asked about his vision for ending the conflict with Israel, he expressed his support and sympathy to the two-state solution with words that seemed literally identical to what Paul Wolfowitz said in the previous Pentagon meeting. He was evidently another neo-conservative politician in the Republican party. The meeting ended in disappointment, when Samer asked him to sign his copy which he promptly obliged with, "my best wishes," but, when I gave him the remaining two copies he asked: "Any particular names?" I replied in a humorous tone, "One to Yasser Arafat, the second to Sheikh Ahmed Yassin!" He looked at me sarcastically and said, "I also wanted you to live in peace with the Israelis."

He signed one copy without mentioning names.[39]

The PBCPR members were invited that evening for dinner by Daniel Abraham at his "Center for Middle East Peace". When we were told that he was the founder and chairman of the "*Slim Fast*" weight loss company, I asked him discreetly about how effective the product was, as my wife wanted to buy it.

He asked me, "Which city in Palestine are you from?" When I told him Gaza, he laughed and said: "Your wife doesn't need *Slim Fast*. There will always be shortages of food there.."

I didn't tell him that my wife actually lived in London. Then he added, "Because you are from Gaza, I tell you, don't let her buy it!" I took it as indirect advice for myself not to waste money on that product. Ziad Asali was also invited and made a short speech on behalf of the PBCPR.

The former Israeli ambassador Michael Oren made a speech, praising the settlers with great sympathy, and I didn't care much for his words. After dinner, I wanted only to mention a phrase by Noam Chomsky, but Ziad advised me not to in order to avoid any confrontation with Oren. Ziad confirmed after dinner that Daniel Abraham had sold his "*Slim Fast*" business for a large sum. I didn't know whether he wanted to save me money, being a poor Gazan, or because he had already sold the company. On another visit to the centre, we listened to many protracted ideas about peace in the Middle East by the President of the centre Robert Wexler.

The following afternoon we had a meeting with Susan Rice, who was campaigning for Senator John Kerry. She was a sure candidate for the position of Secretary of State, had Kerry won, as she was dreaming of succeeding Condoleezza Rice in that position. She listened attentively to the origins of the Palestine conflict from the other side, and enquired about the current situation in Gaza and East Jerusalem.

Another Democratic candidate, Wesley Clark, who attacked the Bush administration with fiery statements, accusing Dick Cheney, Paul Wolfowitz, Donald Rumsfeld, Richard Perle and other collaborators — we met some of them — of waging a political coup to destabilise the Middle East, by invading more countries in order to achieve their project, which was called *The New American Century.*" George W. Bush was re-elected. [40]

Susan Rice was appointed as US representative to the United Nations by Barack Obama in his first term.

Upon our return to Gaza, exactly three weeks later, the founder of Hamas, Sheikh Yassin was killed in his wheelchair by an Israeli missile after leaving his home for prayer. His successor Abdel Aziz al-Rantisi was also killed four weeks later. In the same year a few months later, Arafat's life ended in a French military hospital.

What a bizarre coincidence; the elimination of three Palestinian leaders in the same year! It seemed that Mr. Perle did not take kindly to jokes!

Builders For Peace ...

"The enemy is a very good teacher."
— DALAI LAMA

Following the historic handshake between Yasser Arafat and Yitzhak Rabin on the south lawn of the White House, Vice President Al Gore happily addressed a group of Jewish and Arab-American businessmen who were invited to witness the historic moment by asking them to help the peace process and work together to stimulate businesses in Gaza and the West Bank.

The arrangements agreed to by Yasser Arafat and three Israeli prime ministers have become synonymous with "peace", the only game in town. To be critical of or dissatisfied with Oslo and its aftermath means to be against peace, and to be roughly in the same disagreeable camps as the *"extremists"* (Hamas and the settlers) of both sides, *"haters of peace"* as Bill Clinton has called them.[41]

The infrastructure in the Palestinian territories, which was under the responsibility of the Israeli occupation, was in a deplorable state, and suffered greatly from neglect, lack of maintenance and expansion, especially in the electricity and telecommunication networks.

Historically, the British Mandate authorities granted the sole concession to generate and distribute electricity throughout Palestine to a group of Jewish investors led by Pinhas Rutenburg. They established the Palestine Electric Company (PEC) in 1923, which was responsible for building the first hydro-electric plant on a plot of land in Al-Baqoura village, near the Sea of Galilee.

Immediately after the 1948 *Nakba*, Israel seized the power plants and changed the name of the company to Israel Electric Company, which incredibly is the same company that supplies the Palestinian Authority territories to this day. As part of its aid program for Palestine, the World Bank had funded a field study of the miserable electricity sector in Gaza and the West Bank; it recommended the construction of new and independent power plants, starting with one in Gaza.

Palestinian businessmen were invited to join in the construction of many projects. Wael Khoury assumed the task of creating an independent facility to meet the urgent need of electricity and future energy for Palestine, as it became his daily obsession. He launched an initiative and invited experienced American and European companies to invest in this vital and promising sector.

Jack Adrian, an American of Armenian descent, was the first to arrive with a serious and comprehensive offer to build a power plant in Gaza. One of his partners was a member of the Builders for Peace group headed by the Arab-American activist James Zogby, who accompanied Vice President Al Gore on his visit to Jericho, which was meant to encourage American companies to invest in Palestine. "What is required is a group of 'builders for peace' and reconciliation in our region that has known precious little coexistence during most of the last century."

Within a few years, Palestinians were able to achieve one of their dreams of building and operating their independent power plant, owned by Palestine Electric Company, thus restoring the original PEC name back to existence.

Fayez Zeidan, who claimed to be an engineer and a pilot, was given the task of establishing a Palestinian Aviation Authority for which he was appointed head. Many businessmen were surprised about such an appointment due to the absence of an airport or Palestinian planes; the wonder soon dissipated when Zeidan asked for help in finding an international company that would finance the construction and operation of a future airport in Gaza on a BOT basis. He also admitted that Israeli approval was pending. Indeed, Wael Khoury headed a committee that conducted a feasibility study, but almost all companies contacted viewed the project negatively for purely commercial reasons, due to the small number of expected passengers. In a surprising, and unexpected move, Israel agreed to Arafat's request, as well as the location of the airport east of Rafah on the Egyptian border, with continuous monitoring of the construction stages by the Israeli army and its commander Shaul Mofaz, who used to meet Arafat during that period in Gaza. People who gathered at the airport were really delighted to witness the completion of the Gaza airport project, immediately followed by the first landing of Arafat's plane on the two-mile long runway. [42]

A week later, the plane of Hasib Sabbagh, accompanied by Abdel Magid Shoman, Said Khoury, Munib Masri, Nabil Sarraf and myself took off in the early hours of a sunny day from Amman, heading to Gaza, to congratulate Arafat on this great strategic achievement, a blessed move on the road to building a sustainable economy for a promising future state. When the plane entered Gaza's airspace, I was overwhelmed with joy. For the first time in my life I was able to see my home city from the air. What a wonderful feeling, being on board that flight. This was my life's dream, which I never expected to come true, as all the passengers on that flight had flown hundreds of flights to hundreds of cities around the world, except for Gaza. But, for the rest of the passengers, their joy was mixed with fear of the unknown that awaited them on the ground; the possibility of the plane or its important passengers being detained by the Israeli army! Their next destination was Riyadh, the capital of Saudi Arabia, and a planned meeting with King Fahd as part of a campaign to support the aspirations of the people of Jerusalem — and promoting the activities of the Welfare Association, which was headed by Shoman. Fear quickly evaporated on landing; on the runway was a group of high-ranking PA officials, headed by M. Zuhdi Nashashibi, Muhammad Dahlan and Muhammad Rashid.[43]

That landing was an impressive and auspicious start to a long stream of dozens of flights from various Arab capitals, one of which belonged to prince Al-Walid bin Talal, who was a partner in the newly constructed Movenpick hotel on the Gaza coast. He generously donated a Boeing 727 to become the nucleus of our new national carrier Palestine Airlines. The Dutch Government also gifted two Dutch-made Fokker aircraft, which enabled the company to operate flights to Cairo, Amman, Abu Dhabi, Dubai and, most importantly, transport Palestinian pilgrims to Jeddah for the first time in the history of the Hajj season.[44]

The first visit by an American president to Palestine was the historic landing at Gaza airport of the plane carrying President Bill Clinton, the First Lady Hillary and their daughter Chelsea in December 1998, a visit that enjoyed worldwide media coverage and gave credence to the status and importance of the airport. Among the most popular visitors was the arrival of the most beloved leader for the Palestinians, due to his profound sentiments for their just cause: Nelson Mandela, who visited refugee camps and called on the Palestinians to be patient and to continue negotiations until achieving their legitimate rights. He repeated his famous saying: "*We know too well that our freedom is incomplete without the freedom of the Palestinians.*" He also advised President Arafat to be wise and careful in dealing with the Israelis, as he admitted that what he got from the racist government in South Africa during negotiations was less than acceptable, but with the passage of time, situations would change for the better.[45]

French President Jacques Chirac laid the cornerstone of the sea port during his visit to Gaza in 1996. France, Italy and the Netherlands announced earlier that year their commitment to fund a modern seaport in Gaza. A contract was awarded to the Dutch company "*Palast Needham,*" in which Prince Walid bin Talal owned a stake. Unfortunately, the project was never completed; with the events of the second intifada, Israel destroyed it before the start of the first phase.

The construction of the American School in Gaza was a significant symbol of that initiative being the first American involvement in the field of education in Palestine. An advisory committee was responsible for the continuous running of the school, headed by James Prince, of the Democracy Council, whose members included: Ann Kerr of UCLA, Martin Indyk, James Zogby, Aron Miller and Ann Lesch of AUC in Cairo. Sadly, the school building was targeted and destroyed by Israeli (American-made) missiles. Moreover, the majority of businessmen who returned during the first years of Oslo had immense desire to participate in building economic and social institutions which would ultimately lead to the establishment of an Independent Palestinian State.[46]

The newly formed Palestinian consortium PADICO, headed by Munib Masri, assumed the responsibility of building the non-existent telecommunication sector which was suffering from neglect and limited services during the difficult years of occupation. Sabih Masri became the chairman of *Jawal* mobile company, headed by Hakam

Kanafani, managing the newly established companies that developed new networks which served many towns in Gaza and West Bank.. In his lecture at Birzeit university, Kanafani shared his professional and technical experiences, with the impassioned theme of "Success, Failure and More Success".

Mahmoud El-Farra, who lived and worked in Los Angeles, returned home to became the first chairman of the Palestinian Businessmen Association, which organized events to promote relations with foreign donors. Events were attended by the American ambassador Ed Walker and Jeffrey Feltman, the US Commercial coordinator, who made regular visits to Gaza. El-Farra's company built the first modern and automated flour mill, including several storage silos in Khan Younis.

The restrictions on trade imposed by the Israelis stipulated that all goods for the Palestinians must be imported through Israeli ports, and a handling charge of 3% must be paid to the Israeli Government. Adam Smith best described the Palestinian dilemma after years of wars and occupation: "Commerce and manufacturers gradually introduce order and good government, and with them the liberty and security of individuals, among the inhabitants of the country, who had before lived almost in a continual state of war with their neighbours and of servile dependency upon their superiors." [47]

Sherene Seikaly states:

> In the 1930s, Palestine's men of capital could emphasize private property, investment, and self-responsibility while featuring self-defined socialist thinkers who preached that a commercial sense would deliver Arab awakening. These cross-fertilization and exchanges are indicators of the multiple discourses Palestinians drew on as they navigated what economic growth meant for social life.

A second and important project was the Gaza International

Hospital, the construction of which was planned to begin at the beginning of October 2007. Unfortunately, Hamas took over the Gaza Strip by force, causing the project to be cancelled.

Enron Palestine: A Failed Partner

The world's interest in Gaza stems, among other things, from its steadfastness in the face of the four wars waged by the Israeli army against it. Attacks on its only power plant did not reveal to the public the fact that the largest energy company in the world was the strategic partner in building that plant. Thus, Gaza had been indirectly associated with the biggest bankruptcy in the world.

The dream of building an independent power supply and the development of a project from scratch needed enormous efforts in terms of legal, financial and technical aspects. There were many difficulties facing a project of such magnitude, most importantly the steps required to obtain Israeli permits or at least the initial approvals for the plant location; any large industrial project required Israeli military approval prior to choosing a site, as Israel controls all land crossings and the sea, and the project would be required to avoid the settlements scattered throughout the Gaza Strip. According to the Oslo Accords, the PA's construction of any infrastructure projects such as a power plant did not absolve Israel of its legal responsibility to provide water, electricity and other basic services to the local population under occupation. An extensive search was necessary to find a global strategic partner with expertise in the manufacture, construction and operation of power plants. A partner who would also be willing and prepared to work in the areas of the newly born PNA.

The search started with several visits to several European and American companies to discuss the possibility of their willingness to work in Palestine. Of course the journey was really arduous. The last stop in the search for a partner was in Houston, encouraged by Wael

Khoury, and negotiation started with Enron, the largest American energy company.

Although I was attending the first meeting at Enron's offices in Houston, Texas, as a Senior Adviser to the Palestine Electric Company, and a member of their negotiating team, it became apparent that Enron's negotiating team consisted of eleven experts, including six lawyers; the Palestinian minister of Energy, sitting alone in front of this experienced and motivated team, was easy prey before them. I subconsciously decided to change sides and sat next to the lonely minister, who was not optimistic about the feasibility of reaching an agreement given the complex demands of Enron's team during the three days of meetings; he decided to return to Gaza. In order to encourage the minister to extend his stay, until their lawyers could agree on a draft Power Purchase Agreement, Enron managed quickly to arrange a meeting with Bill Richardson, the Energy Secretary in Washington, who was a popular figure in the Middle East through his tenure as the US ambassador to the United Nations.

When they arrived, accompanied by Ambassador Hasan Abdul Rahman at the Department of Energy in Washington, they were met by Bill Richardson's deputy, who offered the Secretary's apology for not being able to return on time from a meeting in New York. He expressed his eagerness to provide all possible assistance to improve the electricity sector in Palestine and welcomed Enron's future participation in achieving that goal.[48]

There was another visit to check on Abu Mazen's health, who underwent a successful surgery and was moved from hospital to the hotel. In the lobby, Saeb Erekat was bidding goodbye to Secretary of State Madeleine Albright, who had finished her visit to congratulate Abbas on his recovery.

Abu Mazen was recovering, accompanied by his wife and son, Yasser; he was pleased when informed of Enron's readiness to join in the Gaza project instead of the Israeli company Ormat. He urged the Palestinian minister not to waste this opportunity and remain in order to finalise the agreement. Finally, a power purchase agreement was signed in the Muqata'a by Said Khoury and Dr. Hamad under the auspices of both Yasser Arafat and Mahmoud Abbas, in the presence of Enron's Vice-President David Hague in Ramallah. [49]

The signing of this agreement was also witnessed by the American Consul General John Herbst who succeeded Edward Abington, who himself became an independent advisor to the Palestinian Authority. Enron's lawyers demanded that President Arafat ratify the signatures in his capacity as Chairman of the PLO and not as president of the National Authority.

Of course under normal circumstances, heads of states do not sign commercial agreements, but his advisor, Muhammed Rashid, managed to convince him to sign. The matter did not end there; the lawyers also demanded that the Legislative Council ratify it as well. The Council held a special session the following morning in which the agreement was discussed and approved. Council Chairman Ahmed Qurei also confirmed that the project would be exempted from all local taxes throughout the twenty-year concession period. [50]

Enron's lawyers became actively engaged in changing the legal structure of Palestine Electrical Company (PEC), surprisingly, by establishing eight different companies — two of them in the Cayman Islands, in line with Enron's incredible system of project management, for the same project. They also insisted on replacing the Palestinian auditors Saba & Co. and appointing their own auditors Arthur Andersen. Eventually, a supply and construction contract were agreed upon and awarded to the Swedish company ABB. The founders contacted various international financial institutions, led by the World Bank and its affiliate IFC, the European Investment Bank, the Arab Bank and others to secure funding for the proposed project.

Enron confirmed strongly and firmly that OPIC Corporation, which was backed by the US government, agreed in principle to fully finance the project. When its delegation arrived in Gaza to complete the required documentation about the founders of PEC, they noticed that one of the shareholders of the Arab Palestinian Investment Company (APIC), headed by Omar Aggad — a Palestinian businessman with Saudi nationality — was the Saudi Bin Laden Group. Questions were raised about its relationship with Osama bin Laden.[51]

Attempts to obtain American funding were unsuccessful, and after several months of waiting without a tangible result, the Palestinian founders finally approached Abdel Majeed Shoman, chairman of the Arab Bank in Amman, who expressed the bank's readiness to support projects that helped in building an independent Palestinian future economy. He immediately agreed to provide a loan of ninety million dollars, which enabled the construction of the power plant to proceed.

Enron's management in Houston welcomed the idea of a ground-breaking ceremony at the proposed site of the power plant, and used that opportunity as propaganda for its future projects in the Middle East. They also decided to invite the US Secretary of Energy Bill Richardson and the Swedish Foreign Minister to attend the celebration, alongside Chairman Arafat.

In order to allow ample time for the VIPs to attend, the 26th of October was the agreed date. The American Embassy's security men in Tel Aviv made regular visits to Gaza to secure the site. On October 19, Kelly Kimberly, Enron's director of public relations, arrived from Houston to arrange the schedule of the celebration and ensure the necessary security measures were in place. Suddenly, she demanded a change in the date due to information received that the 26th of October coincided with the anniversary of the killing of the head and founder of Islamic Jihad Movement, Fathi al-Shaqaqi, and the risk of a serious hostile operation was elevated.

Mossad agents had assassinated al-Shaqaqi on the Island of Malta in 1995. President Arafat refused to change the date, claiming that his chief of intelligence, Amin al-Hindi, assured him that no attack would take place; furthermore, his schedule for that day included several meetings in Gaza with Robin Cook, Britain's foreign secretary, Amr Musa, Egyptian foreign minister and Abd al-Ilah al-Khatib,

Jordan's foreign minister. The ceremony took place the morning of that day, without a single incident and without Bill Richardson. [52]

At the start of the second intifada, and on the instruction of the State Department, Enron withdrew all its employees from Gaza and retained a Lebanese engineer named Ed Husami, who kept in touch with Ambassador Indyk, who helped mediate with the Israelis to allow the entry of heavy equipment and turbines to the plant site inside the militarily-besieged Gaza.

During his two terms as US ambassador to Israel, Martin Indyk was incredibly a central figure — not only in helping Enron and PEC to obtain Israeli permits for materials needed for the construction of the Gaza power plant (to be transported to the Strip during the critical period of the second intifada); but he was also credited for his demands for a settlement freeze, calling for an end to attacks on Palestinian areas, and his requests for Israel to abide by the disengagement plan initiated by George Tenet, the CIA director.

His successor, Daniel Kurtzer, did not intervene, as he apparently or possibly wasn't aware of the Gaza power plant.

Unexpected news reached Husami, which descended on him like a thunderbolt: Enron's bankruptcy.

Husami and thousands of employees who took their bonuses and sometimes half of their salaries in Enron shares, were bound to lose all their savings. They were patiently waiting for their unknown fate. The Enron scandal was the biggest in the United States' history, and reverberated around the world.

The giant international auditors "Arthur Andersen" declared bankruptcy a few weeks after Enron's disappearance.

During the trial of its chairman, Kenneth Lay, it was disclosed that he was the largest supporter of the presidential campaigns for both George H. Bush and his son, George W. Bush. Lay was found dead in a hotel room before a verdict was announced.

Enron's young and most cheerful manager of operations in Palestine, Andrew Makk, was in love with local food, especially shawarma and kebab; he sadly died of a heart attack after the collapse of his company and the loss of all his life-long savings.

Some observers and financial analysts covering the scandal agreed that the meeting between chairman Arafat and Ken Lay, Enron's chairman, at the Davos Forum in early 2001, was an ominous omen for both. A few months later, Enron declared bankruptcy that caused Lay's death, and the Israeli siege on Arafat in Ramallah led to his death in more severe but similar circumstances.

Blocked Gaza Gas Fields

The 1996 visit of French President Jacques Chirac to Jerusalem and Gaza was marked by the opening of Charles de Gaulle Street, which was named by Mayor Aoun Shawa in appreciation of the valuable in-kind assistance provided by France to the Gaza municipality. Immediately after that, Chirac and Arafat laid the foundation stone of the Gaza Seaport project, which France, Italy and Holland pledged to finance.[53]

After the ceremony ended, and to the astonishment of many, Chirac led his host Arafat by the hand and asked him to get into his fortified car without escorts; even his translator, a lady of Algerian descent, was standing outside the car, looking puzzled and surprised! Did Arafat really understand French? Or could it be that Chirac spoke Arabic?

Chirac was extremely upset and angry at the heavy-handed way in which Israeli security agents treated him when he visited East Jerusalem the day before. Months later, some people speculated that Chirac had told Arafat a secret about the existence of gas or oil fields off the coast of Gaza, according to confirmed pictures detected by a French satellite.

Several months after Jacques Chirac's visit, a colourful map appeared in Yasser Arafat's office, showing the dark blue sea and close to the shore a few red and green dots. No one understood the meaning or the contents of that map. However, one of Arafat's advisors was heard saying that it indicated a serious possibility of the presence of oil and gas off the shores of Gaza; the photo was produced from a French satellite.

Another account about the nature of the discovery of the gas field was mentioned by a close advisor, quoting the National Geographic magazine,, wherein it was confirmed that its chief engineer, Robert Ballard was in 1997 leading an exploration expedition in the Mediterranean in search of two Phoenician ships which were sailing from Lebanon to Palestine. It was believed they sank at the bottom of the sea close to Gaza beach.

During the search, while diving, he noticed bubbles from some rocks that extended from Gaza in the south to Ashkelon in the north; such an observation increased the belief in the possibility of the existence of a gas field in that region. A close friend of the geologist reported his observation to a Palestinian engineer, who informed the PA.

According to the Oslo Accords, the field, if discovered, belonged to the PA. The Israeli Government was not exactly confident in the existence of gas; since the establishment of Israel in 1948, no oil or gas had been discovered there. Consequently, Israel agreed for the Palestinians to scope international companies for the exploration and bear the high costs of such a complex process, with no guaranteed results.

Despite that fact, Israel rejected all requests to allow the start of exploration off the Gaza shore; Netanyahu's government tried, via specious pretexts, to delay the project for several years, until Ehud Barak became the prime minister. In 1999, an agreement was reached in a meeting between Ehud Barak, Hosni Mubarak and Yasser Arafat in Sharm el-Sheikh, to finally allow the gas deal to go through and a permit for the construction of the Gaza seaport.

At the beginning of 1999, a concession was awarded to the British Gas company "BG" and CCC Energy, to explore for gas in the Mediterranean off the shores of the Gaza Strip — an area that was supposedly under the control of the Palestinian Authority. It was rumoured that Tony Blair's envoy Lord Levy was instrumental in concluding that lucrative gas deal.

Initial results of the preliminary drilling confirmed the existence of natural gas reserves in commercial quantities. The signing of a gas development agreement between the Palestinian Authority and British Gas was celebrated in London in November 1999. [54]

Frank Chapman, BG's president, hosted a special dinner at the luxurious Dorchester Hotel, where he praised this historic event for his company to be awarded the first ever Gas concession in Palestine, and he thanked the efforts of Wael Khoury of CCC.

Tony Blair had promised Arafat that he would personally attend the dinner, which prompted Arafat to bring a special and valuable gift to Blair, on the occasion of launching a campaign called "Bethlehem 2000, — a large model of the Church of the Nativity, made of wonderful Bethlehem mother-of-pearl. Blair apologised and withdrew at the last moment and sent his Minister of State for Foreign Affairs Peter Hain instead. To Arafat's anger and dismay, he gave the gift to Hain, who was shocked and astonished while whispering,

"Is this for me?" [55]

Fortunately, there was good news for the Palestinians: on BG's evaluation, the field was a short distance away from the shore: only 20 miles, a depth of less than 600 metres, compared to the Israeli Tamar field which was discovered 10 years after the Gaza field,70 miles outside Haifa at a depth of 2,200 metres; this doubled the latter's the cost of gas development and transportation.

September 27th 2000 was a memorable day in the history of the nascent Palestinian National Authority. A large gathering of businessmen and foreign diplomats headed by Frank Chapman of BG, Said Khoury, Omar Aggad, Robin Kealy, the British Consul, and Tarek Aggad flocked to the seaside, and set out in Arafat's dilapidated boat heading to light the gas torch for "Gaza Marine 1": the first well in a Palestinian Gas field, west of Gaza, thus declaring Palestine's accession as one of the few gas producing countries in the Eastern Mediterranean.

The field's confirmed reserves and declared estimates promised to generate abundant income of billions of dollars each year, which would tremendously help the Palestinian Authority in funding its badly needed infrastructure projects, including the Gaza sea port.

Unfortunately, the joy was squandered the following morning by Ariel Sharon's provocative visit to the Al-Aqsa Mosque in Jerusalem, which ignited the second intifada.

Despite the Israeli air strikes on various targets in Gaza, including the power plant, BG continued to negotiate with the Israeli government, with occasional direct assistance from Tony Blair, on the process of marketing the gas by delivering it to both Gaza for the operation of the power plant, and further north to Ashkelon to supply the Israel Electricity Company. This much needed gas would be cheaper than fuel and environment friendly, and a deal was urgently needed to develop the field and recover its high costs in a reasonable period. Meanwhile, Israel was conducting secret negotiations with a privately owned Egyptian gas company, backed by President Hosni Mubarak, for a long-term deal to supply Egyptian gas at a very attractive price, which seemed to be an additional reason for their reluctance to agree to BG's requests.

Egyptian Oil Minister, Sameh Fahmy, suggested connecting the Palestinian gas to the nearby Egyptian city of Al-Arish, and then pumping back a limited amount of gas to Gaza through a small pipeline in order to operate the power plant; the rest could be marketed by BG through its operations in Egypt. But Israel rejected the Egyptian offer.

Salah Hafez, the Egyptian oil expert, who served as head of the Environment Agency and was a political figure, played a pivotal role in the arbitration case between Egypt and Israel regarding the ownership of Taba in South Sinai, which was returned to Egypt. He said, "There are no maritime borders in the Mediterranean between Egypt and Israel, the border is with the Palestinian Authority and Gaza Strip only." [56]

A year later, indeed, an agreement was reached to supply Israel with Egyptian gas through a pipeline that crossed the Sinai desert to Israel.

Following the fall of Hosni Mubarak regime in 2011 and the election of Mohammed Morsi — the first ever member of the Muslim Brotherhood to become President — a series of terror attacks suddenly began targeting the Egyptian pipeline in Sinai, to disrupt the supply of gas to Israel, which led to the complete closure of the only pipeline.

Surprisingly, it turned out later that Egypt was suffering from an acute shortage of natural gas supplies for its domestic consumption, so they were forced to import gas to cover this sudden shortfall.

Israel tried to reach an agreement with BG to extract Palestinian gas and pump it to the Ashkelon sea port gas facility, as an alternative to the suspended Egyptian gas, but the negotiations did not lead to any positive results.

After the great discovery of the Egyptian Zohar gas field, the largest in the Mediterranean — and two years after the discovery of the Israeli Leviathan field and the Cypriot Aphrodite — five East Mediterranean countries (Egypt, Israel, Cyprus, Greece and Palestine) announced the formation of a joint council called the "EMG Forum." Jordan joined the Forum despite not being a gas-producing or Mediterranean country.

After more than fifteen years of difficult and fruitless negotiations with Israel, important developments emerged with the announcement that Royal Dutch Shell acquired BG and all its assets, including the Gaza Marine gas field.

Shell tried to re-negotiate with Israel, but it encountered many obstacles, forcing it to turn a blind eye to developing the field, and decided to sell its majority share to the Palestinian PIF and CCEnergy, which they became equal partners in the field.

Some PA officials were warned by Ephraim Sneh, a former minister of health in Rabin's government, about an oil field in the town of Rantis — or as it's called, *Meged*, located on the green line; a Romanian drilling company had completed its work on the Israeli side and was prepared to drill a well on the Palestinian side. [57]

The PA declined to deal with the Romanian company, claiming that the field was dominated by Israel for operation or transportation of crude oil at a future stage. Growing challenges in the East Mediterranean necessitated collective responses — especially in the fields of security and prosperity for the interests of the EMG Forum countries; as stated by the Greek oil & gas expert Antonia Dimou, head of the ME unit at ISDA, and participant in major energy events, jointly with Harry Theocharis, who then served as Greek minister of Tourism.

Finally, after twenty-one years, the latest saga was an agreement signed by Magdy Galal, chairman of EGAS and Mohammad Mustafa, chairman of PIF in Ramallah, and agreed by Marwan Salloum, president of CC Energy. [58]

CHAPTER SIX

Hamas & Iran: A Tearful Choice?

"The enemy is a very good teacher."
— DALAI LAMA

You Resist...You Exist

"The unresolved plight of the Palestinians speaks directly
of an undomesticated cause and a rebellious people
paying a very heavy price for their resistance."
— EDWARD SAID

Pre-*Nakba* Palestinians have always been proponents of separating religion from politics. Religious slogans, regardless of their source, did not seem to concern them or did not exist in the first place, as it was not consistent with the natural secular atmosphere that they were brought up within Palestine in general. Suddenly, new factors intervened that upended all previous concepts, and were important events carrying a clear indication of unprecedented and certain political and social changes coming to the region. "In his resistance to foreign colonialists the Palestinian was either a stupid savage, or a negligible quantity, morally and even existentially." [1]

The turmoil continued with the start of the Iraq-Iran war, and the assassination of President Sadat by an Islamic group in 1981, which was preceded by an Israeli raid on the Iraqi nuclear reactor, greatly helped the emergence and spread of the Islamic movements in the region.

The subsequent and brutal massacre of the Sabra and Shatila refugee camps in mid-September 1982, which killed thousands of innocent Palestinian residents, including children, women, and the elderly. The unprecedented frustration resulting from these tragic events, and in light of these massive and successive defeats of the so-called progressive regimes, made the traditional leaders lose their illusory abilities to convince their shocked people of a completely different future full of victories and prosperity.

There was a glimmer of hope on the horizon: large segments of Arabs were able to see its brilliance. They ran after this luminous ray with all their might, in the hope that it would lift them out of all these defeats, calamities and setbacks.

The magical and angelic solution was to resort to Allah, and thus to embrace the rising Islamic movements who carried a shining slogan *"Islam is the Solution"*. Dr. Mustafa Mahmoud commented that "We must shut that door through which the opportunists, the conspirators and crafty people enter. These people use attractive lies as a Trojan horse to enter our Islamic house through its door to blow it up from the inside while wearing the caliphate's turban and glorifying the saints. It is religious deception… It is the disguise of the new enemies." [2]

People currently live in this incredibly grey age, mixed with the colours of good and evil. The colours of hypocrisy and lies have become so prevalent that the ordinary citizen has become totally confused as they have lost the ability to distinguish between the lies of the hypocritical rulers and the truth around them.

The first intifada was peaceful, children resisting occupation forces with stones; the second intifada was different, with offensive weapons, bombs and missile-launching aircraft, unprecedented killing and destruction.

Doctor Mads Gilbert reflects on what occurred, stating:

> I walk out of the hospital gates, and glance up at the
> pitch-black sky to see if I can spot the drone buzzing

above my head. For them, up there, we are so infinitely small down here. They can see everything, monitoring every movement, tapping every call, and reading every text message or letter. They also have a monopoly on air and sea power. Their F16 fighter-bombers meet no opposition, flying freely and bombing wherever they wish. The same goes for their drones and Apache helicopters.[3]

Neve Gordon and Nicola Perugini wrote about people in the line of fire:

Tom Hurndall, a British member of the International Solidarity Movement, while in Rafah, noticed that three Palestinian children were trapped in an area under attack. He picked up one little boy and brought him to safety. When he went back to shield the remaining two, he was shot in the head by an Israeli sniper. A few months earlier, Rachel Corrie, a twenty-three-old American activist, was run over by an Israeli armoured military bulldozer while shielding a Palestinian home from demolition. [4]

The third Israeli war in 2014 was the deadliest military offensive against Gaza in recent history. The war lasted 51 days and had enduring consequences for the two million citizens. Over 2,250 people died, with more than 12,000 wounded. Moreover, at least 22,000 buildings were destroyed.

Pope Francis raised the question "What does it mean to be 'a people'?" He went on to say, "People may have profound disagreements and differences, but they can walk together inspired by shared goals, and so create a future. Classically, a people gathers itself in assemblies and organises. It shares experiences and hopes, and it hears the call of a common destiny." [5]

During the last Israeli attack, a poor father in Gaza said:

"I did the strangest thing today — I exchanged two of my children with two of my brother's. So, in case I get bombed, two of mine will survive and if he gets bombed, two of his will live on! You know God, we have suffered the brutal bombardment and survived, we left our homes without regretting losing all our possessions and memories. As the Qur'an taught us *staying alive is a sacred duty* and a healthy human being is the most precious thing left in our city."[6]

His story humanises a global tragedy, their characters' inner conflict and the architecture of two nations' disputes. All over the world, there are scenes of startling and unprecedented popular solidarity with the Palestinian people.

Gaza As Larger Than Life: that's how Helga Tawil-Souri described its largeness in its patience and resolve, the resilience that is quintessentially Gazan.

> A steadfastness, religious and cultural roots, that is grand and generous, built on its solidarity. The generosity is in abundance, that is offered to a guest no matter the poor circumstances, sweltering dust, and ruins of one's house.[7]

The end of the fourth war came with more pain, sadness, and tears, as dreams fell and were torn quickly, irrefutable facts and myths emerged in the sky of our minds.

A recurring painful paradox.

After the war, like all wars, they gathered their dreams again from under the rubble, they tried to pave a new way, a road of hope, and they rushed to plant more olive trees, orange groves from Jaffa, Palm trees from Deir El-Balah, and stared anxiously at the fishermen in the ancient blue sea of Gaza. The people of Gaza no longer feared the unseen, for they were in the knowledge of God. The affliction, if it descended on them, descended with its definite kindness. As Sameh al-Qasim eloquently captured the sentiment:

You may deprive me of mother's kisses.
You may curse my father, my people.
You may distort my history.
You may build walls of hatred around me.
You may glue my eyes to humiliations,
O enemy of the sun,
But I shall not compromise
And to the last pulse in my veins
I shall resist .. I shall resist. [8]

Iran's Regional Ambitions

"If you are neutral in situations of injustice,
you have chosen the side of the oppressor."

— DESMOND TUTU

The Iranian popular revolution was plotted by Ayatollah Khomeini from his exile in Baghdad, until early 1978 when Saddam Hussein finally expelled him, at the request of the Shah, after the signature of the Shatt al-Arab agreement. Khomeini asked to go to Kuwait, which did not grant him an entry visa. Surprisingly, he declined the invitation of Arafat among others to come to Lebanon; instead Khomeini chose France and from Neauphle-le-Château conducted his final plot to depose the Shah in February 1979, ending over two thousand years of Persian monarchy. It was later disclosed that a group of Palestinian fedayeen were given the task of guarding the Ayatollah in France, until his triumphant return to Tehran.[9]

Khomeini immediately declared the Islamic Republic of Iran, with the newly revised doctrine of "Wilayat al-Faqih," which to some meant "Guardianship of the religious Jurisprudence," embracing the doctrine of interpreting God's commandments.

The great reward that Khomeini decided to offer the Palestinians was inviting Arafat to visit him in Tehran during the first month of his ascension to the Wilayat seat, and thus, Arafat became the first foreign leader whom Khomeini received in Tehran after his homecoming.

With great gratitude and appreciation for another pleasant surprise, Arafat accepted the keys of the abandoned Israeli embassy in Tehran. That gesture by the Ayatollah was intended to mark the total reversal of the pro-Israel policies of the deposed Shah. Arafat appointed Hani al-Hassan as the first Palestinian ambassador to the Islamic Republic. [10]

During the American hostage crisis in Iran, a significant development was in the making, according to the account of my diplomatic friend Issa Khalil Sabbagh, who worked for many years in the White House as the senior translator for Presidents Nixon, Ford, and Carter; the Administration requested the mediation of Yasser Arafat with Ayatollah Khomeini for the release of the hostages. In return, the US would immediately call for direct talks with the PLO as a step for recognition and the beginning of a serious dialogue to resolve the Palestinian issue.

The Saudi Crown Prince at the time, Fahd Al Saud, assured Arafat of this American desire and promise; he also offered the use of his private plane to transport Arafat with the hostages if the deal was approved by Iran.

Arafat made initial contact, but the Iranian response was not encouraging; he had sent Khalil al-Wazir "Abu Jihad" to Tehran, but Khomeini did not receive him, although the Supreme Leader had issued an order to release 13 hostages as a good gesture (women and African Americans) on the grounds that they were not believed to be American spies!

Arafat's attempt failed and the PLO's relationship with the Islamic Republic worsened, especially after the outbreak of the Iran-Iraq war that year, as Arafat was unable not to stand by Saddam Hussein and support Iraq and its Arab connection.[11]

< Members of the Palestine Prize in Engineering named after Hasib Sabbagh and Said Khoury, headed by Dr. Muhammad Shtayyeh. Amman, October 2015

^ Samer Khoury and Suhail Sabbagh at the Church of the Nativity in Bethlehem, 2018.

> Samer Khoury at the CCC building in Ramallah, 2019.

Jabra Ibrahim Jabra was born in Bethlehem, he wrote novels, poetry and plays. His work was translated into many languages that won him many prizes.

^
Former British Foreign Secretary, Douglas Hurd discussing details of his book 'The Last Day of Summer'.
Alhani London, 1993.

<
Iraqi poets; Jamil al-Zahawi (left) and Maruf Al-Rusafi (right) with Sami Schawa "Prince of Violin" in Jerusalem, 1934.

<
London Arab Cultural Week : Poets, authors and publishers joined to highlight the issues of Palestine.
London, June 1986.

My mother and me with her favourite
jasmin flowers - Gaza, 1958.

^
Muin Bseiso is the
poet of the early
Gaza revolution. His
communist idealogy
in his poetry took him
to the world.

>
Che Guevara calls
on all Palestinians to
continue the struggle
to recover their stolen
homeland during his
visit to Gaza, June
1959.

<
"Fadous" famous brass
band roaming the streets
in the Hijri new-year's
celebrations, 1953.

< Ismail Shamout's iconic painting 'Abeer' wearing her Thobe which represents names of several Palestinian cities and villages. Kuwait, 1986.

Postcard of Banksy's 'Balloon Girl' on the Separation Wall in Bethlehem, 2016.

Postcard of Samson's tomb sent using an Israeli stamp during their short-lived occupation of Gaza during the Suez war in 1957.

Presidents Arafat and Abbas witnessing the signing by Said
Khoury and Dr Hamed of the agreement to build the Gaza power
plant. Enron's vice-president and the US Consul General in
attendance. Ramallah, June 1999.

A group photo of the Palestinian officials on the
final day of their Good-Governance program at
Harvard University - Boston, February 2001.

< Saudi poet and politician Ghazi Algusaibi, a committed defender of the Palestinian cause during his book launch - Alhani London, 1993.

> From right: Author Salwa Jarrah, publisher Samir Shawa, Iraqi poet Ahmed Mattar, Ferial Maktabi and Fatima Ibrahim - Al Hani bookshop, London 1991.

^ Former Syrian Minister of Commerce and Finance Dr. Ghassan Rifaie. Doha, 2017.

^ Mohamed Al Mahrouqi, member of the Omani Shura Council and fierce defender of Palestinian rights in international forums.

> Dr Haidar Abdel Shafi is the reputable leader who headed the Palestinian delegation to the Madrid Conference in 1991. He strongly opposed the Oslo accords.

^
Judge Mazin Sisalem is sworn in before Amr Mousa, Secretary General of the Arab League, as the first Palestinian representative in the Arab Investment Court. Cairo, 2004.

^
Mahmoud Al Ghefari, an outstanding collator of audio accounts and memories of Palestinians in the Southern district.

^
Former Minister of Justice, Freih Abu Middain, proudly claims that he offered his jacket (shown above) to president Arafat during their visit to Madrid, Spain, 1998.

< From right; Adib Alwan, Zaki Shihab, Dr Ali Othman, Laila Shawa, Afif Safieh, Fuad Abu Gheida and Lebanese poet Antoin Raad. London, 1993.

From left: Saida Nusseibeh, General Sir Peter de la Billiere, who led British forces in the first Gulf War to liberate Kuwait, Mona Al Ghussein and Samir Shawa. At the launch of Leslie McLoughlin's book 'A Nest of Spies'. London, 1994. >

< The late Gabi Baramki, founder of the Palestinian Pugwash, being honored. From left: Nabil Shaath, Paolo Cotta-Ramusino and Haifa Tarazi Baramki. Istanbul, 2013.

General Assembly of Members of the Welfare Association 'Taawon', the largest Palestinian lobby in providing assistance for refugees inside and outside Palestine. Amman, 2017.

<
The destroyed offices
of Gaza Electricity
Company after the
Israeli air strikes,
despite the presence
of an American
partner in the same
buidling.
July, 2004.

<
Tarek Aggad, a founding
member of PEC and the
Chairman of Arab Palestinian
Investment Company (APIC).

>
Marwan Salloum, president of
CCEnergy, is working diligently
with PIF and EGAS to resume
work on the Gaza marine field.

^
Dr. Muhamed Mustafa,
the chairman of Palestine
Investment Fund (PIF)

Two lobbyists for Palestine: Omar Abbas (left) in
Doha, Qatar and Muhammed Murrar of the Arab
Bank in London.

< Two entrepeneurs.
Left: Armand
Hamer, founder
of Occidental Oil
and right, Hasib
Sabbagh, founder of
CCC.

> Chief engineer Joseph Hayek in
Concession 103, the largest Libyan
oil field that was producing over
one million bpd.
Libya 1969.

< Engineers and staff
supervising the
construction of pipelines
and facilities at Occidental
oil fields.
Libyan desert, 1970.

> Jaffa-born Walid Abu Ghali showing his award for Environmental Protection. Amman, 2018.

< Charles Zacharia, an architect displaced from Jaffa after his family lost all their flour mills in Palestine.

< Dr. Ali Othman with his wife Dr. Saniyah Naqash, an author and lecturer in AUB, Beirut.

Engineer Saad Alhashwa next to his father's amazing Chevrolet (seized by Jewish Militia in 1948 in Jaffa) and the 73 year-old receipt from the main dealer in Jerusalem.

> Gammal Abdel Nasser with his top military officers during his only visit to Gaza following the February attack by Israeli forces. Gaza, 15 March 1955.

< Malcolm X meeting the first Head of the PLO, Ahmed Shoqari, in Cairo on his way to visit Gaza, 1966.

> Jawaherlal Nehru, the Indian prime minister, at the start of his visit to Gaza in solidarity with the Palestinians and to inspect Indian troops serving in the UN Peacekeeping Force, May 19, 1960.

< Mahmoud Farra welcomes Judith Barnett, Assistant Deputy Secretary of Commerce during her visit to the Businessmen Association in Gaza, 1997.

^
US Ambassador Ed Walker, left, with Samir Shawa and Dr. Mohammed Sabawi at the Palestinian Businessmen Asssociation event in Gaza, 1997.

< Jeffrey Feltman on his farewell visit, receiveing a thank you present from the Palestinian Businessmen Association. Gaza, 1997.

> Popular Tunisian singer/ composer Lutfi Buchnak, who visited Jerusalem and sang for Palestine on several occasions. Photographed with the Palestinian art and music critic, Fatima Ibrahim. Carthage Festival. Tunis, 2014.

< Mohammed Assaf with young Karim Abu-Salim. Since winning the Arab Idol competition, he became the bright and artistic face of Palestine to the world. Gaza, 2017.

Zababdeh Folk Arts Troupe, sponsored by Nazih Khalil, performing Dabkah dance in Madrid, Spain to promote tourism to Palestine, 2015.

> A huge demonstration denouncing the devestating Balfour Declaration on its centenary. Tens of thousands of demonstrators participated in London on 4th November 2017.

^
Among protestors were Salwa Jarrah and Misbah Kamal gathering in front of Parliament.

^
British MPs, holding the Palestinian flag in support of the UN resolution to recognise Palestine including Jeremy Corbyn, Peter Hain, Sir Gerald Kaufman, Lisa Nandy, Jack Straw and David Ward.
London, September 2012.

^
David Watkins, MP and Director of CAABU and artist Lamis Dajani holding copies of his book 'Palestine, an inescapable duty'.
Alhani London, 1990.

Iran continued to maintain a pro-Palestinian policy despite the fallout with the PLO, and explicitly supported Islamic Jihad and at a later stage Hamas. The Shah was the most prominent Muslim leader to recognize Israel in 1950, although the recognition was revoked by the Government of Mosaddeq in 1951. After the fall of Mosaddeq in 1953, the Shah's regime resumed its relations with Israel. From the 1950s until the 1970s, Israel imported 90% of its oil from Iran and exported most of its citrus produce to Iran. Six months after his return to Tehran, Ayatollah Khomeini declared the last Friday of the month of Ramadan as the International Day of Jerusalem *"Yom al-Quds."*

Dr. Fathi al-Shiqaqi, with a group of university students while studying in Egyptian universities, founded the Islamic Jihad Movement, praising Khomeini and his revolution in books he published; he then established Al-Quds Brigades *"Saraya al-Quds"* in Gaza. Through the Iranian embassy in Beirut and Hizballah, Islamic Jihad's leadership received logistical and financial support which cemented the ideological and political bond to the Islamic Republic.

The Iranian nuclear program represented a serious international concern, and not only for Israelis or the neighbouring Gulf states. It was clear that the major global powers, including Russia and China, were seeking to permanently close the nuclear club and not allow new members to join its limited and exclusive membership.

Israel repeated its constant claims that the Iranian nuclear program was a major threat to its existence, and must be eliminated with a sudden and fatal strike, as it did to the Iraqi nuclear program with the destruction of the almost ready-for-testing "Tammuz reactor" in 1981.

President Obama wrote after leaving office:

> Iran posed the least serious challenge to America's long-term interests but won the prize for "Most Actively Hostile." Heir to the great Persian empires of antiquity, once an epicentre of science and art during Islam's medieval golden age…With Turkey and Iraq on its western border and Afghanistan and Pakistan

214 | LOBBYING FOR PALESTINE

to the east, it was generally viewed as just another
poor Middle Eastern country. In 1951, Iran's secular, left-leaning parliament moved to nationalize the
country's oil fields leading President Eisenhower to
green-light a CIA-MI6-engineered coup that deposed
Iran's democratically elected prime minister and con-
solidated power in the hands of the country's young
monarch, Shah Mohammad Reza Pahlavi.[12]

Israel was stretched at the time in many Arab countries, under the
guise of protecting them from Iran. Ironically, Iran had also extended
its presence in four or five Arab countries, under the pretext of protecting them from Israel! It seemed that events were accelerating since
1979: starting with the Afghan Mujahideen, funded by the US and its
allies, against the Soviet Union forces that invaded Afghanistan; the
ill-fated historical visit by President Sadat to Jerusalem; the signing
of the Egyptian-Israeli peace treaty after the Camp David talks; the
success of the Iranian revolution in the toppling of the Shah's Persian
empire; and the establishment of the Islamic Republic in the name of
"*Wilayat al-Faqih*" under the leadership of Imam Khomeini.

Badrakhan, the Syrian journalist commented: Iran did not need
a nuclear bomb or weapons of mass destruction to publicly declare
that it controls four Arab capitals, and that it dominates through its
sectarian militias the governments of those troubled countries and
seeks to control their future.[13]

Iran and all the Arab countries were calling for a zone free of
weapons of mass destruction in the Middle East. At Pugwash conferences Jaynatha Dhanapala and Sergio Duerte observed that "the successful adoption in 1995 of the UN resolution on the establishment
of the free zone was the main element of a package that permitted
indefinite extension of the NPT." [14]

The resolution was repeatedly blocked by the United States:
Washington's continuing sabotage of the effort in order to protect its
Israeli client."

The Israeli participants in most regional conferences were skilfully and repetitively trying to replace any discussion about Palestine with a long debate about the Iranian nuclear program, in a clear, deliberate and malicious effort to eliminate any priority of the central issue in Middle East conflicts, Palestine, and focus on the only danger threatening the region: the Iranian regime, the sponsor of terrorism. [15]

During a recent interview with Mehdi Hasan, Israeli minister Danny Ayalon claimed that he didn't know how many nukes his country owns and insisted that Israel's nukes are "irrelevant" to the debate over Iran's nuclear ambitions![16]

Since the first American nuclear bomb was dropped on Hiroshima in 1945, the bomb had become, for all the countries that managed to produce it, nothing but a paralyzed commodity that was never used or sold or traded.

Bozorgmehr Ziaran, Iran's representative to the IAEA, who replaced Ali Akbar Salehi, confirmed that Iran announced its absolute reluctance to acquire nuclear weapons, and reiterated Iran's commitment to the fatwa issued by the Supreme Leader prohibiting the use of nuclear weapons, as it contradicts the teachings of Islam.

John Kerry spoke of US hopes to achieve a deal with Iran's foreign minister Mohammed Javid Zarif, stating that "Obviously, the *fatwa* of the leader is a very important instrument, and we respect it enormously as a matter of religious edict…But that has to be translated into a lay person's regular document, a legal one."[17]

Iran is a nuclear state with a suspended sentence, after the 2015 Vienna agreement! Ali Asghar Soltanieh, the Iranian envoy to Vienna, resigned his post as he opposed the agreement concluded by Zarif. He once told me that Iran has no intention of producing the bomb as per the Supreme Leader's fatwa, and would like to apologize for the people of Gaza who were hoping and praying for a nuclear Iran in order to break the Israeli monopoly of possessing nuclear weapons in the region.[18]

The current reality manifests an incredibly perplexing fact: Iran and Israel pretend to be providing protection, while they are fighting to control the fate and wealth of those vulnerable countries. It is clearly a dark and abject reflection of the vulnerability and shameful surrender of the failure of Arab national security.

Former Israeli President Moshe Katsav and his chief of Staff Shaul Mofaz are among tens of thousands of Jews of Iranian origin who had settled in Israel. There are lasting and good relations between the Jewish community in Iran and Israel. Israel spun Iran's empty threats against it, just as the former president, Ahmadinejad, declared his intention to remove Israel from the world map: such illusory threats served Israel in consolidating its internal national unity and garnering international support and sympathy.

Soleimani took charge of *Failaq al-Quds* in early 1998. He played an integral role in many crucial operations that cemented the Iranian grip on its operations in Iraq, Syria, Lebanon and Yemen. Soleimani became a popular national figure in Iran, and was regarded as the second most powerful general in Iran, behind Ayatollah Khamenei.

Qassem Soleimani was assassinated on 3 January 2020 by U.S. drone attack near Baghdad airport, by order of President Trump. Also, Abu-Mahdi al-Muhandis, the commander of the Iranian-backed Popular Mobilisation Forces "Al-Hashd al-Shaabi," was assassinated in the same attack.

As Albright recalled:

> When reformer Mohammad Khatami was elected president of Iran, he decided to restore relations with the PLO.
>
> During the Camp David talks, Yasser Arafat showed Clinton a letter he had received from Khatami. The letter backed Palestinian participation in the Middle East peace process, acknowledged Israel's legitimacy, and discussed the possibility of a regionwide peace if the Palestinians were allowed establish a state on the West Bank and Gaza.[19]

Arafat's Death

*"The world's cemeteries are
full of indispensable men."*
— CHARLES DE GAULLE

Since becoming the President of the Palestinian Authority which Israel had recognised, Arafat's repeated requests for an Israeli permit to visit Jerusalem, or any of the 1948 cities, were promptly rejected, including his passionate and sincere request to allow him attend Yitzhak Rabin's funeral, which was officially attended by two prominent Arab leaders: King Hussein of Jordan and President Mubarak of Egypt. His request was turned down by Shimon Perez, citing security objections. He finally managed to visit Tel Aviv, for the first and only time, accompanied by the Oslo duo Abu Mazen and Abu Ala'a, to pay their condolences to Rabin's widow Lea — a visit secretly arranged jointly by a former Rabin advisor, Yossi Ginossar, and his friend, Mohamed Rashid, Arafat's advisor.[20]

Despite the unforgettable failure of the Camp David talks between Yasser Arafat and Ehud Barak, under the auspices of President Bill Clinton — which lasted for twenty days — Arafat's return to Gaza was astonishingly marked by a huge welcoming crowd, cheering him for his determination not to forfeit a single inch of the 1967 occupied land (which is less than 22% of the historic lands of Palestine!)

A few weeks later, Ariel Sharon paid his planned and provocative visit to the Al-Aqsa Mosque in Jerusalem, which immediately sparked a second Intifada, called later the *"Al-Aqsa Intifada"*. As a result, Palestinian casualties of deaths and serious injuries accelerated for several months until Barak's defeat in the elections, which brought Sharon to power. Israeli air attacks continued on selected targets, but surprisingly, the Gaza Power plant was a unique and unexpected one, considering the American company "Enron" owned a third of its equity.

When Ariel Sharon succeeded in his bid to become the Prime Minister of Israel, Arafat seemed desperately anxious and was seeking endeavour and support from other leaders, citing the atrocious credentials of Sharon; one of the foreign journalists described him as a *feral beast*.

Fatah was visibly disintegrating, poisoned by divisions, destroying itself from within and increasingly incapable of grappling with the serious challenges facing its founder.

President George W. Bush made this public speech in the United Nations:

> My vision is two states, living side by side in peace and security… Peace requires a new and different Palestinian leadership, so that a Palestinian state can be born … I call on the Palestinian people to elect new leaders … If the Palestinian people actively pursue these goals, America and the world will actively support their efforts.[21]

A clear call to oust Chairman Arafat! This heralded the inevitable end to Yasser Arafat, whom world leaders were confused how to handle, and were unable to contain or tame him. Remarkably, he had a superior ability to withstand pressure and stay away from danger, as he thrived in crises and increased his steeliness amongst calamity. He also mastered the art of evasion and was not shy about making promises and statements which were often not implemented.

A well-known theory is that a charismatic leader's ability to address the masses could arouse their enthusiasm for accepting his method of demagogic rule.

President Arafat enjoyed using popular terminology in certain situations; for example, to escape the dilemma of not agreeing to certain conditions, or an interim solution offer, he sighed heartily:

يا جبل ما يهزك ريح
"O mountain, no wind shakes you."

And in another situation, whenever being unable to persuade the angry public of a difficult decision he had already made, and to assure that his word should be adhered only to:

اللي مش عاجبه يشرب البحر
"Who does not like it, let him drink sea water!" [22]

Some critics have argued that Arafat's strange and peculiar decisions were due to a gradual deterioration of his mental faculties after he underwent a brain operation in June 1992 in Amman, to remove a blood clot formed after his plane crash in the Libyan desert. His personal physician, Dr. Ashraf Al-Kurd, indicated that the president was in good health and did not suffer from Parkinson's disease, but the tremors in his hands were caused by tension.

The Israeli government demanded that Arafat hand over a group of Palestinian activists allied to the PFLP, whom he was harbouring in his presidential compound. They found in his refusal to their demand a motive to attack the building. Israeli tanks bombarded and destroyed large parts of the Muqata'a building, leaving only a small part containing a few rooms, where the president and some of his aides, headed by Nabil Abu Rudeina, took shelter.

The Israelis allowed a limited number of people to enter the building carrying food, drinks and sometimes medicines. Among the most prominent senior officials allowed were Muhammad Dahlan and Muhammad Rashid.

President Hosni Mubarak, who was trying to mediate Arafat's release to attend the Arab League summit in Beirut, claimed that Ariel Sharon would allow Arafat to leave Ramallah to any destination he wanted as long as he did not return to Palestine.

Arafat rejected this offer and shouted his famous phrase: "They want me expelled, a fugitive, or killed, and I want to become a *martyr, martyr, martyr*".

As the siege continued, Arafat agreed under pressure to American requests, conveyed by Secretary of State Colin Powell on his visit to the Muqata'a to appoint Abu Mazen as prime minister, in the hope of reaching an agreement to end the siege.

Three months passed, during which President George Bush received Abu Mazen — without a solution to Arafat's dilemma — who appointed Abu Alaa Qurei to lead a new government. Arafat's health deteriorated almost daily.

At the end of October, Sharon agreed, with the mediation of President Jacques Chirac, that Arafat could travel to Paris for treatment, and guaranteed his return to Ramallah after his recovery from his mysterious disease. Some senior Palestinian security officers believed that Sharon's approval was based on confirmed Israeli intelligence reports that Arafat had only a few days to live, due to the severity of his illness.

At eleven o'clock in the morning of the eleventh day of November 2004, the ex-Prime Minister, Mahmoud Abbas, announced from a military hospital in Paris the death of Yasser Arafat; this was associated with the second intifada, followed by the election of Mahmoud Abbas as President of the Palestinian Authority. [23]

At eleven o'clock in the morning of the eleventh day of November 1918, the French General Madues announced from a train station in Paris the end of the first world war, which was associated with the humiliating surrender of Germany, followed by the famous Treaty of Versailles.

Indeed, the coincidence of Arafat's death after the failure of Oslo to bring about an independent state, with the declaration of Germany's surrender in Paris at the end of the war and the signing of the humiliating Versailles Treaty, recalls Edward Said's rational description after examining the provisions of the Oslo Accords: "*An instrument of Palestinian surrender, a Palestinian Versailles.*" [24]

The French president, who visited Arafat in hospital, ordered a funeral that was usually reserved for friendly Heads of State. The next day, Arafat's body was brought to Cairo, where an official State funeral was planned. His coffin was draped in the Palestinian flag, a hearse drove to a nearby Cairo air base; marching behind were many high-ranking representatives from over fifty countries: headed by President Hosni Mubarak, the Saudi King Abdallah, King Muhammad VI of Morocco, King Abdallah of Jordan, Presidents Bashar al-Assad, Emile Lahoud, Zeinedine bin Ali, Omar el-Bashir, Ali Abdullah Saleh and Abdel Aziz Boutafliqa.

Leaders of other European and Muslim countries were present; William Burns represented the US, while Foreign Secretary Jack Straw represented the UK.

No one could have imagined the significant presence of so many kings and heads of state at the funeral of this fighter and revolutionary leader. Was that out of love and appreciation for his unique personality, or sympathy for the just cause that he represented, a cause that most governments of those participants had a hand in its past and present tragedies? A paradox that requires an honest answer!

There were scenes of chaos and emotion as tens of thousands of mourners converged on the Egyptian helicopter carrying Arafat's body after it landed in Ramallah.

Then the weeping crowd carried his coffin to his final resting place near the Muqata'a, chanting the virtues of their deceased charismatic leader. As expected, Sharon refused to fulfil Arafat's desire and dream of being buried in Jerusalem.

One of dozens of European diplomats who gathered at the Muqata'a was heard commenting on the amazing scene of the tens of thousands who rose up and came to bid farewell to their president and inspirational leader:

"Where were these people while he was besieged in his destroyed office for over two years? Had a quarter of these people demonstrated, they would probably have saved him and lifted the siege."

One of Arafat's advisors commented on his death: "Of course, I don't rule out accusing someone of putting poison in his food, or a conspiracy theory being the cause of his death. But perhaps his extreme fatal anger and anguish of the Israeli siege resulted in his humiliating imprisonment in a crumbling building with destruction all around him in the partially destroyed Muqata'a. In addition to the bitter and painful truth that no one made a real effort to release him, none whatsoever, not from Arab and World leaders, to exert some pressure on Ariel Sharon to release him. Likewise, sadly none of his senior Fatah members — the movement he founded and headed for over forty years — motivated the masses to rise in a popular movement and storm his besieged headquarters in Ramallah. That was the worst ever situation that he faced in his long and bloody struggle. I think he deeply regretted falling into the trap of the second Intifada, which ultimately claimed his life."

As Madeleine Albright tried to summarise, "There was a warm side to Arafat, but his politics were inflexible and, in the end, very costly to his people." [25]

Election of a President

"The greatest enemy of knowledge is not ignorance, it is the illusion of Knowledge"
— STEPHEN HAWKING

The majority of voters, especially in Gaza, who elected Abu Mazen (I was one of them) agreed that he was the only man capable of continuing the march towards a peaceful outcome and ultimately realizing the dream of an independent state. He was one of the first founders of the Fatah movement; one of the historical leaders of the PLO (he held the position of Secretary General for a long time); the architect of the Palestinian Authority; and he signed the Oslo Accords on the White House lawn.

It all exemplified to his adherence and steadfastness to his immutable principles in renouncing violence, and his repeated calls for dialogue and negotiations as a strategic goal to resolve our conflict. He garnered overwhelming support from most world leaders, especially the respect of successive American Administrations.

In fact, he was the preferred candidate amongst other Fatah

historical leaders; no one could challenge his ability to preserve its leadership role of the Palestinian cause. During his presidential campaign, one of his guards quickly closed the door of his car, without noticing that his boss was holding the door. Unfortunately, the fingers of the president's right hand got stuck in the door's groove, which sadly resulted in the severing of part of his middle finger.

Arafat enjoyed several titles during his long career in the armed struggle, being the founding leader of Fatah since its inception in early 1960s, followed by chairman of the PLO in 1968 — a title that he cherished until his death. The Palestine Declaration of Independence in Algiers was a new title bestowed upon him; he was also the President of the State of Palestine, and finally President of the PNA as a result of the Oslo Accords.

Abu Mazen subsequently inherited not only the four titles but also a torn authority, a devastated infrastructure, a divided Fatah movement, a powerful Hamas armed with weapons and fully trained combatants, the destruction of the only airport and abandonment of the newly approved seaport.

These disastrous and devastating conditions and paralyses afflicted all economic and agricultural aspects; hundreds of thousands of Palestinian workers had lost their jobs, and it was an immensely daunting situation, a major consequence of the second Intifada — which Arafat had encouraged and sometimes even fuelled.

My friend Omar Abbas, the president's younger brother, (they both are married to two sisters), an engineer and graduate of an American university, used to run an office in London; a dear friend, we met regularly, years before my return to Palestine and getting to know his elder brother Abu Mazen. Omar had little interest in politics.[26]

I met President Abbas for the first time in March 1995 at his small office in Gaza, Shehadeh; his personal escort and bodyguard greeted me with a welcoming smile. He continues to do the same job for his boss until today. The president did not dispense with Shehada's services throughout those years, mostly as a sign of loyalty. Such a gesture was a popular custom during the history of Palestine, where people took pride in their simple relationships and social coexistence.

Most families enjoyed sharing knowledge, reading books, arts, music and songs as one of their daily desires and the core of their culture. I thought that Abu Mazen had most of these wonderful qualities from the days of that beautiful era.

Despite a strong belief by many observers who thought that due to the heavy burdens carried by such a position, in addition to its great legacy at that critical time, the Fatah movement was extremely divided: security failure was clearly escalating, the Israeli siege on Gaza continued, Hamas and other armed factions were getting stronger, settlement expansions accelerated, the economic situation was deteriorating rapidly, with countless other political problems internally and externally.

Was Abu Mazen's position envied? Some asserted that whoever held such a position would not hold it for long, and certainly deserved great pity. Their logic was proven wrong; here we are, almost sixteen years later, the President is still in office, maintaining his four official titles with admirable strength and rigour. It's a well-known fact that President Abbas has a short temper; he prefers withdrawal rather than confrontation with others. Sometimes he keeps silent at a distance for a long period of time, an expression of discontent.

It is assumed that a wise leader is the one who never makes emotional decisions, whether in times of anger or joy, as angry decisions may not be reversible, and the happy ones may not be fulfilled. Consequently, the safest option for the Palestinian leadership during those difficult years had been not to make any decision whether emotional or provocative, especially during times of distress.

Thus, Abu Mazen persevered despite all these difficulties and lack of prospect for a reasonable solution to resume the stalled negotiations, freeze the settlements, or end the division and reconciliation with Hamas and other factions. Due to all these, the reasonable action was to do nothing! Wait and see, wait for what wind will bring.

The Way the Wind Blows. [على حسب الريح]. He greatly admired the words of the Dalai Lama, and his favourite saying: *"If there is no solution to the problem then don't waste time worrying about it. If there is a solution to the problem, then don't waste time worrying about it."*

Naturally, President Abbas' first visit abroad was of course to Cairo. I went with Marwan Kanafani, Ziad Abu Amro and Ibrahim Abu Naja to his residence in Heliopolis, to greet him and congratulate him on winning the presidency.

The presence of Nabil Shaath and Nasser Qidwa there was an indication of the hidden competition between them for the foreign ministry portfolio. Qidwa won the race, while Shaath became minister of information and deputy to the nominated Prime Minister, Ahmed Qurei.

In most discussions that took place in private sessions in Gaza with Abu Mazen which I was present in, he always emphasized the significant role of "Abu Amaar" throughout the years of our revolution.

> I was fiercely opposed to many decisions made by him. I wasn't the only one; Abu Iyad, Abu Jihad and Abu Lutuf as well. But we always agreed that he remarkably had carried the Fatah movement and the revolution on his shoulders, and with amazing agility and skill managed to preserve its unity and steadfastly ignited the national struggle from its beginnings. [27]

Abu Mazen made two official visits to Syria and Lebanon where he met with many leaders in the refugee camps. He took the opportunity to explain the difficulty of implementing the right of return for all refugees, as they would be required to become Israeli "second grade" citizens and learn to speak Hebrew, and thus lose their Palestinian identity.

An old refugee responded: "The right of return has been at the heart of our struggle; refugees in the camps are determined to return home, they are emotionally unwilling to accept that our grandparents might have been weak, mean or cowardly."

Abu Mazen maintained his unshaken adherence to the principle of distancing himself from all forms of violence, and his role in sponsoring peaceful negotiations despite the fact that in most cases it didn't achieve the desired results.

From a cultural point of view, many individuals looked at President Abbas with respect, pride and admiration. They shared his love for culture, arts and music.

The Al-Hani Cultural Foundation's editors were collecting historical documents for a book on Said Khoury. Abu Mazen gladly volunteered to write an introduction to the book, which was wonderful in its content and choice of appropriate words. He is a brilliant history reader and writer.

He wrote several books, most important of which is 'The Road to Oslo, Through Secret Channels,' in which he revealed many secrets of his negotiations with the Israelis that led to him signing the Declaration of Principles. Abu Mazen had watched dozens of old Arabic classic films and memorised the most popular songs of famous Arab singers such as Umm Kalthoum and Abdel Wahab.

According to a rare whisper from a friend, President Abu Mazen was responding to Hamas messages, which usually began and ended with Quranic verses, with peculiar replies that ended with a clip from Umm Kalthoum or Fairouz's songs.

In a meeting with a group of Jewish Meretz party members in the Muqata'a, in Ramallah, he told them confidently and proudly that he used to listen daily to songs of a Jewish singer who lived in Syria named Eliyaho. "Moshe Eliyaho" was a singer, born in Aleppo, and his songs were broadcast on Radio Damascus before he emigrated to Israel.

Abbas was listening to Eliyaho's songs during that period like any other Syrian Arab singer.

In the case of highly complex national issues, which had become somewhat sterile, headwinds kept blowing against the authority, every time they believed that they were nearer to striking an acceptable solution to restore historical rights, albeit partial. As paradoxical and perplexing as it may sound, Abu Mazen, supposedly an avowed enemy of Hamas, was always seen by their leaders in Gaza as the best of the worst, the lesser evil in the coming legislative elections.

Some critics and opponents of Abbas repeated a rumour that he was the son of Baha'i parents, in an effort to convince voters that he was not a true Muslim. When Omar Abbas was asked about these reports, he replied with a laugh: "These reports are totally untrue: is being a Baha'i a crime punishable by law?"

Dr. Sawsan Hosni, an Egyptian supporter of the Palestinian cause, who converted to the Baha'i faith, wrote:

> Each one of us begins a journey from a certain position, the one who inherits from his fathers to the letter, and the other who reviews the familiar. The second path is fraught with thorns, contemplation, and reflection. God has endowed us with reason so that we may know the path of truth, which is itself the path of God.[28]

Unlike Arafat, Abu Mazen used to repeat some unpopular statements that never satisfied the masses. For example: *"The resistance is absurd"* and *"The security coordination with Israel is sacred."*

The only phrase that was met with applause, satisfaction and approval by the Palestinian and Arab masses was in his response to President Trump's ultimate deal or what was called "Deal of the Century," wherein he prayed that *Allah* destroys his home! "الله يخرب بيتك" ! Allah duly answered his prayer when Trump was expelled from his White House. [29]

Sharon's Unilateral Withdrawal!

*"Always be wary of someone who answers
a question with a question."*

— UNKNOWN

Following the assassination of Yitzhak Rabin and the surprise victory of Benjamin Netanyahu, which enabled him to form his right-wing government in March 1996, a state of astonishment struck the leaders of the Palestinian Authority, and pessimistic signs about the future became evident on their faces. Fraih Abu Middain, who served as Minister of Justice in Arafat's first government, arrived late for dinner at my house. He said the reason for the delay was because he had a longer meeting than anticipated with the new Israeli Minister of Justice Tzachi Hanegbi, an extremist Likudian, who told him at the end of the meeting that the people of Gaza should expect a day in the future when they crave a cup of tea! That is, to expect the worst, which provoked the wrath of Fraih and my anger as well.[30]

The second Intifada, the Al-Aqsa Intifada, rose from Gaza city, as did the first intifada. Gaza became the cradle of uprisings, amidst numerous requests by the Palestinian Authority seeking an end to the violence and return to the negotiating table; with the failure of international efforts to stop it, the Israeli attacks escalated with missile strikes on new targets that included police stations, security forces and government buildings, forcing the security services to adopt new methods to avoid the apache strikes by camouflaging in civilian clothes, and working from homes as this was safer than the destroyed centres.

The appearance of security forces in the streets with their uniforms had become almost non-existent, which led to the emergence of certain vigilante groups — who became known as the "Security Chaos".

Ariel Sharon's victory with his newly founded Kadima party added to the Palestinian worries and pessimism, but surprisingly, he presented to the Knesset a plan to evacuate Gaza settlements and withdraw the Israeli army unilaterally, without any agreement or coordination with the Palestinian Authority! Implementation of his withdrawal plan began a few months after his success in getting rid of Yasser Arafat, his enemy since the 1982 Lebanon War.

To many independent observers — knowing the position of Sharon among settlers as their champion and hero and the most committed sponsor of the spread of settlements over the occupied Palestinian territories — this must have had a hidden plot behind it. So, what was the real purpose for this unilateral withdrawal?

Sharon's senior adviser, Dov Weissglas, explained the objectives of the plan:

> The significance of the disengagement plan is the freezing of the peace process, to prevent the establishment of a Palestinian state, and prevent a discussion on the refugees, the borders and Jerusalem. Effectively, this whole package called the Palestinian state, with all that entails, has been removed indefinitely from our agenda. All with a presidential blessing and the ratification of both houses of congress! [31]

Indeed, on September 12, 2005, his plan was completed and the Israeli army and around 4,000 settlers withdrew from the twenty-one settlements of Gaza despite loud and continuous objections by settlers' leaders and many religious rabbis, who were praying that their Lord would inflict on him the most severe punishment, including death.

However, Sharon ordered that the government provide all the evacuated settlers with generous cash compensation and alternative housing inside Israel proper.

Sharon and his government considered arbitrarily that the entire Gaza Strip was a free entity, but he maintained a land, air and sea blockade, including Gaza's borders with Egypt which remained indirectly under its control.

Egypt, Israel, and the Palestinian Authority agreed on a new protocol to manage the movement between Egypt and Gaza through the Rafah crossing, and the operation would be monitored by a team from the European Union.

A large and solemn celebration at both sides of the border took place in the presence of General Omar Suleiman, head of Egyptian intelligence and the minister responsible for Egyptian-Israeli-Palestinian relations.

One of the first visitors to Gaza was Mohammed Bassiouni, the ex-Egyptian ambassador to Israel during the years of the Palestinian Authority; he also participated as an army officer in two of Egypt's wars with Israel, and noted that he would have preferred to serve in Sweden or Norway, stating: "I was never happy being ambassador to Israel." What was surprising was his strong assertion that "Ariel Sharon plans to postpone the two-state project and any other solution to future Israeli generations, or even to infinity."

There were scenes of chaos and emotion as thousands upon thousands of people in Gaza were overjoyed celebrating the disappearance of Israeli soldiers and settlers from their city; this made it possible for Gazans to reclaim their land that was confiscated over the past forty years, to build in place of the settlements which occupied more that 40% of Gaza Strip's total area.

"The Gaza cemetery," for British soldiers who had been killed in the three battles that had taken place in 1917, could be visited. At the entrance, there is a large marble sign that read: "The land where the Allied soldiers have been laid is a gift from the people of Palestine."

However, some factions, led by Hamas, had started building training camps for their fighters next to the cemetery, on the *"liberated lands."* The control of the PA's security forces was totally absent over these empty settlements, as their interest was primarily concentrated on preserving the agricultural lands, and the remaining greenhouses, with the intention of continuing their production. Such work was planned in close cooperation with James Wolfensohn, President of the World Bank, who was appointed by Secretary Condoleezza Rice, and quickly visited Gaza and formed a committee responsible for repairing the damaged greenhouses and irrigation systems. The World Bank allocated sums to fund that operation. [32]

Gazans travelling to Egypt felt an indescribable relief as they were met by half a dozen Italian officers of the EU team, and not seeing for the first time any of the occupation soldiers at that crossing. Two months later, Sharon closed the crossing, the EU team withdrew, and Israel imposed a complete and tight blockade on the Gaza Strip. The suffering of the people increased tremendously day by day, until Gaza became widely known as the largest open prison in the world.

On my return to Gaza, a month later, this time through the Erez crossing, I began to recall what Hanegbi had said to Abu Madyan ten years ago to this day! Had they really been planning to besiege Gaza since then? How cruel; those Israelis enjoy inflicting additional collective and inhumane punishment on the Palestinians?

About four months after the Gaza withdrawal, Ariel Sharon suffered a stroke and fell into a deep coma. He never recovered, and died eight years later. Many of the evacuated settlers did not grieve or shed any tears for Sharon, believing that God had responded to their rabbis' calls and punished him with that fatal coma, as well as depriving him of completing his cursed and deceptive plan.

Hamas Takes Control

"The world only respects the strong, you must be strong so that everyone respects you."
— MAHMOUD ZAHAR (A HAMAS LEADER IN GAZA)

The results of the second council elections showed drastic and surprising changes. Contrary to expectations, Hamas won 74 seats, while Fatah, which enjoyed an absolute majority in the previous council, won only 45 of the 132 seats. Hamas won the majority of seats at the national level, but the most shocking result was that it won all the seats in the Gaza Governorate.

Hamas immediately nominated Aziz Dweik, one of its members from Hebron, to head the council, and another member from Gaza, Ahmed Bahr, as first deputy; and the independent member, Hassan Khreisheh, who was covertly supported by Hamas as a second deputy. Thus, Hamas came to control the Council, its presidency, and deputies.

Reactions in the Palestinian street to Hamas' huge victory varied between supporters and opponents; some blamed Fatah's poor performance due to the split by its leaders in both Gaza and West Bank.

The morning after the election, I headed to Cairo with Marwan Kanafani, who lost his seat to Hamas, on the way to Doha to attend the Gulf Enrichment conference organised by Steve L. Spiegel, head of the Middle East Centre at UCLA. Among the keynote speakers at the event were former President Bill Clinton, Prime Minister of Qatar Hamad bin Jassim, and veteran American General Tony Zinni.[33]

At the conference, participants were surprised and intrigued by the Palestinian elections' results; since I was the only participant from Gaza at the Forum, I was showered with a barrage of questions to learn more about Hamas' unexpected victory and its impact on the PA's future.

Was the election fair? What happened to Fatah's majority? Why did Salam Fayyad's party lose, contrary to expectations? Will President Abbas call on Hamas to form a government?

In private discussions with General Zinni and my friend, Judith Kipper, I suggested that the most prudent and best scenario for Hamas was to form, in consultation with Abu Mazen, a cabinet of independent technocrats that would be accepted by the USA and other countries, without participation of its own members. Of course, given that it enjoyed a parliament majority, it could withhold confidence in that government.

Zinni agreed with this scenario; however, he warned that US and European aid to Gaza would stop if Hamas formed a government; the only hope was how Abu Mazen would deal with international and Israeli pressure.

A few days later, Ziad Abu Amr was expecting to meet with Hamas' delegation, upon its arrival from Gaza, for consultation in Cairo with Khaled Meshaal, in order to announce the Technocrat Government — Ziad was a strong candidate to be one of its ministers.

The unthinkable happened: Hamas leaders received an urgent official invitation to visit Qatar and meet Sheikh Hamad, the emir, and a second invite from Turkey to meet Erdogan, followed by an invite to visit Russia and meet Sergey Lavrov.

It seemed to observers that these sudden invitations were an external conspiracy to convince its leaders to envisage that the whole world would follow suit and recognize their Islamic movement. Thus, Hamas formed a government unilaterally after Fatah and the rest of the factions refused to participate in a suggested national coalition.

The government was sworn in before President Abbas in March 2006. This unilateral, reckless step was a devastating start to the suffering of Palestinians, especially in Gaza, which was afflicted by many tragedies of siege, destruction, and heinous wars.

Israel's siege became a relentless attack on the entire civilian population of Gaza. It had destroyed the economy, degraded basic infrastructure, including the Gaza power plant, and isolated Gaza from the West Bank and the rest of the world in general. Sadly, the main resistance factions continued to produce aggressive manifestations of their political opponents in order to turn their rivalry into a justified target for attacks. The result was violence and security chaos: despicable and unforgivable conduct by all the factions.

Mohammad Dahlan, and his associates among Fatah leaders, fled Gaza under cover of darkness. They left a few members of their scattered forces without commanding instructions to defend police stations and government buildings. However, they failed to defeat

Hamas fighters who took over the entire Gaza Strip within a few days. They were reciting verses of *Sourat Fater:* "*Plotting evil engulfs the people who practice it.*[34]

In defence of Abu Mazen's policy of not confronting Hamas' coup by the force of arms, one of his close friends said:

> History will record that the president did not give hasty orders to fight and shoot at Hamas members. He did not seek Arab military support to invade the Gaza Strip. He rejected an Israeli offer for him to take over liberated areas of Gaza during the 2009 and 2014 wars. He also, wisely, did not agree to wage a guerrilla war against Hamas members, or to declare Gaza a 'hijacked territory'. [35]

Marwan Kanafani, Arafat's political advisor, also predicted:

> I am absolutely certain that what Hamas did in the Gaza Strip in the early summer of 2007 was a major political, national and moral mistake. I am filled with sadness and sorrow when my reading leads me to the reality and the predictions — that I do not hope to be realized — are that the Palestinian Authority will not be able in the foreseeable future, nor Fatah movement, nor President Abbas or any other Palestinian president from outside Hamas, to regain control or even have a presence in the Gaza Strip.
>
> The geographical, political, and psychological separation between the West Bank and the Gaza Strip has been entrenched. And it would take a miracle to find just a new formula for a peaceful relationship between these two remaining parts for the Palestinians.[36]

Tunnels existed between Israel and Gaza years before the 1967 occupation; they were used by gangs engaged in the smuggling of Hashish, light weapons and contraband to Gaza as a transit point to be forwarded on to Egypt. The history of the tunnels between Gaza and Egypt dates back to the early 1980s after Israel and Egypt signed the peace treaty. The tunnels were then used to smuggle cigarettes, gold, foreign currencies, drugs, and other goods.

In 1982, Israel divided the city of Rafah into Egyptian and Palestinian sides upon completing the withdrawal from the Sinai desert, after fifteen years of occupation, thus showing its resolve to be identical to what Sykes-Picot imposed in demarcating borders of the Arab countries in 1916.

When the First Intifada broke out in 1987, the tunnels were used to smuggle small arms.

The tunnels ran between houses that lay close to the border. The Palestinian Authority started a campaign against most tunnels in 1995 as part of its security coordination with Israel, as stipulated in the Oslo Accords. One of their internal tunnels succeeded, unexpectedly, in capturing the Israeli soldier Gilad Shalit, who was released after five years of captivity in a deal in which nearly a thousand Palestinian prisoners were liberated.

Following Hamas' unexpected control of Gaza and the kidnapping of Gilad Shalit, Israel destroyed hundreds of houses along the border, forcing the Palestinians to make their tunnels longer.

When Israel imposed the blockade on Gaza in 2007, it had a severe impact on life in the Gaza Strip, forcing the Palestinians to use the available tunnels as a strategic alternative to the official commercial crossings, in order to meet their basic needs of food, fuel, medicines and other commodities. The tunnels also contributed to covering the shortage of raw materials that Israel prevented from entering the Strip.

At the peak of that flourishing business, along the 14-kilometre border with Egypt, one estimate put the numbers of active tunnels at 750, while others put it at as high as 1300; some businessmen were tempted to invest in the construction and operation of tunnels. Most owners of houses on both sides of the border, where tunnels originated or passed underneath their land, made money.

Of course, the trade was conducted in daylight with full knowledge of the policemen guarding the Egyptian side of the border, and very much welcomed by Hamas militants who were charging huge amounts of cash, designating it as tax on smuggled goods. The smuggling tunnels became the most profitable business in Gaza. Young tunnel workers became so rich, they started splashing their dollars by buying luxury cars, houses, and farms. They were looked at as the "*nouveau riche*" or "Tunnel millionaires".

New and wider tunnels were dug to smuggle building materials, livestock, spare parts, cars, communications equipment and other devices. A special tunnel was used for importing diesel and gasoline through a three-inch pipeline. Quite possibly, there were also tunnels for smuggling weapons. Strangely enough, a tunnel was used to smuggle wild animals for a newly constructed zoo, with lions, tigers, monkeys, and ostriches.

The Palestinian workforce grew in numbers and gained more skills at digging bigger tunnels and started using modern technology and machinery, instead of the previous primitive methods. Some Lebanese commentators reported that Hezbollah had used some experienced Palestinians from Gaza to help in digging the resistance tunnels in Southern Lebanon.

The tunnels became more stable, and the time it took to dig a standard tunnel fell to less than three months. Land surveyors appeared on the scene, as well as specialist excavators and engineers who supervised the work. The tunnels became the only channel between Gaza and the outside world and were used to smuggle in Palestinian expatriates who wanted to return home from abroad, previously denied entry by Israel. The tunnels also helped sick patients as healthcare in Gaza had almost collapsed since the siege, and people needed better hospitals. There was always a pending threat that Israel might bomb the tunnels at any moment, or Egypt might flood them with water. Dozens of workers and travellers suffered death and injuries from the collapsing tunnels, some miraculously survived. Following the election of the Muslim Brotherhood's Mohammad Morsi as President of Egypt and the arrest of Hosni Mubarak, work stopped in the vast majority of tunnels as the borders were officially opened. The movement of people and goods on both sides became legal and public.

A historic visit by the Emir of Qatar, Hamad bin Khalifa, and his wife, Sheikha Moza, took place at the end of October 2012. They were received by Ismail Haniyeh, leader of Hamas in Gaza. The Emir promised to invest hundreds of millions of dollars in the long-awaited and overdue infrastructure projects, in addition to residential buildings and a fully equipped hospital. A few weeks later, the Egyptian Prime Minister at that time, Hisham Qandil, headed a large official and popular delegation in a short visit to Gaza, and he pledged to work quickly to stop the Israeli aggression and provide urgent in-kind assistance to all residents.

Shortly after came the imprisonment of Morsi and the election of President Abdel Fattah Sisi, with the intensification of armed attacks on Egyptian army bases between Gaza and El Arish by the Sinai terrorist groups, which led to hundreds of casualties among army personnel and civilians. The Egyptian Government took a drastic decision to evacuate all local residents of Egyptian Rafah to a new town about thirty miles away from the border with Gaza, and eventually destroyed the evacuated houses completely.

After their massive and unprecedented demolition, the border tunnels' activity of the workforce and its skilled workers, with their technical expertise, shifted to digging tunnels inside Gaza, for the use of Hamas as Islamic Jihad fighters. This eventually became an essential hideout for their commanders, shelters for their families, and storage for weapons and homemade rockets.

There were unconfirmed reports that the Egyptian Government was planning to build on the Egyptian side of Rafah, in place of the demolished houses, a new city that the Palestinians of the Gaza

Strip could enter without a visa, without a search or inspections, no barriers or checkpoints. It was rumoured that the city would contain several hotels, restaurants, shopping malls, swimming pools and amusement parks. A huge investment with Gulf States' financing and Egyptian implementation, including Israeli approval with Hamas in return for a long-term truce. This city would replace the destroyed "Tunnels for Freedom".

Hamas' illegal seizure of power in Gaza was met with overwhelming rejection by many countries of the world. And Israel took advantage of this by tightening its siege on the poor people of the Gaza Strip. It was a clear double standard. Samuel P. Huntington poignantly said the following in his rejection of double standards:

> Hypocrisy, double standards, and 'but nots' are the price of universalists' pretensions. Democracy is promoted but not if it brings *Islamic fundamentalists* to power, non-proliferation is preached for Iran and Iraq but not for Israel. Double standards in practice are the unavoidable price for universal standards of principle.[37]

Following every war on Gaza since Hamas took control of the Strip in 2007, questions were being repeatedly asked by the present Hamas Leader in Gaza, Yahya Sinwar: "Will the precarious ceasefire hold? Or will it give way to renewed fighting? What will it take to end the oppressive, abhorrent and criminal siege? How can someone end the crippling blockade on Gaza?"

More fundamentally, could Hamas be integrated with a genuine and consensual welcome into legitimate Palestinian politics, the PLO? Would the United States, and international community, acknowledge Hamas as a political reality?

Palestine: A Nuclear Deterrent?

*"We Must Abolish Nuclear Weapons,
or They Will Abolish Us."*

— JOHN F. KENNEDY

In the early months of 1945, nuclear bombs (or weapons of mass destruction) did not mean anything special or dangerous to most inhabitants of the world including Palestinians, as their priorities were focused only on saving their homeland from the clutches of Great Britain, who occupied their country and was in a hurry by force of arms to fulfil its ominous and hostile promise of the "Balfour Declaration" to establish a homeland for Jews in Palestine. They shed tears when they heard about the dropping of a nuclear bomb on Hiroshima in Japan, and they definitely grieved Britain's victory which would not have been achieved without America's bombs and active participation in that war.

The first experience that added more information to my limited knowledge of nuclear power was during my early years of study in London. Salah Jamil, my cousin, was studying law at SOAS, University of London, and was proudly credited with founding the first Palestinian Student Union (PSU) in the UK in the 1960s. There were over two dozen students from Gaza and twice that number from the West Bank and Jerusalem, who became Jordanian citizens due to the annexation of the remaining part of Palestinian land, to the Kingdom of Jordan in 1951. They were afraid or unwilling to join the new Palestinian student union, with the exception of a single British/Jordanian student named Faris Glubb, a red-haired young man with blue eyes, the son of Sir John Glubb, the British general who was the founder of the Jordanian Army and its commander for several years, until King Hussein dismissed him following the Suez war in 1956. Amazingly, out of the twenty-five students from Gaza, seven were family members including the only woman: Umayia. Salah and Faris were actively engaged in lobbying for Palestine on all cultural, social and political events; they also succeeded in enrolling and integrating the PSU into the Arab Student Association (ASA), which had more than 20,000 members, most of them students from Iraq and Egypt; and surprisingly, among them were quite a few Iraqi and Egyptian Jewish students who fled their countries. Its president was an Iraqi "Baathist" student of engineering, named Talib Shabib; upon his return home, being one of the leaders who plotted to oust General Abdul Karim Qassem in the 1963 coup, Shabib was rewarded by his new leader, Abdul Salam Aref, to the post of Foreign Minister of Iraq.

One of ASA's main events was the 1962 annual general meeting to elect its president. The significance of that particular meeting was that after the election result was announced, thousands of students took part in the largest demonstration held in London, organised by the Campaign for Nuclear Disarmament (CND), headed by its leader, Bertrand Russell.

A few weeks later, another event was organized by the two cousins Salah Jamil and Ali Maher, Faris Glubb, and Elias Farah, at the Egyptian Cultural Centre with two keynote speakers Erskin Childers and Ethel Menen, in support of the Palestinian refugees. Addressing the Egyptian students, Faris talked in Arabic about the necessity of collective student efforts in clarifying the justice of our common cause, he ended his short speech with: "We must lobby for Palestine."[38]

At the time I didn't pay much attention to the word "lobby" because I didn't know its meaning then. There was overwhelming support for the Palestinian cause among Arab and African students; a prominent participant was an Iranian medical student named Mehdi Isfahani, his father was a minister in the nationalist Mosaddeq government which was overthrown in a plot by Britain and America. According to his logic, there was a congruence between our two cases in blaming Britain, which carried out its promise to the Zionists and what it did to Iran by restoring the Shah.

Two Egyptian postgraduate students were preparing for a doctorate in physics from the University of London: Abdel Rashid Mahmoudy, who was translating into Arabic a novel by Colin Wilson "The Outsider" for a Lebanese publisher called Suhail Idris, and Rashad Amer, who was the younger brother of Abdel Aziz Amer, my French teacher in Gaza high school. I always suspected he was a close relative of Field Marshal Abdel Hakim Amer, the supreme commander of the Egyptian Army, although Rashad shyly denied it.[39]

Both Egyptians were worried about rumours or unconfirmed reports that Israel had tested a nuclear bomb with the help of the apartheid regime in South Africa. Naturally, this would cause great anxiety and fear in Egypt and, consequently, with the Palestinian people of Gaza. Rashad explained the Egyptian position regarding the worries toward Israel's nuclear bomb: "Our President, and the Egyptian people, deplore all efforts that are helping Israel become the sole nuclear hegemon in the Middle East. Israel is an existential threat not only to Egypt, but to the rest of the Arab world."

A few weeks later, Rashad met an English journalist, a follower of Israeli news and its military and political developments there, who confirmed the reports and added that France, after its humiliating defeat in the Suez War, had provided Israel with a nuclear reactor ostensibly for peaceful uses, but also capable of enriching the necessary quantities of uranium to produce a nuclear bomb. France became the fourth country three years earlier, after the USA, USSR and Britain, to conduct a nuclear test, followed by China.

Significantly, according to a political analyst, Britain, despite its historical role in the establishment of the state of Israel starting with the Balfour Declaration till the end of the mandate, refused to provide Israel with a British-made reactor. It seemed that following Britain's defeat in the Suez, it was afraid of Israel becoming a great power, which might rival it in its ambition for control of the British protectorates and emirates in the Arabian Gulf. Israel would undoubtedly become the sixth country in the world to possess the bomb, despite its very small area and meagre population and natural resources.

Nasser made several requests to the Soviet leadership for the supply of a Soviet nuclear reactor to produce some sort of a regional balance between Israel and the Arab states, and possibly to satisfy his own ambitions. The Soviet Union refused and finally he was dissuaded from the idea of nuclear bombs. But, typically, Israel never confirmed nor denied its possession of the bomb. The influence of such significant information in those early years made my interest focus mainly on studying the peaceful uses of nuclear energy, with my support for Bertrand Russell and his courageous campaign for nuclear disarmament (CND).

The UN Secretary General announced that the State of Palestine submitted its instrument of accession on 29 December 2017. Palestine was to become the 193rd party to the Chemical Weapons Convention CWC, confirmed by Jean Pascal of French Pugwash. [40]

Faris and I became great followers of peace movements in Europe, we used to discuss ideas of many influential writers regarding the need for youth to get involved in freeing the world from all weapons of mass destruction.

Peace is the most powerful deterrent to ALL wars.

Dimona and its Proximity to Gaza

Once the shocking rumours were confirmed that Israel had the French reactor and was in the process of developing a nuclear bomb, Nasser's concerns were mainly focused on Israel, becoming the sole nuclear hegemony in the Middle East, creating an existential threat to Egypt and to the rest of the Arab world.

By producing warheads from its reactor base in the Negev desert village of Dimona, twenty-eight miles east of Gaza, I felt a deep and shocking sense of anxiety and bewilderment mixed with anger in the event that Israel launched a nuclear attack on Egypt or had a nuclear accident that would definitely impact the neighbouring Gaza Strip.

The work on the Dimona reactor started in 1958, two years after the end of the failed Suez campaign, and was completed in mid 1963. Israel did not hurry to announce its possession of the nuclear bomb, such an announcement would act as a powerful deterrent to any attempt by an Arab leader to launch a military campaign, or even threats of attack by the Arab armies — especially those of Gamal Abdel Nasser and his army, which became greater in number and armed with advanced military equipment, relying on supplies from the Soviet Union.

Contrary to all expectations, Israel did not declare its possession, but never denied it, and thus this state of ambiguity continued to dominate worries in Egypt and the Arab world.

In the mysterious game of international politics, France agreed to supply and construct a modern nuclear reactor, more powerful than the Israeli Dimona, to oil-rich Iraq, after Saddam Hussein seized power in 1975. No one knew or guessed Saddam's apparent purpose and desire in wanting to possess the nuclear bomb. He probably wasn't thinking of attacking Israel or liberating Palestine, but his undeclared goal was to get rid of the Shah of Iran; who saw him as a real threat, with his ambitions in the Shatt-al-Arab after building a powerful naval fleet and occupying three small Arab islands in the Gulf. Saddam also had his mind set on the spiritual leader, Ayatollah Khomeini, who had taken refuge in the holy city of Najaf in Iraq, and who aspired to overthrow the Shah.

Construction of the Osirak reactor, which the Iraqis named Tammuz, began in 1979, followed by Iraq signing the NPT and allowing AEA teams to inspect the program. Despite Iraq's declarations and commitments that the reactor would be used for peaceful purposes, Israel saw other possibilities and decided to blow it up.

The opportunity came during the start of the Iran-Iraq war, while the two sides were distracted by fighting each other. Six F-16 warplanes attacked the reactor on June 16, 1981 and it was completely destroyed. Israel never allowed AEA inspectors into Dimona, as it is one of five non-signatories to the Treaty on the Non-proliferation of Nuclear Weapons (NPT).

In April 1986, the Chernobyl nuclear power plant's accident became public, considered to be the worst ever nuclear disaster in history, both in material and human casualties. It released airborne radioactive contamination that precipitated onto parts of the USSR and Western Europe. While people all over the world were watching the media coverage of the accident, the horror of the nuclear devastation of Hiroshima and Nagasaki came to light again.

A few months later, Mordechai Vanunu, an Israeli technician who worked at the Dimona nuclear reactor, fled to London in September 1986 and agreed to sell his story to a British newspaper, where he would reveal details of the secret Israeli nuclear weapons program.

Vanunu, who was born to Moroccan parents, emigrated to Israel in 1963 from Marrakesh. He managed to work in the Dimona Nuclear Reactor for nine years, in its underground facility dedicated to the production of Plutonium and Lithium. He was able to smuggle a camera and secretly photograph parts of the reactor in a covert manner. Vanunu enrolled at the university and studied philosophy, which served as a turning point in his life as he became more attached to politics and joined the ranks of the anti-war movement at that time. He began to feel remorse and suffering because of his work in a reactor that secretly produced nuclear weapons. When his superiors discovered his left-wing opposition ideas, he was dismissed.

The British newspaper's attempts to verify the authenticity of his information reached Israeli intelligence agencies. The Sunday Times of London finally published Vanunu's story on 5th October that year: he divulged that Israel had produced more than 100 nuclear warheads and 20 hydrogen bombs. The Mossad sent a female agent who lured Vanunu to Italy, where he was kidnapped, drugged and smuggled to Israel aboard a ship. He was tried and sentenced to eighteen years in prison.

The fear was that a similar accident to Chernobyl in Dimona would have devastating effects on the population of Gaza Strip, which had no recognized facilities to treat potential casualties. There were over fifteen countries, including small ones like Finland, that operated nuclear reactors, some for peaceful use in nuclear power stations. The Middle Eastern countries had been deprived of that advanced and complex technology.

The unfortunate nuclear accident that struck the Japanese city of Fukushima in March 2011 was triggered by an earthquake and tsunami, a natural disaster, unlike Chernobyl which was caused by human error. In the days after the disaster, radiation in the atmosphere forced the evacuation of all residents within a 30-kilometre zone. There was concern around the world about the safety of nuclear power plants.

Lessons learned from the Fukushima disaster led to a discussion on the serious risks of nuclear power generation at the Pugwash conference in Berlin, where some experts called for a cautious approach in response to the meltdown and reduction in nuclear power usage.

During a coffee break in the Berlin Pugwash meeting, a comical and fascinating discussion took place between an Iraqi academic and an Israeli scientist about the ease of obtaining nuclear weapon technology *via* the internet.

The Iraqi added: "You know, it is possible that a Palestinian scientist in Gaza builds a small nuclear bomb, if he can get three kilograms of uranium!"

The Israeli asked contemptuously: "Will he get some enriched uranium from Iran?"

"Of course not, it is possible he gets a small quantity from the black market in Africa, maybe from Chad! Possibly smuggle it into Gaza from the nearby Dimona!" replied the Iraqi.[41]

Of course, talking about the Israeli nuclear issue would not preoccupy public opinion much and would not cause a local uproar either, as it remained shrouded in mystery and was deliberately kept silent in all languages. We must continue to play the same chord until the truth emerges and to obtain clear answers in the end.

Senator Dianne Feinstein from California wrote:

> During the Cold War, the United States and the Soviet Union were mired in an arms race. The antagonism led each side to stockpile more than 3,000 nuclear weapons to prevent the other from gaining an advantage. America's nuclear arsenal is unnecessarily and unsustainably large. [42]

Pugwash: Conflict Resolution

"The release of atomic power has changed everything except our way of thinking ... the solution to this problem lies in the heart of mankind."

— ALBERT EINSTEIN

Pugwash drew its inspiration from the famous 1955 Bertrand Russell-Albert Einstein Manifesto, which urged all leaders of the world to think in a new way; namely, to renounce nuclear weapons and to find a peaceful means for all matters of dispute.

The first Pugwash conference was held in 1957 in the village of Pugwash, named after its indigenous inhabitants in Canada, to discuss the threat posed to civilization by the advent of nuclear weapons; it was a catalyst for the formation of a unique and innovative organisation. From that humble beginning evolved a continuing series of meetings at locations all over the world. Pugwash and its co-founder Joseph Rotblat were awarded the Nobel Peace Prize in 1995.

Resolving the Palestinian conflict was a central issue in almost all of Pugwash conferences during the past 25 years. Palestine Pugwash group was headed by Gabi Baramki, a Jerusalemite, who was head of Birzeit University and a professor of chemistry. His wife, Haifa Tarazi, was an active member. Pugwash's standard statement on Palestine stated:

Pugwash, and all its members across the world, were urged to contribute to engaging policymakers and politicians in Europe and elsewhere to raise the issue of Palestinian statehood and the rights of its people.

At a global level, the Palestinian narrative is in the shadow of the Israeli narrative. In large part this is because of the amount of money put into propaganda by Israel, a key direction for Palestinians must be to overcome this narrative battle of "two sides in conflict" and instead highlight to the world the massive power disparity and illegal occupation. [43]

My first participation was made possible by the invitation of its Director General, Paolo Cotta, an Italian professor of physics at Milan University. The invitation was to attend its 56th conference to be held in Cairo, and join the plenary session as a speaker along with: Riad Malki, who is currently the Palestinian foreign minister; Henry Siegman, the influential American Jewish civic leader; and Ron Pundak, the Israeli academic who participated in the secret talks with Abu Alaa Qurei in Norway, which eventually concluded the Oslo Accords.

Amr Mousa, Secretary General of the Arab League, opened the conference, followed by Egyptian Foreign Minister Ahmed Aboul Gheit, with a welcoming speech. On the third day was a generous invitation to visit the Grand Egyptian Museum in Tahrir Square by Minister Zahi Hawass, to enjoy the splendour of King Tutankhamun, his amazing furniture and his precious golden mask. The visit was followed by a working dinner, an invitation from the Egyptian entrepreneur Naguib Sawiris. During dinner we viewed a valuable presentation about ancient Egyptian civilization, and we were handed a Sawiris souvenir gift of a copper cup with the name of each participant engraved in Arabic, English and Hieroglyphic — a lovely gesture.

In April 2009, the Pugwash conference was held in The Hague, the headquarters of the newly established International Criminal Court. Attention was focused on the presence of many active personalities in the field of human rights, international law and distinguished former defence ministers, among them William Perry and Malcolm Rifkind. And two former UN inspectors of WMD in Iraq, Rolf Ekeus and Hans Blix, a former foreign minister of Sweden.

Judge Richard Goldstone was having lunch at our table, and when I told him that I am from Gaza and wished to give him some information about Gaza prior to the attacks, he turned to the other side and refused to talk. When I complained to Paolo, he explained that Judges are not supposed to talk about their work to others. The judge headed the UN Fact Finding Mission on the Gaza Conflict. Israel, as usual, refused to cooperate with the investigation team and rejected its findings, even denying the members' entry to Gaza via Tel Aviv airport. The mission conducted two field visits to Gaza, entering through the Rafah border crossing from Egypt.

The report concluded that the Israel Defence Force and Palestinian militant group had committed war crimes and possibly crimes against humanity. Netanyahu, arrogantly and indifferently, said: "The Goldstone Report is a field-martial, and its findings were pre-written."[44]

Participants questioned the ICC prosecutor Luis Moreno-Ocampo about opening an investigation of war crimes committed during the Gaza War. He evaded a direct answer, arguing that this war was not one of his competencies, and his focus was on bringing Sudanese President Omar al-Bashir to The Hague to be tried on charges of crimes against humanity.

The Omani member Mohammad Mahrouqi insisted that our main aspiration had been to find ways to eliminate the existential threat posed by the Israeli nuclear reactor at Dimona, and its 200 nuclear bombs. "Why is nothing being said about Israel's nuclear weapons?" Iran's representative to the IAEA in Vienna asked pointedly.

William Perry gave a lengthy but enjoyable speech warning

against the spread of nuclear weapons and the dangers of other states seeking to acquire the bomb, mentioning North Korea and Iran. He gave us a report on his recent work in forming the Nuclear Security Project, jointly with Henry Kissinger, George Shultz and Sam Nunn.

Malcolm Rifkind gave a frightening account of regional tension and confirmed that there were over 13,000 nuclear weapons in the world, in nine countries "including Israel" and some 22 countries with weapons-usable nuclear materials potentially vulnerable to theft. The dangers were real, we must create a safer world.

In another Pugwash meeting in the Italian city of Bari, a strong presence of Palestinians was visible, including Nabil Shaath, and on the other side among the Israeli delegation were Galia Golan and Ephraim Halevy, the former head of Mossad. A verbal altercation occurred as Halevy directed his words to the Iranian ambassador to Austria, who was also participating in the nuclear discussions, asking him to convey a message to the Iranian government that Israel will arm and assist the Iranian Kurds, as it did in the past with the Kurds of Iraq. The ambassador's response was: "Please give me your arms. I represent my government, but also I am an Iranian Kurd!" The hall erupted with laughter. [45]

In the Pugwash conference that was held in Istanbul, the participants were invited for a luncheon at the *"Adile Sultan Palace"* with President Abdullah Gul, who made a keynote address that seemed to be his last official engagement before handing the presidency over to Ragep Tayeb Erdogan.

Gul talked about his university years in Britain and his work in Jeddah, Saudi Arabia. His speech was followed by two lengthy ones from Mohammad Jawad Zarif, Iranian foreign minister and Ahmet Davutoglu, the Turkish foreign minister.

During lunch by invitation of President Gul, while tasting authentic local cuisine — sitting between Sinan Mahmet, a former diplomat who served at the Turkish Foreign Ministry for over thirty years, and Dr. Bakhtiar Amin, an Iraqi Kurd who served as Minister of Human Rights in the Federal Iraqi Government — discussion was concentrated on the Palestinian human rights abuses by the Israeli army and the sufferings of Kurds elsewhere. Sinan added in praise of Pugwash that "in order to follow world events you need to understand people of different nationalities, their ideas and movements — but if you don't know geography, you'll never have the full picture. But, these Pugwash meetings across the world give us the opportunity to be included in the picture." [46]

Nabil Shaath, Husam Zomlot, Taghreed el-Khodary and Mukhaimer Abu Saada, a professor at Al-Azhar university of Gaza, were also representing Palestine in the Istanbul meeting.

The 2015 conference was held in Japan, marking the 70-year anniversary after the destruction of Hiroshima and Nagasaki, under the slogan *"Remember Your Humanity — Let Nagasaki be the Last,"* recalling the Russell-Einstein Manifesto: as long as nuclear weapons and other weapons of mass destruction exist, their catastrophic consequences cannot be avoided.

Another conference was in Astana, the newly built capital of Kazakhstan that suffered enormously from the nuclear testing conducted in the polygon of *Semipalatinsk* that was shut down by its president Nursultan Nazarbayev; he also ensured that all Soviet nuclear weapons and testing sites were withdrawn from the country after 1992.

The conference was attended by Kassym Tokayev, chairman of Parliament; Paolo Cotta and Sergio Duarte of Pugwash; Sergey Ryabkov, deputy foreign minister of Russia; former UK defence minister Desmond Browne; Sam Nun, Talaat Masoud, Saideh Lotfian and Ali Asghar Soltanieh of Iran, who served as Iranian ambassador to the UN Office at Vienna for three terms between 1983 and 2014; and Hussain Al-Shahrastani, former Iraqi Deputy Prime Minister.

Pugwash called for a nuclear and WMD-free zone in the Middle East. Pugwash also considered that Gaza was a disaster zone, and was seriously concerned with the humanitarian situation of its population. The conference called on all relevant regional parties including Egypt, Israel, the Palestinian Authority and the *de facto* government in the Gaza Strip to overcome their political differences and to intensify cooperation, in order to find solutions to urgent problems, and to resume investments in infrastructure; to allow the unhindered movement of goods and people and to lay immediate foundations for sustainable development.

A memorable and special visit was scheduled to the Gallery of Karipbek Kuyukov, the armless artist who painted using his teeth and lips; he was born with no arms as a result of the intense nuclear radiation that occurred from the nuclear tests that the Soviet Union was conducting in Kazakhstan for many years. President Nursultan Nazarbayev decided to denuclearize the land of his country forever.

When you meet this great artist, you feel the urgent need to work hard on destroying all nuclear weapons. He said there were thousands of deformed babies at birth, and he was determined to continue his work in arts to warn future generations of the scourge and dangers of nuclear weapons. The words of this amazing anti-nuclear weapons activist were expressive, moving and an unforgettable experience. He insisted that he wanted to fulfil his mission to be the last victim of nuclear arms tests.[47]

At the close of the conference, participants headed to Astana's Expo 2017. The theme of the exhibition was nuclear disarmament. The last activity in Astana was a farewell visit to president Nazarbayev's palace.

The majority of Pugwash members and participants in its annual conferences show sympathy for the Palestinian issues, calling for an end to the Israeli occupation. Among the greatest and most sincere Pugwash sympathisers for Gaza is the Italian Paolo Cotta, its Director General.

CHAPTER SEVEN

In Search of an Honest Broker

"In the end, we will remember not the words
of our enemies but the silence of our friends."

— MARTIN LUTHER KING JR.

The "Two-State" Delusion

"Sometimes people don't want to
hear the truth because they don't
want their illusions destroyed."

— FRIEDRICH NIETZSCHE

The 'two-state solution" was originally suggested by the Peel commission following the 1936 Palestinian strike that lasted for six months. As stated in the Peel commission, "An irrepressible conflict has arisen between two national communities within the narrow bounds of one small country. There is no common ground between them. Their national aspirations are incompatible. Neither of the two national ideals permits combination in the service of a single state." The only workable solution was the creation of two sovereign states. "Partition", the commission argued, "seems to offer at least a chance of ultimate peace.[1]

Whenever negotiations of the two-state solution faltered, it seemed impossible to achieve and was finally and publicly met with complete rejection by the newly-formed Israeli government headed by Naftali Bennett. This takes us directly to Paul Wolfowitz's words and statement to the Palestinian Businessmen delegation at the Pentagon; that the idea of a two-state solution was based on his initiative, which made many people question realistically: was it possibly a well-articulated plan by the neo-conservatives, similar to their "WMD" plot in Iraq? Was the end of such an initiative the inevitable failure? What was the perception and understanding of the two-state solution? What was the Palestinian Authority's perception of the real solution in its political, economic, security and international dimensions?

The two-state solution is "the only way forward", this familiar myth is typically delivered with an affirmative voice claiming there is a solution to the Israeli-Palestinian conflict, and that is waiting for us just around the corner. However, the reality of the current colonization of vast parts of the West Bank by Israel renders any two-state solution an improbable vision. At best, the most one can hope for is a Palestinian Bantustan".[2]

The first years of the second intifada coincided with the first term of President George W. Bush (2000-2004), who showed little interest in finding a solution to the Palestine-Israel conflict, especially after the September 11th attacks.

The Palestinian Council on Foreign Relations witnessed extensive visits by European political envoys after the US administration decided to ban its citizens from entering the Gaza strip, thus all Americans, including journalists, withdrew. UN special coordinator, Terje Rod-Larson, EU special Representative, Miguel Moratinos, and Russian representative, Alexander Saltanov continued to visit the Gaza Strip periodically, despite the intermittent explosions and the massive destruction of infrastructure and many public buildings of the Palestinian Authority. They were watching structures implode and crumble razed to the ground with iniquitous force.

But, people's steadfastness was heroic. In a brave gesture, the former US envoy to the Middle East, the veteran Dennis Ross refused to heed to the imposed ban and broke it by coming to Gaza to participate in a political seminar about the two-state solution organized by Ziad Abu Amro, with participation of two Quartet members and EU ambassador Marc Otte.

The meeting was distinguished by the unusual public appearance of some of Hamas' leaders, including Mahmoud al-Zahar and Ismail Haniyeh, who later succeeded Khaled Meshaal to become the leader of Hamas, among the audience.

Dennis wrote an article about how the public in Gaza did not object to his speech:

"Afterward, when I expressed surprise that neither the audience comments on violence nor my reference to the Palestinian obligation to dismantle the terrorist infrastructure drew rebuttals. Ziad and Samir Shawa (a leading Palestinian businessman) expressed no surprise. In their words, Palestinians wanted to see the violence end." [3]

After the meeting, there was lunch at Jawdat Khudari's, where I was carrying a newly published book in Arabic, which Dennis asked to borrow. To my surprise, Jawdat whispered

"I think Dennis can read Arabic!"

When talking about the future of the two-state solution, ending the occupation, or lifting the siege on Gaza, the behaviour of the Israelis was completely unpleasant: their faces were often frowning, indicating a lack of interest, their view of others with utmost condescension and arrogance when asked about Israel's next borders.

We must exclude Galia Golan, a member of Meretz and an activist in the *Combatant for Peace*, as she was sincere in her sympathy with the children of Palestine and in her defence of the two-state solution so that both peoples could enjoy peace and security. She believes that "At some point, a leadership will arise in Israel that wants to end the conflict, mainly to avoid a binational state."

Aaron David Miller, a veteran American diplomat, and expert on the Middle East conflict, speaking about the remote possibility of achieving that goal: "No human can divine the future… Israelis and Palestinians have a proximity problem that tethers them together. For the foreseeable future, they'll remain trapped by a two-state solution impossible to implement on the one hand but too important to abandon on the other." [4]

Daniel Kurtzer, the former US Ambassador to Israel stated that the "pursuit of a diplomatic settlement, including a two-state outcome, suffers from a lack of leadership on all sides… There is no alternative to two states for two peoples."

Ali Jarbawy, a former Palestinian minister, wonders: "Consecutive Israeli governments' acts in the West Bank and Jerusalem make the realization of the two-state solution rather impossible. To realise this, pressure on Israel is needed." [5]

The possibility of achieving the long awaited two-state solution has significantly diminished. It seems likely that the only option left is the one-state solution despite the claims of a state of apartheid. Some people, politicians, artists and activists around the world tried to propose realistic ideas for a just solution, including the elusive "two-state solution" but their fear of retaliation was palpable.

For Ehud Yaari, an Israeli journalist and fellow of the Washington Institute, "the two-state solution is a "lost cause". As he put it, "a lost cause is usually associated with a hopeless cause; that is, a few years ago, they supported and believed in its happening. It will take time …." [6]

Dennis Ross commented on the two-state solution; "As you can see, I don't have great confidence that it is still viable."

Martin Indyk is confident that "There is no other solution that can actually resolve the conflict."

Mansour Abu Rashid, a retired Jordanian General, a military expert in regional security, a regular participant in Pugwash conferences and a formidable lobbyist for a permanent solution, believes strongly that the two-state solution is the only way out for stability in the region.

"The killing of Palestinian demonstrators by Israeli forces in Gaza is tragic. It is the right of all people to protest for a better future without a violent response. We must treat the Palestinian people with dignity" stated Senator Bernie Sanders .[7]

Many Palestinians who dreamed of achieving at least the establishment of two states, despite the extreme unfairness of losing three-quarters of their historical land, were shocked by the evaporation of such a humble solution. They felt that their leadership had lost the compass; that they had fallen into a long and dark tunnel, and began swimming backwards in a world that has no apparent connection to reality and its great challenges and the successive fundamental changes. Those who build their houses in illusions, will eventually be destroyed by the truth. Those who set their lives in the wind, will inevitably be robbed by the storms.

The final analysis of the dilemma of the two-state delusion came from Edward Said in his essay featured in *From Oslo to Iraq and the Roadmap.*

> How damaging and how tragic this collective *delusion* has been is more evident with the passing of each day, and which the coming to power of such anachronistic and ill-suited a figure brings to a garish, bizarre new light.
>
> How long will the awakening take, and how long much more pain will have to be felt, before the opening of eyes is fully accomplished?"

We'll Meet in Jerusalem?

Al-ard-al-Muqaddasah.
The holy land.
Eretz Hakodesh

When mentioning God, Al-Aqsa, the Church of the Holy Sepulchre, Sheikh Jarrah, and Mount of Olives, Jerusalem immediately comes to mind. In the distance, the national dimension of Palestine shines through.

The Catholic Father Manuel Musallam stated:

"Jerusalem is the city of God, in which the Old Biblical Testament, Gospel of the New Testament, and the Qur'an in the Isra and Mi'raj are historical scenes around which religious believers gather. Jerusalem in religious beliefs is the city of the "*Day of Resurrection*", the great day of the return of Jesus Christ, as stated in the prophecy of Zechariah".[8]

This ancient city is the cradle of religions and remembrance. In the eyes of millions, Jerusalem always served as a beacon of hope, a pinnacle of spirituality of the three monotheistic religions. But, as stubborn fate would dictate, its unique high position and divine holiness could not protect her from the great tragedies and many wars that befell its people from invaders, tyrants and those who were inspired to seize its charming religious treasures.

In the words of Palestinian-American author Yousef Khanfar:

> As long as there is life, there will always be Jerusalem, and as long as there is Jerusalem, there will always be jealousies, and as long as there are jealousies, there will be blood. The colonised souls sleep painfully in refugee camps, while the colonisers sleep peacefully in stolen homes. And beneath the crest of this noble

land, the ashes of the powerful and the powerless are all mixed together; the voices of the deities and laities breathe no more. While war belongs to the day and sun, religion belongs to the night and noon. [9]

Defending Jerusalem was a sacred responsibility, but Eugene Rogan believed that the Arab states hoped to rely on the newly established Arab Liberation Army (ALA) to defeat the Jewish forces in Palestine without having to send in their regular armies. The plan, as is now known, was to have:

> …Fawzi al-Qawuqji in charge of the northern front, and the charismatic Abd al-Qadir al-Husayni to lead the Jerusalem front…Unlike the Jewish soldiers in the Hagenah, who had enjoyed British training for over a decade and had gained combat experience fighting with the British in World War II, the Palestinian had not had the opportunity to build up an indigenous militia. [10]

With the rise and frequency of violence by Israeli settlers and their idiotic far-right groups towards the civilian Arab citizens of East Jerusalem, came the demolition and confiscation of homes in the Sheikh Jarrah neighbourhood and the continued storming of the Al-Aqsa mosque's courtyards.

But, what do you know about those houses in Jerusalem? Are they not inhabited by their real owners in a land whose people have been absent and expelled?

Raja Shehadeh, a Jerusalemite lawyer, notes:

> …to have seen writ on the land the fanaticism of its settlers, who deluded themselves by creating a land of make-believe where the history of one people had been utterly erased from the landscape and replaced by messianic fantasy, all this was edifying. Their presence

was untenable, just as the Ottomans, after a 400-year presence here, also had to leave. [11]

The late Faysal Husayni was proud of belonging to his hometown, and warned against abandoning Jerusalem, which would affect the entire region:

> Jerusalem can be either a shining sun with its warmth over the Middle East, or a black hole that swallows everything.[12]

Gabi Baramki, a prominent academic and educator, became the dean of Birzeit College, and assumed the post of acting president of Birzeit University by proxy following the unjust and arbitrary expulsion by the Israeli occupation forces of its president, Hanna Nasser. He represented Palestine on the Council of Pugwash for many years, and was highly respected for his views:

"We all carry Jerusalem on our heads, it's definitely immersed in our conscience, we will not rest, we will not compromise and will not normalise with Israel." [13]

One of the first requirements and miracles of prophecy and its permanence is that the prophets and their immediate followers who believed in their heavenly message, were ordained to suffer various kinds of physical torment. They were chased, escaped, migrated and crucified.

Strangely enough, God ordered Abraham to slaughter his son. *Ayoub* (Job) endured torment and disease for many years in order to please his Lord. Moses and his people fled from the pursuit of the Pharaoh, they wandered in the desert for forty years. Jesus and the Virgin Mary were chased until it ended with Christ carrying the cross, walking on the path of pain in Jerusalem to be crucified.

Prophet Muhammad emigrated from Mecca to Medina at night to escape from the infidels who fought him in several battles for many years. Finally, the persecution of the Jews throughout the ages from Nebuchadnezzar to the pogroms and Holocaust in Europe.

All these events indicate that the person or people whom God chooses to carry his message has to endure very severe and almost eternal types of torment. Is there a similarity to what the Palestinians have endured and still are enduring? Or is it His wish for them to be part of *The Chosen People*? (Despite my firm belief that such a term is exclusivist, but, it is permissible for the Palestinians in dreaming to be ordained by God to make them part of that people!)

But rational consideration and realism are necessary to understand what surrounds us. If we do not understand first, how can we infer the path and options for solutions to our problems?

Now we can see the extent of global solidarity with Palestine and Jerusalem's "Sheikh Jarrah" as something unbelievable, it is the most prominent fruit of our steadfastness, courage and patience that our people presented to the world. It really looks like a coup by all standards in world public opinion, which reiterated its solidarity with our just and humane cause. It's quite a wonderful and rare moment to watch these huge popular demonstrations in several major capitals of the world. We should cherish and preserve it and it should be exploited in the right way so as not to go to waste.

When protests flared in East Jerusalem, protesters gathered at Damascus gate. A foreign journalist who was covering the protest, was injured by an Israeli solder's fire, was carried by protesters to a Palestinian medical team next to an ambulance, when the doctor asked him, "How do you feel Mister?" He replied while smiling and said,, "Considering the alternative, I feel fantastic!"

Tamim al-Barghouti, the young poet of Ramallah who is nicknamed *"the poet of Jerusalem"*, (son of Murid Barghouti also a poet and Radwa Ashour, a famous Egyptian author), calling on his followers wrote:

> … in our wills , we leave before our death, each Palestinian should absolve himself or herself of the agreements signed under their name that give up the land

of historic Palestine, and stress that these agreements
are void and ephemeral. [14]

What complicates matters further in finding a common formula
for peaceful coexistence in the eternal and holy city, the forged allegations continue to deepen the gap between the two parties of the
conflict. Yuval Noah Harari, the Israeli writer explains:

> For example, one of the major obstacles for any peace
> treaty between Israelis and Palestinians is that the
> Israelis are unwilling to divide the city of Jerusalem.
> They argue that this city is 'the eternal capital of the
> Jewish people' — and surely you cannot compromise
> on something eternal. What are a few dead people
> compared to eternity? This is of course utter non-
> sense... In contrast, the city of Jerusalem was estab-
> lished just 5,000 years ago and the Jewish people are at
> most 3,000 years old. This hardly qualifies as eternity. [15]

It happened that Edward Said had refuted these Israeli allegations
several years ago at Birzeit University, where he confirmed that there
are "all sorts of invented history. The Israeli government says that
Jerusalem represents 3000 years of history, but, in my opinion, to say
this is a historical fact is to enter into invention and mythology...The
same can be said about Palestine." [16]

To those who believe in the existence of God, as the Ruler and
Director of all things, such a system may appear as a manifestation
of divine wisdom, tending towards the slow and ultimate perfec-
tion of humanity. Unfortunately, Jerusalem remains the insidious
obstacle on the way to a solution. All its places of worship are waiting for the day when peace will prevail despite the real pessimism
that accompanied previous negotiations, that day remains reeling
in the wind.

How many roads must a man walk down
before you call him a man?
The answer, my friend, is blowin' in the wind.
And how many ears must one man have
before he can hear people cry?
Yes and how many deaths will it take 'till he knows
that too many people have died?
The answer, my friend, is blowin' in the wind.[17]

Samia Khoury, a Palestinian writer, elected to improvise new words on Bob Dylan's to suit our new situation:

How many years must we stay under siege
Before we regain our freedom?
And yes how many more lives need to be lost
Before justice and peace will prevail?
The answer, my friend, is blowin' in the wind.[18]

But, the great messages do not come randomly or inevitably and blind, they do not come for people waiting for a faithful prophet like the one who waits for Godot, who does not come.

The Impossible Dream!

"To dream the impossible dream.
To fight the unbeatable foe.
To bear the unbearable sorrow.
To run where the brave dare not go.
To reach the unreachable star."

— JOE DARION

People who enjoy a normal life find their lives interspersed with rosy dreams. As for the Palestinians who have been forcibly expelled from their lands and homes, their dreams come to the fore in the images of their original homes and the proximity of their return.

Remarkably, such a process is completely reversed in the dreams of the children of Gaza. Most nights they watch houses collapsing over their heads, while remains of the victims, usually their relatives or friends, are scattered amongst the detritus, as the terrifying whizz of rockets fly above high towers. Persistent and bitter nightmares keep haunting them night after night.

For Palestinians, dreams represent hope; dreams of returning home, dreams of having a choice where to live, dreams of seeing their parents. Dreams have become deeply attached to every Palestinian in the diaspora and an essential part of daily life. But, why is it that everything has to be a dream? Why is there no realization of Palestinian dreams?

Looking back at some historical events that occurred in the recent past, one can feel hope: the fall of Berlin Wall led to a young East German woman Angela Merkel serving as the Chancellor for over 16 years; with the end of apartheid rule in South Africa, Nelson Mandela assumed power as the first African president; and the election of Barack Obama as the first non-white president of America.

People in our region should be optimistic in their outlook to think logically and realistically that the impossible becomes possible in the end.

Dr Iyad Sarraj, a leading psychologist explains that commonalities between dreams and everyday life provide clues as to how our consciousness operates that gives us the ability of the mind to turn pure information into a dynamic multidimensional reality. Spiro Sayegh, a native of Beersheba and a graduate of Damascus University in dentistry, used to ask the clients of his clinic to tell him about their previous dreams while he extracted their teeth without anaesthesia. [19]

Pope Francis confirms that God is also dreaming for us,

> Discerning in the midst of conflict requires us sometimes to pitch camp together, waiting for the skies to clear. Time belongs to the Lord. Trusting in Him, we move forward with courage, building unity through discernment, to discover and implement God's dream for us, and the paths of action ahead. [20]

While Noam Chomsky reminds us that:

> The Israeli-American military historian Amos Perlmutter wrote: "Begin and Sharon share the same dream: Sharon is the dream hatchet man.
> The dream is to annihilate the PLO, douse any vestiges of Palestinian nationalism, crush their allies and collaborators in the West Bank and eventually force them into Jordan and cripple, if not end, the Palestinian national movement. [21]

Walid Abu Ghali, a refugee from Jaffa was studying agricultural engineering in Cairo University and sharing a flat with another refugee, Fuad Abu Gheida, a footballer with Al-Ahly Football Club. Both were friends since their parents' exile to Damascus in 1948. Walid used to dream about Fuad and his team's performance and predicting the results of each game. Almost all his dreams were amazingly fulfilled; the club decided to invite him to attend for free all its matches in Egypt.

There are many Israeli activists who work for peace and reconciliation; Peace Now, Combatants for Peace, Jerusalem Peacemakers, Galia Golan, Gershon Baskin, Gideon Levy and others. What if Palestinians woke up one day and found their country free and independent without wars, tragedies, arrests and injustice from tyrants and occupiers, and without foreign interference? With its new and free culture, concepts overlap and intertwine, questions arise, doubts abound, and certainty emerges from the heart of doubt. There is a lot of questioning about for how long and where to, and research on future directions. The desired result is the self-actualization of a community of citizens, who think progressively, and find independence stemming from within.

A new state is established on the basis of the common public interest, everyone cooperates in aiding each other, hatred disappears, almost disappears for those who disagree with free opinion, religion, sect or ethnicity, religion will witness a radical transformation. A society that accepts others, accepts differences, not out of tolerance but in the sense that difference is a cultural wealth and that the culture that closes in on itself dies. Anyone who does not tolerate difference or hates the diversity and plurality of society will find himself isolated in this new high society. The new nation will not be an imaginary metaphysical entity, but rather a will for the future, whereby every citizen is guaranteed the right to think and act on the basis of their conscience. A society that relies on itself and depends on its own resources and cohesion, and does not fear external schemes of interference or attacks.

There are many factors that bring together the components of our *Dream* state, young and old, especially their incredible attachment to football, the universal language that brings everyone together. Fortunately, the coach of *Club Palestino* in Santiago, who led his team to the final of the Copa America Championship, became the new manager of the State's National team. He selected top players, who qualified with amazing ease to the World Cup finals in Doha.

The Israeli writer Eshkol Nevo wrote in his book "*World Cup*":

...I was a kid...just following orders, naturally, what can a soldier do except follow orders?

Even Rabin himself said, 'Break their bones', the Rabin of the Rabin assassination! ... In Jenin, a Palestinian who was hit by a rubber bullet was lying in the middle of the street and my commander told me to leave the bastard there, let him die, but I screamed that I was a medic and had to treat him, and I kneeled next to him and managed to stop the bleeding and saved him, and I didn't care that, afterwards, the whole unit called me Yuval-bleeding-heart. But I too sat in the Nablus Family house and watched England-Cameroon.[22]

When Muneer Abu Salim left his refugee camp in Gaza, after his success earning a scholarship to study in Germany, he lived in a room in an old lady's house in Heidelberg. Every evening she would shout at him:

I wish you happy dreams,
"Muneer, *glückliche Träume*"
"*Ebenfalls meine gute Dame*" [the same to you.]

Before going to bed, he used to wonder: isn't there anyone wishing us a beautiful and happy reality? What will I do with a sweet dream, while my family and friends in our camp are living in a miserable reality?

Our dreams will not mature unless they are touched by painful or cruel experiences.

The impossible simply takes a little longer.

Peace and Reconciliation

"How can you find the TRUTH
about JUSTICE in an age of lies?"
— THE SECRET BARRISTER

In April 2001, after seven months of violent acts and devastation between Israel and the Palestinians, President George W. Bush sent his envoy, George Mitchell, to head a reputable European fact-finding mission to occupied Palestine. Their recommendations became known as the "Mitchell Report".

The Mitchell Report clearly stated that:

> Both parties meet to reaffirm their commitment to signed agreements and understandings. The parties are at a crossroad. If they do not return to the negotiating table, they face the prospect of it being out for years on end. Israelis and Palestinians have to live, work and prosper together. History and geography have destined them to be neighbours. That cannot be changed.

Signed by:

Suleyman Demirel, former President of Turkey.
Thorbjoern Jagland, foreign minister of Norway.
George Mitchell, former majority leader of the US Senate.
Javier Solana, former Foreign Minister of Spain and EU Representative. [23]

Many serious questions are raised, more than a quarter of a century after the interim solutions that led to the frozen Oslo Accords by many parties. For example, how much longer must we wait to achieve the promised two-state solution? Will millions of Palestinians continue to live in refugee camps and millions more in the Diaspora forever?

Edward Said had anticipated this, telling us that;

> … Therefore the "peace process" has become the only game in town: governments work with and for it, so do institutions like the World Bank, the UN, and an impressive number of donor countries, and of course the media treat it as an undisputed fact. But what if, according to all the signs and indications of unrequited nationalism and mountain hostility, this isn't and cannot be the peace to bring peace between Palestinians and Israelis? What if the "peace process" has in fact put off the real reconciliation that must occur if the hundred-year war between Zionism, Jewish nationalism, and the Palestinian people is to end? [24]

We are living in times of a global pandemic, severe climate crises, and unprecedented international consensus protests against racism and the appalling crimes of Israeli settlers. Lasting peace needs leaders of great capacity and noble hearts. What are we to expect from a future Palestinian generation born of crowded narrow street in their camps, the darkness of prisons and the oppression of the occupation's soldiers? How can this generation accept the idea of peace?

The US claims to be a mediator in the Israeli-Palestinian conflict, it is clear that the US is complicit in Israel's violations of international law and it undermines any prospect of a just peace.

It is noted that during October 1947, when the UN was debating partition, "Truman favoured a division of Palestine that would give the Arabs a proportionate majority of the lands. Truman was a genuine liberal who had moral qualms about Zionism. He was the last American president to express them." [25]

A forcible annexation of any land in the West Bank, and especially the Jordan valley along with its absorption into Israel, could give large numbers of non-Jewish citizens the right to become an addition to the Arab Palestinians living under Israeli law. Many Arabs view the new "*World Order*" in which America seeks to guarantee the continued Israeli domination of power over countries in the Middle East, as a major blow to their moral, social and economic aspirations and their national independence.

Real peace was never to be achieved with the thousands of conditions and many hours of absurd negotiations that went into all the unimaginably complicated conditions that Israel attached to every small step. "Yes, Israelis deserve security. But so do Palestinians. So do the people of the wider Muslim world," noted the journalist Robert Fisk.

Rashid Khalidi, who was chosen by Faysal Husayni to serve as an adviser to the Palestinian delegation also noted that "James Baker was gone ten months after Madrid. The new team were all men to them "the peace process was a career. They generally had academic expertise. Dennis Ross, Martin Indyk, Daniel Kurtzer, and Aron Miller all had PhDs." [26]

President Jimmy Carter boldly outlined the policy needed to achieve peace for Israel and Palestine:

> Steps that must be taken for the two states to share the Holy Land without a system of apartheid or the constant fear of terrorism. There will be no substantive and permanent peace for any peoples in this troubled region as long as Israel is violating the UN resolutions, official American policy, and the international "road map" for peace by occupying Arab lands and oppressing the Palestinians. U.S. government leaders must be in the forefront of achieving this long-delayed goal of a just agreement that both sides can honour. [27]

During the 2002 Arab League Summit held in Beirut, which was not attended by Yasser Arafat (for the first time, as he chose not to leave

Ramallah due to a serious threat by Ariel Sharon that if he left, he would not be allowed to return), the Saudi Crown-Prince Abdullah declared his historic Arab Peace Initiative (API), that was unanimously approved, and was intended to offer full recognition of Israel by all Arab States in return for the establishment of a Palestinian state on the 1967 borders according to the UN resolutions.

At the time it was regarded as a substantial concession from the Arabs. It was met by complete silence from Sharon and his cabinet.[28]

A year or two later, two Israeli activists, Yuval Rabin, the son of the late Yitzhak Rabin, and Koby Huberman, jointly formed a group that included some public figures including Amnon Shahak, Akiva Eldar, Adina Bar Shalom and Aliza Shenhar. It responded to the API by launching an Israeli Peace Initiative (IPI), Shahak and other members had a meeting in Cairo with the Arab League Secretary at the time, Nabil Al-Arabi. They met to promote the terms of their initiative, but their efforts were unsuccessful with Netanyahu, who rejected both initiatives. [29]

Marc Lamont Hill and Mitchell Plitnick correctly note that the "idea of an American 'honest broker' in the Middle East has been a joke for decades. Only a real debate over U.S. policy can change that… We must be willing to embrace, or at least consider, any solution that will yield freedom, justice, safety, and self-determination for everyone." [30]

The policies of the great powers are controlled by money which led to the aggravation of the *power of money*.

Sadly, in our regional environment, those who decide the fate of our people have contracted the disease of *the power of money*, and are the least concerned with the fate of their people.

John B. Judis explained:

> When Obama took office, he declared that Israel has to stop expanding into the West Bank and agree to the existence of a Palestinian state. Obama eventually backed down. He was heeding Israel's wishes to focus on the

threat from Iran rather than the settlements, and was opposing a Palestinian effort to win recognition at the United Nations. [31]

In conclusion, it is not the most intelligent people with scientific and moral competence who take leadership positions in this world. In the words of Mohamed El Baradei, a Nobel Peace Prize winner and a former vice-president of Egypt:

> "For those who talk about the right of Israel to defend itself, does this mean by extension: the right to occupation? The right to establish settlements? The right to racial discrimination? It is time to stop juggling with facts and rhetoric if we are serious about reaching *real peace*."

America's Ageing Symptoms

At what point then is the approach of danger to be expected?
I answer, if it ever reaches us, it must spring amongst us.
It cannot come from abroad. If destruction be our lot,
we must ourselves be its author and finisher.
As a nation of freemen, we must live through all time,
or die by suicide.

— ABRAHAM LINCOLN

At the end of the second world war, the world was divided by two powers; and with the collapse of the Soviet Union in 1991, America remained the only superpower.

Following the death of the prophet Muhammed (pbuh) in 632, the Arabs burst out of their desert peninsula, and simultaneously attacked two world superpowers, the Romans and the Persians. Within twenty years, the Persian Empire had ceased to exist. The Arabs had established their own empire extending from the Atlantic Ocean to the plains of Northern India and the frontiers of China.

Every collection of people on earth has distinctive characteristics. If the same nation were to retain its domination indefinitely, its peculiar qualities would permanently characterise the whole of mankind. Under the system of empires lasting for 250 years, each of the innumerable peoples of the world enjoyed a period of greatness, during which its peculiar qualities are placed at the service of humanity.

The Assyrians, marching on foot, could only conquer their neighbours, who were accessible by land. The British, making use of ocean-going ships, conquered many countries and subcontinents, which were accessible to them by water-North America, India, South Africa and Australia — but they never succeeded in occupying their neighbours, France, Germany and Spain.

"The terrifying realisation by the leaders and the people of the superpowers is that they do not expect that their power has finite limits, and ultimately will end." [32]

It was clear that the United States could not continue to drain its strength and potential in endless marginal wars. Is the United States in the process of decline? No one should be under the illusion that America has lost its strength and capabilities, on the contrary, it is still the dominant superpower in the world. But the issue is largely due to the state of political confusion and the increasing societal divisions in the last two decades.

What is happening now is a clear expression of the erosion of American resolve. It is a definite confirmation of the golden rule of the cycle of time that previous empires underwent, and caused their ageing and their invertible collapse, as expressed by General Glubb: "The average lifespan of empires was 250 years, but has been decreasing in the last century. Of course, there is no exception in the context of cosmic norms and rules. The Soviet Union collapsed only after seventy years." [33]

Money is the agent of gradual decline; excessive wealth injures the nation as money begins to replace the honour and adventure of the founding fathers. Moreover, men do not normally seek money for their country or their community, but for themselves. Therefore, the age of affluence silences the voice of duty.

Decadence is a moral and spiritual disease, resulting from too long a period of great wealth and power, producing cynicism, decline of religion, pessimism and frivolity. The powerful states which appeared impregnable, ultimately fail due to their inherent instability and internal contradictions.

Aaron Miller is questioning the increased polarisation in American society, asking, "How can America give advice to other nations on how to resolve their differences or their problems, while it cannot figure out how to resolve its internal problems?" And concluded that reality is missing now. [34]

Samuel P. Huntington once argued that as America is the leader of western democracies:

non-Westerners also point to the gaps between Western principles and Western action. Hypocrisy, double standards, and "but nots" are the price of universalist pretensions. The overriding lesson of the history of civilizations, however, is that many things are probable but nothing is inevitable. [35]

Ali Othman, who lived in New York, and who witnessed the awful face of racism against ethnic minorities, stated:

> The world can expect a satisfactory resolution to the problem of racism where intolerance and discrimination are due to colour or race. But where racism is the expression of a cardinal doctrine in religion, then the evils born of it will persist as long as that doctrine remains alive in the hearts of the followers of that religion. This kind of racism is lasting because in being a religious requirement, it is devoid of the redeeming sense of guilt associated with racism.[36]

Time was not far away from when African Americans were prevented from riding buses with white passengers, and were barred from entering restaurants or clubs that were reserved to whites only. None of those white people ever imagined that millions of their own children would elect Barack Obama to become the first black president of America.

Despite this, violent racism prevails across America. A hateful example was the deliberate strangulation by the US police officer of the African American citizen George Floyd. That was clear evidence of the cruelty, hatred and racial superiority that the world suffered from in the past.

Tony Zinni is questioning the absence of inspiration:

> What happened? ..how come we can't inspire people to join us? How come we created hatred and distrust

in many situations despite our good intentions?…we must face the reality that just as we don't know our own power or how to use it, we are not aware of the ways we actually touch, affect, or influence the environment. [37]

Marc Lamont Hill echoes this sentiment, stating, "To be nobody is to be subject to state violence. In recent years thousands of Americans have died at the hands of law enforcement, a reality made even more shameful when we consider how many of these victims were young, poor, black, or unarmed." [38]

Frank Barat wrote in his introduction to *Gaza in Crisis:* "I sincerely believe that what is happening in Palestine would never have lasted this long if the public were properly informed about what had been really taking place in this part of the Middle East. Noam, Ilan, and I worked on the dialogue, now titled: *"The Ghettoization of Palestine".* [39]

Will these ageing symptoms have an impact on Palestine-Israel conflict resolution? Nadim Shehadi, *claims that* Arab-American relations could yet return to former glories! On balance, modern US policies in the region have been catastrophic. America as a post-Second World War superpower is not the same country as before and it has different values. [40]

When Trump's followers, mainly extremists and right-wing militias, stormed the Capitol on January 6, 2021, it gave a clear signal of a divided society that, perhaps, is preparing for more turmoil and instability.

The Curse of Normalisation

*"What does it profit a man if he gains
the whole world and loses his soul ?*

— MATTHEW 16:26

In 1922, the British archaeologist, Howard Carter, discovered the most important archaeological find of pharaonic antiquities, the tomb of King Tutankhamun with its most precious and wondrous contents, especially the amazing golden mask. In the years following the discovery, several members of the team who participated in the excavation process with Carter died in mysterious circumstances; since then, that phenomenon became known as *"the Curse of the Pharaohs"*.

Zahi Hawas, a former Egyptian minister of Antiquities, confirmed the occurrence of several mysterious events, such as the death of his brother-in-law as he was entering the tomb of Tutankhamun, a Japanese film crew fled the scene as floods suddenly covered the area, the Culture Minister Farouk Hosni had a severe heart attack and many more related accidents, although, he personally doubts these phenomena.[41]

In a recent discussion about the normalisation of relations between three Arab states and Israel which was taking place at an accelerating pace, and to decipher what was going on, with the narration of Howard Carter's curse, a veteran Egyptian diplomat explained:

"Since the establishment of Israel in 1948, the Arab states collectively agreed to take a unique and unified stand against any attempt to recognize the Jewish State. Moreover, they also agreed to boycott all companies that deal with Israel in what has become known as the *"Arab boycott"*.

Similarly, all Muslim states and some newly independent countries in Asia and Africa, Greece, Spain and the Vatican followed suit in refusing to recognize Israel. The first Muslim country to recognise Israel was Turkey, in March of 1950, its Prime Minister Mehmet Gunaltay who approved the decision to recognise Israel lost his job two months later, and died of cancer. He would be succeeded by Adnan Menderes, the first Turkish prime minister to visit Israel after nine years of its recognition. He signed trade and cooperation agreements; a year later, he ended up being arrested, tried, and hanged.

The Shah of Iran was the second Muslim leader to recognize Israel also in late 1950. From then until the late 1970s, Israel imported 90% of its oil from Iran. Unfortunately, during the people's revolution against his rule, Britain and the U.S. abandoned him. Israel and his US allies couldn't save the throne of their most loyal Muslim ally. Worse still, he was denied residence in America; they left him to die in Egypt, after being welcomed by Anwar Sadat.

The first Arab leader to visit Israel was Anwar Sadat in 1977 following the October 1973 war. He was received by Menachem Begin and Golda Meir, and spoke before the Knesset. Two years later, a peace treaty was signed which was facilitated by President Carter.

Following the signing of the treaty, Sadat and Begin were awarded the Nobel Peace Prize.

Henry Kissinger claimed that in 1981, during his last visit to Washington, President Sadat invited him to come to Egypt the following spring for the celebration when the Sinai Peninsula would be returned to Egypt by Israel. Then he paused for a moment and said, "Don't come for the celebration-it would be too hurtful to Israel. Come six months later, and you and I will drive to the top of Mount Sinai together, where I plan to build a mosque, a church and a synagogue, to symbolise the need for peace." [42]

Anwar Sadat was assassinated during the victory celebration crossing the Suez Canal on "The Glorious 6th October". The assassination squad was led by Khalid Islambouli, a member of the Muslim Brotherhood, whose imprisoned leaders Sadat had pardoned. Neither the Peace Treaty nor his visit to Jerusalem nor the Nobel Prize saved him.

During the 1982 Israeli invasion of Lebanon, Bachir Gemayel secretly agreed to recognize Israel and enter into a peace deal similar to

Anwar Sadat's Egypt-Israel treaty. Three weeks after becoming president, a huge explosion destroyed his Falange headquarters. His Israeli friends did not provide him with the necessary protection, he died a few hours later in hospital.[43]

The Israel-Jordan peace treaty that was signed in Wadi Araba in late October 1994 led to Jordan becoming the second Arab country, after Egypt, to sign a peace accord with Israel. King Hussein, who shook hands with Ezer Weizman, the President of Israel, was hoping that his people would approve his vision of normalising relations with the enemy usurping the land of Palestine. Sadly, he was disappointed to observe that the vast majority of his people rejected the idea of normalisation, and the unpopular treaty did not extend more years to his life. He died of a malignant disease.

On the other hand, there were non-Arab leaders who refused normalisation with or recognition of Israel, despite their friendship and sometimes dependence on the United States. General Zinni in his meeting with General Pervez Musharraf, President of Pakistan: "The first issue on Musharraf's agenda was the peace process — the Israeli-Palestinian dispute — an issue is far from number one with President Bush." [44]

During his mediation efforts General Zinni explained:

> As I travel through the Middle East asking what it would take to stabilise the region, I hear a litany of issues.. The United States must commit fully to the Israel-Palestine peace process. It must clearly be involved in the mediation and bring its power to bear on both sides to reach a resolution.[45]

General Anwar Al-Eshki was the first high-ranking Saudi official to openly visit Jerusalem and Tel Aviv and meet publicly with Israelis there. He was among the moderate Arabs calling for dialogue with the Israelis in an attempt to peacefully end the conflict with Israel, based on the Saudi initiated Arab Peace Initiative of

2002. Al-Eshki worked for Prince Bandar Bin Sultan, while serving as the Ambassador to the USA, and the Head of Saudi General Intelligence.

We met several times at conferences in European cities as well as in Doha, during most of those meetings, he used to repeat a gripping narrative about Islamic Sharia law:

> The fourth Caliph, Ali Ibn Abi Talib, left his old shield with a Jewish jeweller for repair, who seized the shield claiming to own it. The caliph filed a complaint with Judge *Shareeh*, who was recently appointed by the Caliph.
>
> The judge summoned both the plaintiff and the defendant, who stood before him and asked Ali: Do you have witnesses?
>
> The Caliph replied: "Yes, my son Al-Hassan and my servant Qanbar", the Judge immediately rejected the witnesses as they were too close to Ali, and asked him again: do you have other witnesses? The answer was categorically no.
>
> The Judge ruled that the shield belonged to the jeweller, despite his firm knowledge that the Caliph does not lie, but according to Sharia law, possession is for the jeweller.
>
> After a short while the jeweller returned to the court holding the shield, addressing the judge: "Oh my God, this religion that makes me stand with the Caliph equals in front of you, rejecting his claim for lack of evidence, is undoubtedly a religion of justice and tolerance." Then he declared his conversion to Islam. [46]

In August 2001, Sheikha Fatima Bint Mubarak, the wife of Sheikh Zayed Bin Nahyan (the first president of the United Arab Emirates), and the mother of Sheikh Mohammed Bin Zayed, called on all women throughout the Arab world to donate to the Palestinian Intifada, which she began with a personal donation equivalent to one million US Dollars.

Sheikh Zayed was among the top Arab leaders loyal to the cause of Palestine. [46]

Sheikha Fatima's eldest son, Mohammad, chaired the Abraham Accords campaign that was launched by Donald Trump and Benjamin Netanyahu, which was designed by Jared Kushner. Sheikh Mohammad quickly accepted the proposal to inaugurate the new Abrahamic religious group that combines Islam, Christianity and Judaism.

As explained by Mahmoud Ghefari: "Muslims do not object to the naming Ibrahim or Abraham, the believers among them pray and bless Abraham and his family in their prayers twenty times a day." [47]

But, their objection is for Donald Trump and his son-in-law Kushner using "Abraham Accords" as a new religion under a normalisation plan, which is being religiously rejected by the majority of the Islamic nations.

It is not surprising according to the theory of *"the Curse of the Pharaohs"* that the first victim of the *"Deal of the Century"* and *"Abraham Accords"* was President Trump himself, who lost in his attempt to be elected for a second term, in which he was relying on Jewish votes in return for his incredible help to Israel. Astonishingly, the majority of Jewish voters gave their support to President Biden. Trump's son-in-law Jared Kushner, who was dabbling in the Gulf States mainly for his own personal gain, and his wife Ivanka Trump, lost their prestigious positions in the White House! And finally, Netanyahu followed suit by failing in his last attempt to remain in power and was evicted with his wife Sarah from the Prime Minister's residence. Could this be the beginning of the Curse of Normalizations?

The Egyptian poet Hisham Algakh recited his poem in Dubai, *The Last Letter in The Torah:*

*What do you say...My land? Who has shackled you
with mud? Was I in Hittin? Wasn't Salah other than
me?*
When I become Hisham the Zionist..
*When I get married, I will give my daughter to a
Zionist.*
*I am afraid an Arab groom will make her work in
prostitution; He didn't care about his homeland.*
Would he care about my daughter?
*O Gulf Arab nations, recite the name of God who cre-
ated Theatres, Resorts, Restaurants and Women.*
*In Jerusalem, I have land, palm trees .. and my lover
was hiding all the secrets of love. I don't ask for Al-Aq-
sa Mosque,*
I want my lover back. God will protect his house." [48]

As Gershon Baskin put it,

Many Israelis may think that the problem was swept
under the carpet by unilateral recognition of Jerusalem
as the capital of Israel, or peace and normalisation
agreements with some Arab countries. Israel's most
existential problem was never in Dubai, nor in Khartoum, nor in Rabat. Israel's most existential problem is
in Jerusalem, in the West Bank and in Gaza [49]

An angry Lebanese journalist commenting on the Abraham
Accords:

The frivolous in the Arab world have won the social
battle in their favour. They have seized everything with
all their pettiness and corruption.
They want to rob the Palestinians of their right to protest this egregious injustice. In the absence of authentic

values and principles, they float their programmed corruption. It is the time of the descending tramps. [50]

Shrinking the Conflict

"As man is the best of the animals when perfected,
so he is worse when separated from law and justice.
For justice is most dangerous when it is armed,
and man armed by nature with good sense and virtue,
may use them for entirely the opposite ends.
Therefore, when he is without virtue
man is the most unscrupulous and savage of animals."

— ARISTOTLE

Shrinking the conflict, is it really a new Israeli term? Naftali Bennet promised to take steps to reduce the "conflict", comparing it to traffic accidents. As Bennet put it, "it's impossible to eliminate them entirely but, it is possible to take steps to reduce the problem" adding that "better economy and more dignity for the Palestinians can improve the situation." [51]

Incredibly, Martin Indyk replied by stating that, "Dashing all hopes of political progress while raising economic expectations- as PM Bennett is doing- can lead to an increase in conflict rather than its reduction. What sounds like common sense could end up being very dangerous." [52]

The current Israeli government is planning to ban raising the Palestinian flag in Jerusalem. This recalls what Hillary Clinton remembered from these meetings that she attended between Abbas and Netanyahu in Jerusalem: "The next day the conversation continued at Netanyahu's home in Jerusalem, where he displayed the *Palestinian flag* as a sign of respect to Abbas… That night in Jerusalem was the last time Netanyahu and Abbas would sit and talk face-to-face." [53]

Palestinians are trying to predict the upcoming actions of Naftali Bennett, who shows open hostility to the Arabs on several occasions. Will his meetings with the "normalised" Arab leaders reflect positively on his future policies toward the Palestinians? Although the *Abraham Accords* have been characterised by empty promises to the Palestinians and a lack of public Arab support.

Will there be confidence building measures as was the case during President Obama's second term?

Mustafa Barghouti questions the future intentions of the new Israeli government, asking;

> Is there anything more insolent than the Israeli Government's Deduction of millions of dollars in taxes that we pay from the sweat of our brow, equal to what is provided to the families of martyrs and political prisoners, and then brazenly providing the same stolen money as loans to the Palestinian Authority, and considering all of this as an indication of good intentions and confidence building measures! [54]

Hanan Ashrawi holds that we "are people seeking freedom, peace and justice; any attempt to deny the inspirations and negate the rights of an entire nation living in captivity and under occupation is ethically and morally repugnant." She also commented in Newsweek Magazine that "we are guilty of being Palestinians, of aspiring to freedom, of refusing to surrender to a military and colonial occupation." [55]

The latest declared Israeli policy which claims that dealing with Arab governments first is the key to solving the problem of Palestine, thus returning to the early Zionist policy of purification, as Nur Masalha analyses the extreme ideology behind the policy of expelling the Palestinians:

> Zionists adopted the same approach of dealing with Arab leaders to seek a solution outside Palestine. At the

root of this notion — that the Palestinians did not have to be dealt with directly — was the denial of a distinct Palestinian identity or any resemblance of Palestinian nationalism. Thus the attitudes of Chaim Weizmann and David Ben-Gurion. [56]

Ahmad Sarraf, a well-known Kuwaiti Journalist sent me a message with an article by Thomas Friedman that started with the following:

> Princess Diana once famously observed that there were three people in her marriage, *"so it was a bit crowded."* The same is true of Israelis and Palestinians. The third person in their marriage is Mother Nature — and she'll batter both of them if they do not come to their senses.
> Gaza is built on the exact same sand as Jaffa/Tel Aviv, where many Gazan families originally came from…
> I appreciate the Gazans' sense of injustice. Why should they pay with their ancestral homes for Jewish refugees who lost theirs in Germany or Iraq? The only answer is that history is full of such injustices and of refugees who have reconciled with them and moved on. [57]

The answer was clear and profound:

> Israel can only maintain — if it so desires — itself as an ethnocracy by perpetuating the displacement of the refugees and their descendants. No matter how difficult it seems, we must believe that justice will one day be achieved. [58]

It is apparently clear that present Israeli leaders do not learn the lessons of history, not even the recent ones. Time is not on their people's side.

When Prime Minister Yitzhak Rabin, the renowned army General among their leaders, courageously tried to protect the future generation of Israelis by signing the reconciliation accords and the recognition of the PLO, while giving them a limited self-rule, the extreme right promptly assassinated him.

Gideon Levy wrote:

> Damn them all…One of the most unfortunate tendencies which permeate successive Israeli leaders' thinking is the reliance on coercion. If no one agrees with their demands or point of view, they force them to comply, incredibly and regularly by threat of force.[59]

Jeremy Corbyn, the former Labour leader, commented on the change of government in Israel:

> An independent Palestine looks no nearer in spite of moves to install a new government in Israel. Nothing suggests that Naftali Bennett would support an end to the occupation, the siege and the settlements which have been condemned by the UN. [60]

Among the proposed projects that will shrink the conflict is a scheme of building a city on the Gaza-Egyptian border with huge Gulf State funding as part of the *"Deal of the Century"* as dreamt by Jared Kushner and proposed by his father-in-law Donald Trump. The dream aims to improve the life of the Palestinians in exchange for their consent and acquiescence to the continuation of the Israeli occupation.

Israel's position in the world during the Trump presidency lost millions of its traditional supporters, especially among university students, professors and youth in general. One poignant example was the announcement by Stephen Hawking, the world-renowned physicist, of his decision to join the academic boycott of Israeli universities, by pulling out of a conference in Jerusalem to celebrate Shimon Peres' birthday, as a protest at Israel's treatment of the Palestinians. Hawking's refusal had caused a great deal of interest in the education community world-wide.

At a conference organised by an American institute in a European capital to discuss settlers' activities, boycott of settlement goods and the BDS movement, which enjoyed a rapid spread in Europe, a participant was sitting next to me. I thought he was from Spain; when it was his turn to introduce himself and give a brief overview of his work, I was shocked that I was sitting next to one of the hardline settlers, who was in fact their leader in the West Bank and absolutely rejected the two-state solution. His name was Dani Dayan. I had read some time ago that he was nominated by Benjamin Netanyahu as Israel's ambassador to Brazil, but President Dilma Rousseff refused to accept him due to his extreme views as she was influenced by ex-president Lula de Silva in their sympathy for the Palestinians.

I asked him with clear astonishment, "Are you the one rejected by the Brazilians?"

He replied, "Are you the Shawa from Gaza?"

I said jokingly, but with a louder voice, "There is a good alternative, I think Gaza would welcome you as the new Israeli Ambassador there." The hall exploded with laughter. And he laughed too.

The discussion ended by emphasising that the real danger is not only the boycott of settlements' produce, but the academics and university students' boycott. There is a fast-growing trend of increasing hostility to settlements and Israel's racist policy towards the Palestinians.

This newly invented novel with a satanic title, *Shrinking the Conflict*, was coldly met by those interested in ending the conflict. But, of course, there are parties who are drumming up this narrative as the only alternative to the two-state or an internationally legitimate solution. There are some who give interpretations as they please, the truth is not in this title, but rather what is happening in America at the local level that may ultimately affect the future of its relations with

Israel and the countries of the religion in general. Thomas Friedman recently explained such a possibility and its impact:

> The incredibly massive traditional support for Israel and almost everything it does was not limited to members and supporters of the ruling party, but it was full and comprehensive support from both Republicans or Democrats.
>
> After four tumultuous years of Trump's rule, in fact, the majority of the younger generation and mainly college students have become staunch opponents of Trump and, consequently, the Republican party.
>
> Therefore, they do not grant Israel the support with sincere attachment, as was the case in the past. For example, if a university like Wisconsin invited Netanyahu as a former prime minister of Israel, to speak, he must be protected by a large police contingent because of the apparent student hostility to Israel. There is a real fear of internal unrest in the 2024 elections from Trump's extremist cult. [61]

A survey of US Jewish voters taken after the Israel-Gaza conflict in May 2021, commissioned by the Jewish Electorate Institute, 34% agreed that "Israel's treatment of Palestinians is similar to *racism* in the United States, 25% agreed that "Israel is an *apartheid state*" and 22% agreed that "Israel is committing *genocide* against the Palestinians." [62]

Protecting Netanyahu as suggested by Friedman, is not confined to the United States only. Numerous universities in European cities witnessed the expulsion of Israeli ambassadors and diplomats who were prevented from speaking by large groups of students, which indicates a clear signal of their future vision of Israel's disgusting policies.

A former American diplomat once stated:

> Of course, if the two-state solution becomes feasible, then the settlers are the biggest losers. As for the alternative to the two-state solution by establishing one state, then Israel is the loser in the long term. As for the current situation remaining as it is for several years to come, the Fatah and Hamas movements will be the losers. Now, take your pick!

Some diplomats argued the significance that Israel is not the state of its citizens but of all the Jewish people, while the United States, for example, is most assuredly only the state of its citizens. Egyptian Ambassador Hesham Youssef, in an article in the United States Institute of Peace wrote:

> Without progress toward a comprehensive solution to the conflict, we may see more proposals toward transitional arrangements-either as steps taken to advance and preserve the two-state outcome, or interim arrangements without guarantees pertaining to achieving a two-state solution.[63]

It's a Matter of Time

"The strongest of all warriors are these two:
Time and Patience"

— LEO TOLSTOY

Freedom is the most precious thing in a person's life. But in the lives of colonialists, the issues of freedom, human rights, and the rights of others appear to them as a kind of incomprehensible hallucination. A person usually tends to improve their general life's conditions and satisfy a certain passion for a specific topic; this may be connected to scientific research, a study in historical subjects or a militant orientation to a cause they believe in. Among them there are the champions of freedom who stand up to the perversions of governments and often sacrifice their material advantages, which may also put their lives at risk.

Today, indeed, the feeling of insecurity among Israelis emanates more often from the vicissitudes of daily life than any fear of outside threats. Decadence is a moral and spiritual disease, resulting from too long a period of wealth and power, producing cynicism, decline of religion, pessimism and frivolity. The citizens of such a nation will no longer try to save themselves, because they are not convinced that anything in life is worth saving. Yuval Noah Harari writes:

> The tightening web of international connections erodes the independence of most countries, lessening the chance that any one of them might single-handedly let slip the dogs of war. Most countries no longer engage in full-scale war for the simple reason that they are no longer independent. Though citizens in Israel, Italy, Mexico or Thailand may harbour illusions of independence, the fact is that their governments cannot conduct independent economic or foreign policies,

and they are certainly incapable of initiating and conducting full-scale war on their own. [64]

The myths of Zionism have been repeatedly refuted by Israeli,
European, American and Arab Jewish historians; by the scholar Ilan
Pappe, for example.

Writing in Haaretz, Dan Ben-David believes that the covid-19
pandemic is a mere preview for the eventual demise of Israel from
internal pressures and tensions: the highly insulated orthodox Haredi
share of Israel's population has risen sharply (they are in contrast
to "*Neturei Karta*" Jews, who show solidarity with Palestine.) The
real story in Israel is no longer one of left-right, religious-secular or
Arab-Jews.[65]

Ephraim Halevy questioned the necessity of establishing a
Palestinian state in the years between 48 and 67. The West Bank,
East Jerusalem and Gaza Strip were not under Israeli occupation,
why did no one declare a State of Palestine then? History testifies
that powerless people are often shocked and paralysed in the face
of terror and oppression, and are unable to organise and resist; the
horrors of the Holocaust during the second world war are a tragic
reminder.

There is a real concern amongst Israelis about the decline in the
support of evangelical Christians in the U.S. Despite Trump's overtly
pro-Israel stance, he lost Jewish votes, indicating the declining support for Israel amongst American Jews.

Some indicated the arrival of the current pandemic as a rehearsal
for the horrific apocalypse; it starts with a weak virus that mutates
after each pandemic. Perhaps it will end the problem of the earth and
thus all our complex troubles, especially since all known religions talk
about the *Day of Resurrection* with great certainty.

On the other hand, what is the point of the Palestinian leaders
continuing the unendurable suffering of their people, in exchange
for fleeting positions and gains? Do they have no dignity and no
sense of their own history? There seems to be a similarity between

the Palestinian Authority and *Tantalus*, both are subjected to eternal punishment. *Tantalus*, the Greek mythological figure, was doomed to stand in a pool and stare at fruits and refreshing water for eternity but never able to taste it.

It is time to think differently about Oslo. As we should close the Oslo chapter. We must at some point provide a new strategy with partners of the international community and indeed like-minded Israelis and Jewish figures around the world who object to injustice and oppression. Israel's arrogance and disavowing its implementation for more than twenty-five years has altered everything.

There are serious discussions by a group of Palestinian academics and scholars in an attempt to define a clear political road map for the future, in light of the accelerating changes on the Arab, regional and international arena — especially regarding how to deal in any future negotiations with the Israeli side.

The consensus was based on the following psychological analysis: The truth no longer has a place in the minds and hearts of the Israelis, almost all the facts they present to the world are hypothetical and illusory. Of course, when the truth has no place, deception becomes the basis of their leaders' policies, a game that Benjamin Netanyahu has perfected for many years. Israeli society, including Palestinians living inside the green line, suffer from constant anxiety, fear for their fate, fear of self and fear of their fellow countrymen.

The Jewish community who produced geniuses in science, arts, commerce and cultures years before the establishment of the State of Israel, were extremely disappointed to watch the Israelis in their own state became oblivious and stupid, possessed by the old dead and buried guilt complex, they could not get rid of the inherent suspicion of others, they see what is going on in the world as a conspiracy against them, and thus their lives are filled with contradictions.

The present state of division in Israeli society invariably marks the transition from the age of conquest to the age of affluence. Money becomes the agent of gradual decline, as Israelis have the highest per capita income in the Middle East, wealth injures the young nations, money replaces honour and the adventures of their pioneers. The age of affluence will ultimately silence the voice of duty.

Following the visit to AIPAC office in Washington, a visit by Daniel Levy, for a working breakfast at the Willard, he talked about a new Jewish Lobby in the US called J Street, he was one of its founders, its main aim was to lobby for an end to the Israeli-Palestinian conflict through direct negotiations and to vigorously promote the two-state solution. He also confirmed that a J Street delegation is planning to meet with President Mahmoud Abbas. Many Israelis of the right-wing Likud claimed that J Street is an anti-Israel front for Iranian or Palestinian interests.

Ilan Pappe described the fallacies of the past:

> The Zionist historical account of how the disputed land became the state of Israel is based on a cluster of myths that subtly cast doubt on the Palestinians' moral right to the land. Palestine was an Empty Land. The Jews were a people without a land. Zionism is Judaism…etc. Setting the historical record straight might have an impact on the chances for peace and reconciliation in Israel and Palestine. [66]

Nabil Fahmi, the former Egyptian foreign minister, also asks, "How can the Palestinians get out of this dangerous predicament… from this darkness? How is it possible to develop an agreed vision to confront these rapid developments? They must form an effective framework as a real "crisis cell" that should discuss ways to resolve the dilemmas." [67]

Galia Golan, a leader of the peace movement, is an active member of *Combatants for Peace*. "To be pro-Israel is to stop the occupation and these violations of human rights. Apartheid cannot be in the interests of decent people, Israelis or the state of Israel." [68]

Romi Khosla reported on a recent study of the geomorphological threat in the region. "The gradual rise in sea levels resulting from global warming will transform settlement patterns in coastal Gaza, Israel, and the West Bank. An estimated three million Israelis will be uprooted, and Gaza will lose its fresh water aquifers."

A new generation of Palestinians is arising that no longer respects the old taboos and will not tolerate the status of its leaders as a question mark rather than a beacon of hope. There was a strong belief that still exists in the old theory of "*The Rise and Fall*" of the human race throughout history. It tells us about the rise of the great leaders and their empires to the highest conquests and domination of the world population that was followed by decline and oblivion.

In the Palestinian case, it is a matter of time, although the waiting may seem long, but patience and steadfastness that has become a national slogan that adheres to the Palestinians in Gaza and the West Bank, to this day, is clear evidence that their dream will eventually come true, sooner or later.

Surely the time has come for the Palestinians to start thinking of themselves as a people with a common history and goals. They must stop blaming each other, since they are all Arabs. They are the victims of a terrible conquest. They must seize the moral high ground and keep pressing their case against the injustice of a prolonged military occupation.

Rashid Khalidi charts a path to a united future:

> A rejuvenated, unified, democratic Palestinian national movement led by a new generation and built around a robust set of political goals would multiply that impact on Israeli, U.S., and international public opinion. The communication of an authoritatively presented Palestinian political message rooted in the principle of equality and backed by political, diplomatic, and mass action would decisively prove the unsustainability of Israel's continued oppression of the Palestinians. [69]

In the end, the words and thoughts of the Palestinian thinker Jabra Ibrahim Jabra follow us gently through his remarkable historical epic journey.

> "I wished that memory had an elixir that would bring back to it everything that happened, in its chronological sequence, the actual facts that are embodied by words pouring out on paper. Our memory, no matter how much we resist its conclusions and its victims, together control us. It makes bitterness sweet, evading us, right or wrong. Is there a definitive outcome for any event in life?
>
> I must sift through the facts and data and isolate it from the misinformation, innuendos and illusions. Are the facts always material, settled and rationalised? Evidence is not always consistent, and contradictions may appear in the smallest parts of things. Wherever there is life, it is a continuous struggle, and a continuous challenge. [70]

A collective passion.
A collective struggle for the future.

Bibliography

Abu-Lughod, Ibrahim. 1963 and 2001. *The Arab Rediscovery of Europe. A study in Cultural Encounters*. New York: Princeton University Press.

Abu Sitta, Salman. 2016. *Mapping My Return A Palestinian Memoir*. Cairo: The American University in Cairo Press.

Albright, Madeleine. 2003 and 2013. Madam Secretary, a memoir. New York: Harper Perennial.

Algosaibi, Ghazi Abdul Rahman. 1989. *Roses on Sana's Braids. Poetry*. (Arabic). Beirut : Arab Foundation for Studies.

Barr, James. 2011. *A Line In The Sand, Britain, France And The Struggle That Shaped The Middle East* .London: Simon & Schuster UK.

Bayoumi, Mustafa and Rubin, Andrew. 2019. *The Selected Works of Edward Said 1966-2006*. New York: Vintage Books.

Ben-Halim, Mustafa. 2014. *Libya's Hidden Pages of History, a memoir*. Limassol: Rimal Books.

Black, Ian. 2018. *Enemies And Neighbours, Arabs and Jews in Palestine,1917-2017.* London: Penguin Books.

Blumenthal, Max. 2015. *Goliath, Life and Loathing in Greater Israel.* New York: Nation Books.

Brown, Dan. 2017. *ORIGIN*. London: Transworld Publishers.

Butt, Gerald. 1995. *Life At The Crossroads, A History of Gaza*. Nicosia: Rimal Books.

Cansiz, Sakine, 2019. *Sara, Prison Memoir of a Kurdish Revolutionary*. Translated and edited by Janet Biehl. London: Pluto Press.

Carter, Jimmy. 2006. *Palestine, Peace Not Apartheid.* New York: Simon & Schuster.

Chomsky, Noam. 1999. *Fateful Triangle, The United States, Israel & The Palestinians.* London: Pluto Press.

Chomsky, Noam. 2016. *Who Rules The World ?* London: Penguin Books.

Chomsky, Noam & Pappe. Ilan. 2010. *Gaza In Crisis Reflections On Israel's War Against The Palestinians.* London: Hamish Hamilton

Clinton, Hillary Rodham. 2004. *Living History.* New York: Simon & Schuster.

Clinton, Hillary Rodham. 2015. *Hard Choices.* London: Simon & Schuster.

Cossali, Paul & Robinson, Clive. 1986. *Stateless in Gaza.* London : Zed Books.

Ellis, Marc H., 1994. *The Renewal of Palestine in The Jewish Imagination.* London: Alhani International Books.

Eshki, Anwar Majed. 2016. *Shariah (The Law of Islam) and the American Constitution.* Jeddah: ME Strategic Studies Centre.

Eshkol Nevo. 2010. *World Cup Wishes: Four friends, three wishes and one Story...* London: Chatto & Windus.

Eshkol Nevo. 2018. *The Last Interview.* New York: Other Press.

Espanioli, Hala. 2009. *The Secrets of Proverbs.* Nicosia: Rimal Books.

Fanon, Franz. 2001. "first published in France 1961 by Francois Maspero" *The Wretched of the Earth,Preface by Jean-Paul Sartre.* London: Penguin Books.

Fisk, Robert. 2006. *The Great War For Civilisation, The Conquest Of The Middle East.* London: Harper Perennial.

Fukuyama, Francis. 2018. *Identity, Contemporary Identity Politics and the Struggle for Recognition.* London: Profile Books Ltd.

Ghabra, Shafeeq. 2018. *The Nakba and the Emergence of the Palestinian Diaspora in Kuwait.* Doha: Arab Centre for Research & Policy Studies.

Gibran, Khalil, 1926. *The Prophet.* London: William Heinemann.

Gilbert, Mads. 2015. *NIGHT IN GAZA.* London: Skyscraper Publications Ltd.

Glubb, Sir John. 2002. *The Fate Of Empires and The Search for Survival.* London: Windmill press.

Graham-Brown, Sarah. 1980. *Palestinians and their Society 1880-1946.* London: Quartet Books.

Gordon, Neve and Perugini, Nicola. 2020. *Human Shields, A History of People In The Line Of Fire.* California: University of California Press.

Habayeb, Huzama. 2019. *Velvet.* Cairo & New York: Hoopoe.

Habibi, Emile. 1969. *Sudasiyat al-Ayyam al-Sittah "The Sextet of the Six Day War"*. "Arabic". Haifa: Arabesque Publishing House.

Habibi, Emile. 1975. *The Secret Life of Saeed: The Pessoptimist.* "Arabic". Haifa: Ibn Khaldun Publishing.

Harari, Yuval Noah. 2019. *21 Lessons for the 21st. Century.* London: Vintage Books.

Harari, Yuval Noah. 2011. *Sapiens, A Brief History of Humankind.* London: Vintage Books.

Hasib Sabbagh, *From Palestinian Refugee To Citizen Of The World.* (1996). Edited By: Mary-Jane Deeb And Mary E. King. Maryland: University Press of America.

Herzl. Theodor. *The Jewish State.*

Hill, Marc Lamont. 2016. *Nobody, Casualties of America's War on the Vulnerable, from Ferguson to Flint and Beyond.* New York: Atria Books.

Hill, Marc Lamont and Plitnick, Mitchell. 2021. *Except For Palestine, The Limits of Progressive Politics.* New York : The New Press.

Hirst, David. 2010. *Beware of Small States, Lebanon, Battleground of the Middle East.* London: Faber and Faber Ltd.

Hosny, Dr Sawsan. 2018. *Journey from Faith to Certainty.* (Arabic). Cairo: Bardia Publishing Co.

Huntington, Samuel P. 2002. *The Clash Of Civilizations and The Remaking of World Order.* London: Simon & Schuster.

Hurd, Douglas. 1993. *The Last Day of Summer.* London: Alhani International Books.

Hurd, Douglas, 1994. *A Suitcase Between Friends.* London: Alhani International Books.

Isaacson, Walter. 2003. *Benjamin Franklin: An American Life.* New York: Simon & Schuster.

Jabra, Jabra Ibrahim. 1978. *In Search of Walid Masoud.* (Arabic). Beirut: Dar Al Adab.

Jabra, Jabra Ibrahim. 2005. *Princesses' Street.* Translated from Arabic by Issa J. Boullata. Fayetteville: The University of Arkansas Press.

Judis, John B. 2015, *GENESIS, Truman, American Jews, and the Origins of the Arab/Israeli Conflict.* New York: Farrar, Straus And Giroux.

Kanafani, Fatenn Mostafa. 2020. *"Modern Art in Egypt, Identity and Independence,*

1850-1936" London : I.B. Tauris- Bloomsbury Publishing Plc.

Kanafani, Ghassan. 2015, *Political Studies. The Fifth Volume. (Arabic).* Limassol: Rimal Books.

Kanafani, Marwan. 2007. *Years of Hope.* "Arabic". Cairo: Shorouk Publishing.

Kawar, Widad. 2010. *Threads of Identity.* Limassol: Rimal Books.

Khalidi, Rashid. 2020. *The Hundred Years' War On Palestine. A History of Settler Colonial Conquest and Resistance.* London: Profile Books Ltd.

Kissinger, Henry. 2014. *World Order. Reflections on the Character of Nations and The Course of History.* New York: Penguin Press.

Kurtzer, Daniel C. and Lasensky, Scott B. 2008. *Negotiating Arab-Israeli Peace: American Leadership in the Middle East.* United States Institute of Peace Press.

Lawrence, T.E. 1940. *Seven Pillars Of Wisdom. A triumph.* London: Jonathan Cape.

Masalha, Nur. 1992 & 2009. *Expulsion of the Palestinians. The concept of "transfer" in Zionist Political Thought, 1882-1948.* Beirut: Institute for Palestine Studies.

Masalha, Nur. 2012. *The Palestine Nakba: Decolonising History, Narrating The Subaltern, Reclaiming Memory.* London : Zed Books.

Masalha, Nur. 2018. *PALESTINE, A Four Thousand Year History.* London: Zed Books Ltd.

McLoughlin, Leslie. 1993. *"A Nest of Spies".* London: Alhani International Books.

Nashashibi, Nasser Eddin. 1990. *Jerusalem's Other Voice.* London: Ithaca Press.

Obama, Barack.2020. *A Promised Land.* London: Penguin-Viking.

Othman, Ali Issa. 1993. *Islam and The Future of Mankind.* London: Alhani International Books.

Othman, Maher. 2016. *Jordan in British Secret Documents,"1953-1967".* *The First Five Years Of King Hussein's Reign.* "Arabic". Beirut: Arab Studies Publishing.

Pappe, Ilan. 2006. *The Ethnic Cleansing of Palestine.* Oxford: Oneworld Publications Ltd.

Pappe, Ilan. 2017. *Ten Myths About Israel.* London: Verso.

Palestine + 100, *stories from a century after the Nakba.* Edited by: Basma Ghalayini. (2019). London: Comma Press.

Pope Francis. 2020. *Let Us Dream, The Path To A Better Future.* London: Simon & Schuster UK.

Regan, Bernard. 2017. *The Balfour Declaration. Empire, the Mandate and Resistance in Palestine.* London: Verso.

Rogan, Eugene. 2010-2018. *The Arabs, A History*. London: Penguin Books.

Rooney, Sally . 2018. *Normal People*. London : Faber & Faber Ltd.

Ross, Dennis. 2004. *The Missing PEACE, The Inside Story of the Fight for Middle East Peace*. New York: Farrar, Straus and Giroux.

Rush, Alan.1987. *Al-Sabah, History & Genealogy of Kuwait's Ruling Family*. London: Ithaca Press.

Sabbagh, Issa Khalil. 1991. *From My Notes. 50 Years in Media and Diplomacy*. "Arabic". London: Alhani International Books.

Said, Edward. 2004. *From Oslo to Iraq and the Roadmap*. London: Bloomsbury Publishing.

Said, Edward. 2000. *The End of the Peace Process, Oslo and After*. London: Granta Books.

Said, Edward. 2003. *Orientalism*. London: Penguin Books, a New Preface.

Said, Edward.1993. *Culture & Imperialism* . London: Chatto & Windus Ltd.

Sartre, Jean-Paul. 1962. *Sketch For A Theory Of the emotions*. London: Routledge Books.

Seikaly, Sherene. 2016. *Men of Capital, Scarcity and Economy in Mandate Palestine*. New York: Stanford University Press.

Sharabi, Hisham. 2008. *Embers and Ashes, Memoirs Of An Arab Intellectual*. Translated from Arabic by: Issa Boullata. Northampton: Olive Branch Press.

Shawa, Samir. 2018. *Gaza, Where to ?* "Arabic". Limassol: Rimal Books.

Shehadeh, Raja. 2019. *GOING HOME A Walk Through Fifty Years of Occupation*. London: Profile Books.

Shehadeh, Raja, 2017. *Where The Line Is Drawn. Crossing Boundaries in Occupied Palestine*. London: Profile Books.

Shevardnadze, Eduard. 1992. *The Future Belongs To Freedom*. London: Alhani International Books.

Shibli, Adania, 2017. *Minor Detail*. London : Fitzcarraldo Editions.

Smith, Adam. 1904 & 2010 *The Wealth of Nations, The Economics Classic*. London: Capstone Publishing Ltd.

Sorkin, Michael and Sharp, Deen "Editors" 2021. *Open Gaza, Architectures of Hope*. Cairo, New York: American University in Cairo Press.

Tawil-Souri, Helga and Matar, Dina. 2016. *Gaza as a metaphor*. London : C. Hurst & Co.

Watkins, David. 1992. *PALESTINE, An Inescapable Duty.* London: Alhani International Books.

Wells. H.G. 1933.*The Country of the Blind.* London : Penguin Classics.

White, Ben. 2009. *Israeli Aparthied, A Beginner's Guide.* Foreword by John Dugard. London: Pluto Press.

Zinni, Tony. 2006. *The Battle For Peace, A Frontline Vision of America's Power and Purpose.* New York: Palgrave Macmillan.

Notes

Introduction

1. Ziad Abdelfatah Wafa. *History of the PLO*. 2006
2. Ibid

Chapter 1

1. "The Stones' Intifada", broke out in December 1987 in Jabalia camp in the Gaza Strip. It was an unarmed uprising, children throwing stones at the Israeli armoured vehicles.
2. PLO negotiated with the US through mediators headed by Hasib Sabbagh that led to the UN Geneva meeting in November 1988.
3. Ahmed Ben Bella served as the first President of Algeria following its independence from France on 5 July 1962. Arafat's request, as told by Ambassador Dajani.
4. Yitzhak Shamir intended to prolong the Madrid negotiations for at least ten years!
5. Abdelsalam Majali became prime minister and was given the task of signing the Wadi Araba peace treaty with Israel in October 1994.
6. Visited Nashashibi in his house in the Sheikh Jarrah neighbourhood in Jerusalem. He regretted the lack of progress on a solution.
7. Mark Ellis was the first Rabbi I met, his book sold a few copies; "What does it mean for Jewish history and theology to continue oppressing the Palestinian people?"
8. Rabin courageously confirmed his commitment to peace at the joint session

of Congress in July 1994.

9. The curse of the Nobel Peace Prize was also shared with Yitzhak Rabin and Shimon Peres.

10. Arafat rarely mentioned his father publicly or visited his grave in Khan Yunis.

11. Marwan Kanafani in his book *The Years of Hope*, 2007. The plane crashed on 7/04/1992.

12. Among leaders who visited Gaza were King Hussein, John Major, Jacques Chirac, Tony Blair, Bill Clinton and Nelson Mandela.

13. Many foreign channels have permanent correspondents in Gaza including Turkish, Russian, Iranian and Lebanese.

14. Was actively engaged in meetings with foreign organisations, diplomats and public figures.

15. The Agreement on Economic Relations between the PLO and Israel, signed in Paris on 24 April 1994.

16. Edward Said from: The End of the Peace Process, Oslo and After.

17. Nur Masalha, *PALESTINE, A Four Thousand Year History*.

18. Ibid.

19. Edward Said, Culture & Imperialism.

20. The All-Palestine Government was opposed by Jordan and Egypt.

21. Hisham Sharabi in his book *Embers and Ashes, Memoirs of An Arab Intellectual*. Translated by: Issa Boullata.

22. During the reign of Al-Mamoun, the scientific renaissance flourished, the translation of the heritage of Greek civilization, and his encouragement of scholars such as Al-Khawarizmi in all fields, especially astronomy and geography.

23. The Swiss team made another significant discovery of a collection of rare coins minted in Gaza.

24. Nur Masalha, from his book *PALESTINE, A Four Thousand Year History*.

25. The Geneva Exhibition lasted for six months with a large turnout of interested citizens.

26. The project proposal was not implemented after Hamas seized control of the Gaza Strip.

27. Sheikh Mustafa served as the Imam of Al-Sayed Hashim Mosque in Gaza where Hashim bin Abd Manaf, the grandfather of Prophet Muhammad is

buried.

28. Gerald Butt, who was BBC's Middle East correspondent, *Life At The Cross-roads, A History of Gaza*.

29. It was Nasser's only visit to Gaza, which accelerated the completion of the Czech arms deal and the start of a trend by most regimes in the region to acquire Soviet arms.

30. Maher Othman in his book *Jordan in British Secret Documents, 1953-1967. The First Five Years Of King Hussein's Reign*. Arabic.

31. Rashid Khalidi on Palestinian society; *The Hundred Years' War On Palestine. A History of Settler Colonial Conquest and Resistance*.

32. Elia Abu Madi was a Lebanese-born American poet, this poem is part of (Al-Talasem) Puzzles, "I came, not knowing from where, but I came. And I saw in front of me a path, so I walked. I shall remain walking, whether I want to or not. How did I come? How did I see my path? I don't know." Lastu Adri.

33. Haidar turned into politics after my treatment, he played a pivotal role by heading the Palestinian delegation to the Madrid conference and Washington talks. He was highly critical of Arafat's policies. On the contrary, Mustafa stayed away from politics and preserved his medical practice.

34. The United Nations Peace-keeping Force "UNPF" entered Gaza following the withdrawal of Israeli forces on March 7, 1957 and remained there for over ten years.

35. Wijdan joined the popular struggle and was elected Vice-President of the Palestinian Women's Union.

36. Bassam's poem was kept by his wife who gave birth to a baby boy seven months after his tragic death.

37. Rafik Hariri was elected prime minister of Lebanon in 1992, he was assassinated on February 14, 2005. Nazih managed to expand his ambitions by building a solar power plant in the West Bank.

38. Saad Alhashwa, now living in Canada, is still holding the receipt hoping to recover his father's stolen Chevrolet.

39. Ibrahim Touqan' poem *Mawtini* was the popular melody during the Palestinian resistance to the British Mandate, and amazingly became the official national anthem of Iraq.

40. Asmahan's drowning was not an innocent accident, and it was believed that

it was a conspiracy by the British due to their suspicions at the time of her assistance to the Palestinian revolutionaries.

41. Umm Adnan sadly died in Lebanon with the key in her pocket. Her oud was inherited by her young son, Muhammad who plays with it masterly and tenderly Farid's songs. He also graduated from the American University in Beirut with a political science degree.

Chapter 2

1. Dan Brown in his book *Origin*.
2. JFK, in his inauguration speech, January 1961. It was believed that he borrowed the quote from Khalil Gibran, and the rest of it is written near Kennedy's grave in Arlington.
3. Armand Hammer, a Russian immigrant, played a major role with the Soviet leaders during the cold war.
4. CCC was registered in Beirut as a Lebanese company.
5. Joseph continued to work for CCC in Kuwait and Jordan for over four decades.
6. Ziad Rahbani was a communist sympathiser.
7. Typically, how Arabs viewed Americans in the 1950s.
8. Barr, James. 2011. *A Line In The Sand, Britain, France And The Struggle That Shaped The Middle East.*
9. Theodor Herzl, *The Jewish State*. It was also reported that the Sultan rejected his requests on two occasions, for the purchase of land in Palestine.
10. T.E. Lawrence wrote in his book *Seven Pillars of Wisdom*. "The ruin of high hope: A stalemate, was an intolerable prospect. We schemed to strengthen the Arab Army. If this drew off one division from the enemy in Palestine it would make possible a British ancillary attack. After a month's preparation this plan was dropped. It was clear that the British did not favour the entry of Sharif Hussein's Arab forces into Palestine, and had set their destination for Syria."
11. Gerald Butt, in his book *Life At The Crossroads, A History of Gaza.*
12. Source: Public Record Office, Cab.24/24, Aug. 23,1917. Lord Edwin Samuel Montagu was Secretary for India, 1917-22.
13. Bernard Regan: *The Balfour Declaration. Empire, the Mandate and Resistance in Palestine.*

14. Winston Churchill, in his article *Zionism versus Bolshevism* in Illustrated Sunday Herald, (8 February1920).

15. Gerald Butt, *Life At The Crossroads, A History of Gaza.*

16. An open letter signed by Albert Einstein, published in the N.Y. Times on December 4,1948.

17. As reported in the Jewish Virtual Library, Modern History of Israel: The assassination of Count Bernadotte (Sept. 17, 1948).

18. Ian Black, 2018. *Enemies And Neighbours, Arabs and Jews in Palestine, 1917-2017.*

19. Douglas Hurd in his books. *A Suitcase Between Friends* and *The Last Day of Summer*, 1993.

20. Ghazi Algossaibi, Saudi Ambassador in London: 1989. *Roses on Sana's Braids.* Poetry. (Arabic).

21. Tony Benn in an interview with American film director, Michael Moore:

22. Ali Issa Othman in his book *Islam, The Future of Mankind.*

23. Layla Moran, a Liberal Democrat MP in her Bill to recognise the State of Palestine to the House of Commons.

24. Tony Blair who served as head of the Quartet for 10 years. from his article, Feb 10, 2020 on PS.

25. Crispin Blunt, a Tory MP and British Foreign Office official.

26. President Jimmy Carter in his book *Palestine, Peace Not Apartheid,* 2006

27. Francis Fukuyama, 2018. *Identity, Contemporary Identity Politics and the Struggle for Recognition.*

28. Gaza was not annexed, but given the name "Areas under the Administration of the Egyptian Forces."

29. Nur Masalha in 2012. *The Palestine Nakba: Decolonising History, Narrating The Subaltern, Reclaiming Memory.*

30. Azmi Bishara, a former Arab Knesset member, now living in Doha, Qatar.

31. Ilan Pappe 2006. *The Ethnic Cleansing of Palestine.*

32. General Tony Zinni, *The Battle For Peace, A Frontline Vision of America's Power and Purpose.*

33. Ghada Karmi is a Doctor of Medicine and political analyst. From an article in "World Literature Today" Summer 2021 in Palestine Voices issue.

34. Haroun Hashem Rashid, a poet born in Gaza, his poem was made a National

Anthem "A'idoun" (We shall return), sung in schools of the Gaza Strip during 1950s and 60s.

35. Abahir Sakka, *Gaza, A Social History under British Colonial Rule, 1917-1948.*
36. Prince El-Hassan bin Talal wrote a letter to The Guardian in May 2020.
37. As reported by the British MP David Ward.
38. Prime Minister Boris Johnson in his UN speech, September 2019.
39. Leslie McLoughlin in his book *A Nest of Spies.*
40. Event arranged by Sanaa Al-Aloul, head of the Palestinian Community in London.
41. During an Atlantic Ocean conference in Istanbul, 2017.
42. A meeting was held at the Royal Liberal Club in London, (5 Aug. 2014).
43. In a Tweet by Senator Bernie Sanders, dated 20 March 2020.
44. An amazing prediction?
45. Zuhdi Tarazi kept his post at the UN until 1991.
46. Guantanamo prison is still in operation.
47. His promises for the Palestinians were blown in the wind.

Chapter 3

1. Don't complain to people about your pain. By the Iraqi poet, Kareem Al-Iraqi
2. From the book *Palestine + 100, stories from a century after the Nakba.* Edited by Basma Ghalayini.
3. Widad Kawar, in her book *Threads of Identity.*
4. The Tripoli bombings resulted in the killings of Gaddafi's daughter. Also, another daughter of Palestinian engineer Basim Al-Ghussain.
5. Richard Gere in a video appearance at the annual Israeli-Palestinian Memorial Ceremony to mark remembrance day. April, 2021.
6. From Banksy's website.
7. Mikis Theodorakis, in a program by Al Mayadeen English, 02 September 2021.
8. Michael Moore in a tweet on 10 April 2018.
9. A poem from the *Almond Blossoms and Beyond* collection. Translated from the original Arabic by Mohammesd Shaheen. Interlink Books 2010.
10. Sally Rooney in her book *"Beautiful World, Where Are You".* Edward Said's remarks in his article.

11. Sarah Graham-Brown in her book *Palestinians and their Society 1880-1946*.

12. Lutfi Bushnaq visited Jerusalem several times after the establishment of the PA.

13. David Watkins' book *Palestine, an Inescapable Duty*.

14. Hala Espanioli in her book *The Secrets of Proverbs*.

15. Ben Halim's book *Libya's Hidden Pages of History* was published in Arabic and printed in Cairo, an English copy was published by Rimal Books in 2014 in Cyprus.

16. Ibrahim Abu-Lughod, *The Arab Rediscovery of Europe. A study in Cultural Encounters*.

17. Ramzi Baroud, editor of the Palestine Chronicle, Arab world books. From an article in "The Arab American News", June 2016.

18. Che Guevara during his visit to Gaza in 1959, while meeting Palestinian youth at the high school.

19. Emile Habibi in his novel *Sudasiyat al-Ayyam al-Sittah* "The Sextet of the Six Day War".

20. Badri was also imprisoned with Muin in 1959.

21. Adania Shibli, in her novel *Minor Detail*.

22. Dan Brown in his book *Origin*.

23. Ilan Pappe, *The Ethnic Cleansing of Palestine*.

24. Barbari owned and edited "Al-Salam" (Peace) newspaper from 1959 until his death in the 1967 war by Israeli forces. He wrote the Indira quote in his newspaper after her visit to the U.S. in March 1966..

25. What Sartre gave to the doctor was a copy from his book: "Sketch For a Theory of Emotions". Simone de Beauvoir also warned the refugees in the Shati camp: "The oppressor would not be so strong if he did not have accomplices among the oppressed."

26. The Bseiso family kept a framed photo of Malcolm X shaking hands with Sheikh Kholusi Bseiso and that quotation.

27. Philippe Lazzarini in his statement to the UN General Assembly's Fourth Committee, October 5, 2021.

28. Salman Abu Sitta in his book: *Mapping My Return. A Palestinian Memoir*.

29. Edward Said describing Hasib, *From Palestinian Refugee To Citizen Of The World*.

30. Jimmy Carter writing the foreword of *From Palestinian Refugee To Citizen Of*

The World.

31. As told to the author by Ghassan's younger brother Marwan.

32. Habibi's body was removed from Nazareth in accordance with his will and buried in Haifa, where I visited a year later and wandered through the splendid Baha'i gardens.

33. Ian Black in his book *Enemies And Neighbours, Arabs and Jews in Palestine, 1917-2017.*

34. Zababdeh is located in the Jenin Governorate in the West Bank, its Christian residents proudly coexist with others.

35. Huzama Habayeb in her novel "Velvet."

36. Ruddani Li Biladi "Take me Back Home" a song by Fairouz, lyrics by Said Akl.

Chapter 4

1. Alan Rush in his book *Al-Sabah, History & Genealogy of Kuwait's Ruling Family.*

2. Shafeeq Ghabra, a Palestinian-Kuwaiti professor, in his book *The Nakba and the Emergence of the Palestinian Diaspora in Kuwait.*

3. Ibid.

4. Ibid.

5. Alan Rush, *Al-Sabah, History & Genealogy of Kuwait's Ruling Family.*

6. Ibid.

7. Arafat and Khalil al Wazir visited China for the first time in March 1964, China agreed to open an office for Fatah and promised to support their Liberation Movement. His second visit included a trip to North Vietnam and North Korea. "Fatah, the Beginnings", Palestine Studies Magazine, 2015.

8. Khartoum's Arab League Summit in the aftermath of the 1967 defeat in the six-day war, became famous for "The Three No's": No peace with Israel, no recognition of Israel, and no negotiations with Israel.

9. Sherifa Dina's second marriage was approved with the blessings of King Hussein and her daughter Princess Alia.

10. Salah Khalaf "Abu Iyad" the second in command after Arafat, was assassinated on 14 January 1991, some reports suggested that his killing was ordered by Saddam Hussein as Abu Iyad was against Iraq's invasion of Kuwait.

11. Rashid Khalidi in his book *The Hundred Years' War On Palestine. A History of Settler Colonial Conquest and Resistance.*

12. Ibid.

13. Fraih was a member of the Palestinian delegation to Madrid and Washington negotiations, accompanied Arafat to the Oslo signing ceremony in the White House in 1993.

14. Edward Said in his book *From Oslo to Iraq and the Roadmap*, 2005.

15. The Tarazi family is one of the oldest Christian families in Gaza.

16. 28 October,1994 witnessed the first armed clash between the PA and Hamas.

17. George Tenet made two visits to Gaza and Ramallah and met with Arafat and Hindi.

18. Muhammed Murrar and Hisham Alami spent years of their childhood in Jerusalem walking behind the wooden cross on Via Dolorosa Street.

19. It was reported by Basil Akl that in most years, the number of Palestinian students exceed that of other nationalities at the AUB.

20. Walid Khalidi in Hasib Sabbagh's book *From Palestinian Refugee To Citizen Of The World.*

21. The first Taawon meeting was held in Geneva on 15 April 1983.

22. Records from Taawon's archive of its first meeting.

23. Jaweed was later removed from his membership of the PLO, Arafat ordered his arrest in Gaza a year later.

24. During the 2013 Pugwash conference in the city of Bari, Italy.

25. Hamami's last telephone call, minutes before he was shot, was to our office in London asking about his friend Maher Othman.

26. Naim Khader, a lawyer born in Zababdeh town, was shot dead while walking to his PLO office in Brussels on 1st June 1981, exactly a year after the Venice Declaration.

27. Naji was carried, unconscious, to hospital by Afaf Ibrahim, who worked with him in the London office of Al-Qabas. He died a month later.

28. Hillary Clinton also called Ehud Barak "the most important voice for peace in the Israeli government of Netanyahu" in her book *Hard Choices*, 2014.

29. Atallah Hanna, is the Palestinian Archbisop of Sebastian, who is famous for rallying both Christians and Muslims against the settlers and Israeli occupation.

30. Dr. Rifai resigned from the Syrian cabinet in 2004. Mohammad Mahrouqi sadly died in 2019 after a short illness and couldn't fulfil his dream of visiting Jerusalem.
31. Nur Masalha from his book *The Palestine Nakba: Decolonising History, Narrating the Subaltern, Reclaiming Memory*.
32. Ibid.
33. Franz Fanon from his book *The Wretched of the Earth*.
34. Abu Naja was Minister of Agriculture and a leading member of Fatah in Gaza.
35. Pope Francis from his book *Let Us Dream, The Path To A Better Future*.
36. Marwan Kanafani from his book *Years of Hope*.
37. Meeting with Al Hourani at his office.
38. Ibid
39. Khalid Jarrar tweeted after the death of her daughter.
40. *Sara: Prison memoir of a Kurdish Revolutionary* by Sakine Cansiz. Pluto Press, 2019.

Chapter 5

1. The committee was formed in early 2003.
2. Both senior partners served for many years at the State Department.
3. Ambassador Kawar held several meetings with committee members during their stay in Washington.
4. EFE is still working in Palestine and other MENA countries.
5. PLO office in Washington is still closed despite President Biden's promise to restore relations with the Palestinian Authority.
6. Salam Fayyad was replaced by Rami Hamadallah as prime minister in June 2013 after six years in office.
7. "Unofficial Diplomats" title was given by Clovis Maksoud, the former Arab League Ambassador to the UN and a friend of Samer.
8. "There is always something in the knowledge of the unseen".
9. Ross did write about it in detail in his book *The Missing Peace, The Inside Story of the Fight for Middle East Peace*.
10. Madeleine Albright in her book *Madam Secretary, a memoir*.
11. Hillary Clinton in her book *Living History*.

12. Meetings at the Aspen Institute offices in Washington.

13. The Aspen "IDEA" magazine, Winter 2005 / 2006.

14. Enjoying reading Walter's book on our way back to Gaza, Isaacson wrote several historical books.

15. Some Non-UNRWA schools operate three daily shifts due to lack of buildings and shortages of teachers in Gaza.

16. Iyad received the Physicians for Human Rights Award in 1998 and the Olof Palme Prize in 2010.

17. Henry Kissinger also mentioned his last meeting with Sadat in his book *World Order, Reflections on the Character of Nations and the Course of History*

18. Toni Verstandig, a cheerful lady, also invited other Palestinian members of the MESG.

19. Liz Cheney was elected as a Republican member of Congress, she courageously denounced Donald Trump's claims of a rigged 2020 presidential election.

20. JFK letters to Arab leaders, from the White House Archive.

21. After presenting her with a donation for the John F. Kennedy Memorial Library, March, 1965.

22. President George W. Bush speech in the United Nation, September 2002.

23. In 2005, Scooter Libby resigned from his White House position, as he was accused of lying. He was sentenced for imprisonment, but commuted by Bush, then pardoned by Trump in 2018.

24. Ofer is the most notorious Israeli prison located inside the West Bank, not far from Ramallah.

25. The visit took place in 2014, shortly after the multilateral meeting called by President Obama, with the participation of Presidents Abbas, Mubarak, King Abdullah 11 and Prime Minister Netanyahu, which did not lead to any significant results.

26. Marc-Lamont Hill in his book *No Body: Casualties of America's War on the Vulnerable, from Ferguson to Flint and Beyond*.

27. Barack Obama in his *A Promised Land*.

28. Ibid.

29. Ibid.

30. Ibid.

31. Hillary Clinton in her book *Hard Choices*.

32. Barack Obama; *A Promised Land.*

33. Ibid.

34. During Wolfowitz's first visit to Baghdad, a few months before our meeting, his hotel was hit by two rockets that destroyed several rooms, but he survived.

35. Dennis Ross in his book *The Missing Peace, The Inside Story of the Fight for Middle East Peace.*

36. The Palestinian delegation was impressed by Senator's Hagel sincere rejection of wars and violence, especially the Iraq war and the suffering of Palestinians in Gaza.

37. Hagel resigned his top Pentagon position two years later, due to disagreements with Obama.

38. Barack Obama in his book *A Promised Land.*

39. Sheikh Ahmed Yasin was assassinated one month after the petty meeting with Perle. Of course, no connection.

40. Wesley Clark failed in his bid for nomination.

41. Edward Said in his book *The End of the Peace Process, Oslo and After.*

42. The Gaza Airport Terminal building was donated by Morocco with an Islamic-style design that is evident in its windows.

43. At the runway, Israeli officers in civilian clothes, examined and kept the passports of all passengers on board the flight.

44. Zeidan ordered four Canadian "Bombardier" passenger planes to be added to the Palestinian Airlines, unfortunately, the airport was bombarded and destroyed a few months before their delivery.

45. The symbolic landing of Mandela's plane on the almost free Palestinian soil was an inevitable and important indicator of people's ability to triumph over apartheid, no matter how long it took.

46. Iyad Sarraj and I were also members of the American School's advisory committee.

47. Adam Smith in his legendary book *The Wealth of Nations, The Economics Classic.*

48. The Palestinian minister was astonished at the lobbying power of Enron and its chairman in the corridors of power.

49. After his return to Ramallah, Abu Mazen and Arafat co-sponsored the signing of the agreement to build the first independent Palestinian power plant in

June 1999.

50. Ahmed Qurei was appointed by Arafat to fill the position of Prime Minister vacated by Abu Mazen in 2003.

51. All inquiries and concerns about Osama Bin Laden and his alleged or possible involvement in the construction of Gaza power plant, were made two years before 9/11 attacks!

52. Despite Arafat's busy schedule, he insisted on inviting the foreign participants in the plant's ceremony to dinner at his presidential residence.

53. The three European countries pledged seventy million Euros towards the construction of the Gaza sea port.

54. Gas concession agreement was signed at London's Grosvenor House hotel in November 1999.

55. Arafat was sullen throughout the dinner.

56. Salah Hafez also played a pivotal role in the arbitration case between Egypt and Israel regarding the ownership of Taba in South Sinai, which was returned to Egypt on 19 March 1989.

57. Ephraim Sneh had talked about Rantis Oil Field on several occasions, but Palestinian officials did not heed to his warnings.

58. An MOU was signed in the presence of President Abbas and the Egyptian Oil Minister in Ramallah on 21 February 2021.

Chapter 6

1. Edward Said in his acclaimed book *Orientalism*, p.306.

2. Mustafa Mahmoud, the Egyptian writer in his book *The Road to Hell*, 1992.

3. Mads Gilbert in his book *Night In Gaza*.

4. Neve Gordon, and Nicola Perugini, in their book *Human Shields*.

5. Pope Francis in his book *Let Us Dream, The Path To A Better Future*.

6. As a result of the the indiscriminate violent Israeli bombings, several families were completely exterminated, including Abu Hatab, Al-Qolaq. Al-Masry, and Abu Al-Awf. The teacher, Atta Zaki on May 20, decided to exchange two of his sons with two nephews.

7. Helga Taweel-Souri and Dina Matar in their book *Gaza as a metaphor*.

8. Samih Al-Qasim is considered to be the great Palestinian resistance and

intifada poet,

9. Was organised by General Amin al-Hindi.

10. Hani Al-Hasan was appointed by Arafat as minister of interior in Ramallah in 2003.

11. As confirmed by Issa Sabbagh in his book *From My Notes. 50 Years in Media and Diplomacy*.

12. Barack Obama in his book *A Promised Land*.

13. Badrakhan article in the Lebanese newspaper "Al-Nahar".

14. Dhanapala, ex-foreign minister of Sri Lanka, was the president of Pugwash, and was succeeded by Duarte, the ex-foreign minister of Brazil.

15. Noam Chomsky in his book *Who Rules the World*.

16. Mehdi Hasan, from his interview on Al Jazeera English.

17. Kerry made his remarks after meeting King Abdullah II in Amman, Jordan, on November 13, 2014 (cns news).

18. Since 2010, Soltanieh has become a regular participant in all Pugwash conferences.

19. Madeleine Albright confirmed the event in her book *Madam Secretary, a memoir*.

20. Arafat's visit took place at night on 10 November 1995.

21. President George W. Bush, on June 24, 2002 in his speech at the United Nations.

22. Arafat was famous for repeating both phrases at Fatah rallies.

23. Abu Mazen, since his resignation, moved to live in Gaza, and had never met Arafat in Ramallah, until he announced his death in the Paris military hospital.

24. Edward Said, "The Morning After" in LRB 21 October 1993

25. Madeleine Albright in her book *Madam Secretary, a memoir*, commenting on Arafat's photo in the garden of her house.

26. Sadly Omar Abbas died in Doha in 2016, before visiting Gaza.

27. In a meeting with Abu Mazen in March 2004 in Gaza.

28. Dr Sawsan Hosni in her book *Journey from Faith to Certainty*.

29. Abu Mazen rejected Trump's "Deal of the Century" by voicing his phrase on TV, "Allah Yekhreb Beitak".

30. In a clear confirmation that Likud's strategy was against peace since the beginning of the negotiation phase.

31. It was reported in Haaretz by Ari Sharit on October 6, 2004.

32. The World Bank plan never materialised. The farms were seized by Hamas a year later.

33. The Doha Forum conference started on 28 February 2006.

34. At a Fatah rally in Yarmouk stadium, Mohammad Dahlan issued a stern warning that he would suppress Hamas if it tried to seize Gaza by force, which he considers Gaza as his main stronghold. 2007.

35. As quoted by Gaza Governor Ibrahim Abu Naja.

36. Marwan Kanafani in his book *Years of Hope*, 2007.

37. Samuel P. Huntington, in his book *The Clash Of Civilizations and The Remaking of World Order*.

38. Both Childers and Menen visited Gaza in solidarity with the Palestinians in 1963. Faris Glubb went to work as a journalist in several Arab countries, supporting Palestine until his death in Kuwait in 2004.

39. Field Marshal Amer was publicly blamed for the humiliating June 1967 defeat, it was rumoured that he committed suicide a month later.

40. Jean Pascal was a member of French Pugwash, confirmed CWC on Palestine in an email to the author.

41. The Iraqi physicist's joke was meant to illustrate the ease of transfer of technology that could reach hostile hands.

42. Dianne Feinstein article in the Washington Post, 3 December 2014.

43. Pugwash Organisation is a pioneer in the fight for nuclear disarmament. Its activities and annual conferences are welcomed by many cities around the world.

44. Netanyahu: Goldstone Report's comment, Archived 22 September 2009 at the Wayback Machine, Ynet News 16 September 2009.

45. Ambassador Reza confirmed that there were many Iranian Kurds working in the diplomatic corps.

46. Amin and Sinan were constantly participating in discussions of the Palestinian issue in support for its just resolution.

47. The Participants of the Astana conference were determined to spread the Artist's work and embraced Karipbek Kuyukov's ambition to be the last victim of nuclear radiation. 2017

Chapter 7

1. Ian black, in his book *Enemies and Neighbours.*

2. Ilan Pappe from his book *Ten Myths About Israel.*

3. Dennis Ross in an article "Palestinian Stirrings" The Washington Institute, 2 Jan, 2005.

4. Aron David Miller speaking in a webinar 2021.

5. In Foreign Affairs article August 24, 2021.

6. Ibid.

7. Senator Sanders on a tweet dated 31 March 2018.

8. Father Manuel Mussalam in a speech in Ramallah, March, 2021.

9. Yousef Khanfar, an award-winning Palestinian author, from his article in "World Literary Today" of which he is the Executive Editor.

10. Eugene Rogan, in his book *The Arabs, a History.*

11. Raja Shehadeh in his book *Going Home: A Walk Through Fifty Years of Occupation.*

12. Faisal al-Husayni, article in Al Quds newspaper, December, 2000.

13. Gabi Baramki was honoured by Pugwash and the PA in Istanbul.

14. Tamim Barghouti, in an interview on Al Jadid.

15. Yuval Noah Harari in his book: *Sapiens, A Brief History of Humankind.*

16. Edward Said, in a lecture at Birzeit University. November 1998.

17. Bob Dylan wrote his song "Blowin' in the Wind".

18. Samia Khoury in a tweet on her website.

19. Spiro Sayegh, a dentist living in Cairo, is well known for his research in the science of dreams and horoscopes.

20. Pope Francis from his book *Let Us Dream, The Path To A Better Future.*

21. Noam Chomsky, in "Foreign Affairs,"

22. Eshkol Nevo in his book *World Cup.*

23. The Mitchell Report was produced following a fact-finding mission in the Palestinian Authority, visiting cities: including AlKhalil, Jenin and Ramallah in April 2001.

24. Edward Said in *The End of the Peace Process, Oslo and After.*

25. John Judis *GENESIS, Truman, American Jews, and the Origins of the Arab/Israeli Conflict.*

26. Rashid Khalidi in his book *The Hundred Years' War On Palestine. A History of Settler Colonial Conquest and Resistance.*

27. President Carter in his book *Palestine, Peace Not Apartheid.*

28. Arab Initiative also known as "Crown Prince Abdullah's Initiative".

29. Details of the Israeli Peace Initiative were introduced to us by Koby Huberman and Yuval Rabin in2015.

30. Marc Lamont Hill, from his book *No Body: Casualties of America's War on the Vulnerable, from Ferguson to Flint and Beyond.*

31. John B. Judis, *GENESIS, Truman, American Jews, and the Origins of the Arab/ Israeli Conflict.*

32. Sir John Glubb, in his book *The Fate of Empires.*

33. Ibid.

34. Aron Miller in Foreign Affairs interview..

35. Samuel P. Huntington, *The Clash of Civilizations and The Remaking of World Order*

36. Ali Othman in his book *Islam, the Future of Mankind.*

37. General Tony Zinni, *The Battle For Peace, A Frontline Vision of America's Power and Purpose".*

38. Marc Lamont Hill and Mitchell Plitnick in their book *Except For Palestine*: *The Limits of Progressive Politics*

39. The foreword for *Gaza In Crisis Reflections On Israel's War Against The Palestinians*, by Noam Chomsky and Ilan Pappe.

40. Nadeem Shehadeh, in a Chatham House article.

41. Zahi Hawas, as told in a live interview on Egyptian TV.

42. Henry Kissinger in his book *World Order. Reflections on the Character of Nations and The Course of History.*

43. Bachir Gemayel was assassinated on 13 September 1982, while Israeli forces were present in Beirut.

44. General Tony Zinni in his book *The Battle For Peace, A Frontline Vision of America's Power and Purpose.*

45. Ibid.

46. As reported in Al-Quds newspaper

47. Anwar Eshki in his book *Shariah (The Law of Islam) and the American Constitution.*

48. Poem delivered by Al-Jakh at the Arab Poetry Festival in Dubai in 1997.

49. Gershon Baskin in an article published by Al-Quds newspaper.

50. Faded Chalq in an article in Al Nahar newspaper July 2021.

51. Naftali Bennet in a speech in Jerusalem on 02/09/2021..

52. Martin Indyk in a tweet on 3 September 2021,"Dashing all hope of political progress..."

53. Hillary Clinton in her book *Hard Choices.*

54. Mustafa Barghouti from an article in Al-Quds newspaper.

55. Hanan Ashrawi, after resigning from the Executive Committee of the PLO.

56. Nur Masalha in his book *Expulsion of the Palestinians. The concept of "transfer" in Zionist Political Thought, 1882-1948.*

57. An article by Thomas Freidman on May 22, 2018, sent to me by Al-Qabas author Ahmed Sarraf.

58. Ibid.

59. Gideon Levy (A translation in Al-Quds newspaper).

60. Jeremy Corbyn, in a Tweet dated 31 May 2021.

61. Friedman in his interview with Al-Jazeera Arabic Channel.

62. A survey as reported by Ron Kampeas, July 13, 2021 in JTA (Jewish Telegraphic Agency).

63. Ambassador Hesham Youssef, in an article in the United States Institute of Peace, Jan14, 2020.

64. Yuval Harari in his book *21 Lessons for the 21st. Century.*

65. Dan Ben-David wrote in Haaretz on February 5, 2021 his article "Pandemic" was the promo.!

66. Ilan Pappe in his book *Ten Myths About Israel*

67. Nabil Fahmy in the Foreign Affairs survey.

68. Ibid

69. Rashid Khalidi in *The Hundred Years' War On Palestine. A History of Settler Colonial Conquest and Resistance.*

70. Jabra Ibrahim Jabra in his book *In Search of Walid Masoud* (Arabic)

Acknowledgements

My thanks go to those who helped create this book, some prefered to remain anonymous. The stories by Charles Zacharia, Nazih Al-Khalil, Marwan Kanafani, Fuad Abu Gheida, Norman Baron, Walid Qattan, Muhammed Murrar, Anwar Mobasher, Mohammed Ayoubi, Mohammed Gabala, Joseph Hayek, Walid Abu Ghali, Fraih Abu Middain, Ramzi Kayed,, Martin al-Ghussein, Sami Sayegh, Maath Alousi, Anwar Eshki, Ghassan Rifaii, Ahmad Youssef, Emile Jouzy and others.

A debt of gratitude to dozens of scientists, physicists, historians and diplomats whom I met in several conferences and events around the world, whose ideas, insight, experiences, vision and friendship deeply impacted this book.

I owe gratitude to many colleagues and friends on social media, whose writings, messages and remarkable views were a source of inspiration to me, among them:

Nur Masalha for his encouragement and historical advice, Nasri Sayegh, Abdel Badrakhan, Maher Menzalji, Talal Salman, Ribhi Hamdouna, Gershon Baskin, Ilan Binyamin, Jonathan Wright, Gideon Levy, Salah Hafez, Salim Nassar, Ahmad Zikra, Saida Nusseibah, Ahmad Youssef, Raja Coumine, Hend Khoury, Ghania Malhees.

Many thanks for the tremendous effort of Nadeem Zikra, in London for his dedicated and great work in editing the manuscript.

To my dear cousins: Nora (the distinguished publisher), Omar, Haya, Jado, Azzam, Nadia, Laila, Samira, Lima, Haifa, and special thanks to Jason and Najla for sending old family photos.

I always wondered why many writers acknowledged their families last. During the last three years, my son and daughter offered unflagging support and affection; in helping to improve the book, Hani with his sharp eye provided numerous suggestions and valuable advice. Lena brought her artistic design expertise that added a sparkling expression to the photo sections. Special thanks go to Lamis for allowing me the time to pursue this venture.

I am always grateful for the profound influence of my late mother, for her teachings appear clearly on the pages of this book, she taught us the art of life, the meaning of faith and the respect for the opinions of others.

Photo Credits

Most photos in this book are from the author's collection, Al Hani Books photo archive and family albums.

My thanks goes to everyone who provided valuable information and amazing photos:

Father Manuel Mussallam, Saad Alhashwa, Zaki Al-Ridwan, Fraih Abu Middain, Fatenn Mustafa Kanafani, Khaled al Ghussein, Avedis Djeghalian, Khaldoun Abu Salim, Mazen Sisalem, Hind Husseini of PASSIA, Studio Kegham, Studio Morris, Salwa Jarrah, Misbah Kamal, Charles Zacharia, Al-Qidwa family, Pugwash Conferences, Doha Forum, UNRWA, Samer Khoury, Jawdat al-Khudari, President Arafat's office, Suha Ayyad, Sami Sayegh, Gaza Mayor's office, Fatima Ibrahim, P.B.A.Gaza office, PEC, Joseph Hayek, CCEnergy, Al Hani archive, Ray Irani, ArtTalk Egypt, Peter Rodman, the Pentagon, Lena Saba, Nazih al-Khalil, Kanafani Family Album, Mahmoud al Ghefari, Walid Abu Ghali, Jason Shawa, Nabil Shaath, Zuhair Alami, Martin al-Ghussein, the Welfare Association, Alhani Cultural Foundation Gaza, David Ward, and Marwan Salloum.

Edward Said and Ibrahim Abu-Lughod photo (AP photo / Charles Tasnadi) - Shutterstock.

The orchestra for Gaza photo: (ZUMA Press, Inc. / Alamy Stock.)

The music band photo on the back cover by Studio Morris , courtesy of Zaki al-Redwan.

Every effort has been made to identify copyright holders; in case of oversight, and on notification to the publisher's email, corrections will be made in the next edition.

Index